Psychological Warfare in the Arab-Israeli Conflict

Psychological Warfare in the Arab-Israeli Conflict

Ron Schleifer

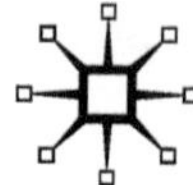

PSYCHOLOGICAL WARFARE IN THE ARAB-ISRAELI CONFLICT

First published in 2014 by PALGRAVE MACMILLAN® in the United States—a division of St. Martin's Press LLC, 175 Fifth Avenue, New York, NY 10010.

Where this book is distributed in the UK, Europe and the rest of the world, this is by Palgrave Macmillan, a division of Macmillan Publishers Limited, registered in England, company number 785998, of Houndmills, Basingstoke, Hampshire RG21 6XS.

Palgrave Macmillan is the global academic imprint of the above companies and has companies and representatives throughout the world.

Palgrave® and Macmillan® are registered trademarks in the United States, the United Kingdom, Europe and other countries.

ISBN: 978-1-137-46702-7

Library of Congress Cataloging-in-Publication Data is available from the Library of Congress.

A catalogue record of the book is available from the British Library.

Design by SPi Global.

First edition: September 2014

10 9 8 7 6 5 4 3 2 1

Contents

CHAPTER 1

Psychological Warfare Theory

Since biblical times, psychological warfare has been a nonviolent weapon used to achieve military goals.[1] Psychological warfare, or psywar, has been employed with varying degrees of success in hostilities, ranging from total war to low-intensity conflicts (LICs), and ideological and organizational struggles. Its implications on political life have been especially felt since the latter half of the twentieth century. Given the media's dominating influence, psywar's role in policy-shaping is expected to increase in both war- and peacetime.

Psychological warfare is based on the idea that enemy troops do not have to be killed or wounded; instead, they can be influenced not to pull (or to hesitate in pulling) the trigger, even convinced to abandon the battlefield, or their leaders can be persuaded not to send them into the combat zone in the first place. In the broadest sense psychological warfare encompasses all nonviolent activity that aims at realizing the state's goals. While regular military operations can have indirect psychological implications, such as the London Blitz in World War II, Intifada's psychological warfare, for instance, stresses nonviolence.

Psywar is a strategic weapon, or force multiplier. The side that applies it wisely gains a distinct advantage over the enemy. Psywar augments the fighting effort, and its benefits far outweigh the costs. Its outlay is much lower than that of violent combat activity, and it assumes the moral high road by avoiding human loss and material destruction and helping the parties end the carnage as quickly as possible. Put simply, psywar saves lives and resources. But it demands continuous, expert application alongside diplomatic activity. This is true for conventional wars as well as the LICs that Israel has faced in the last two decades. Civilian populations on both sides play a critical role as target audiences. Psywar's aims include boosting home front morale, galvanizing the nation's support in a conflict, and undermining enemy home front resistance and convincing it to end the hostilities.

The American communications theorist Harold Lasswell devised a concise formula for the media process: Who's sending the message? What is being said? What channel is being used? And, how effective is its influence? This formula is most useful for analyzing psychological warfare. The topics in this book are arranged according to psywar messages and themes, the party deploying psywar, and, of course, psywar's degree of influence (success).

Psychological warfare's importance is apparent at every stage of the conflict, and this reality has not changed in the last hundred years. For instance, even before hostilities erupt, psywar is used to convince the home audience of the need to go to war. When the enemy is far from the homeland, a different approach is taken as citizens demand to know why valuable resources are being spent in a distant campaign and why citizens are being asked to sacrifice their lives when the enemy is not physically endangering them.

In wartime, psywar has three main target audiences: the home audience, the enemy audience, and the neutral audience. The home audience has to be convinced of the war's justification; the enemy army has to be convinced that its chances of winning are zero, while the enemy's citizens have to be brought to realize the war's futility; and the neutral audience has to be co-opted as its support can be of crucial importance. Psywar units continue operating even after the war is over; their main task at this point is to counter the local population's natural hostility toward an occupation force. The message to be conveyed is that the foreign troops are in their territory only on a temporary basis and have no intention of harming them.

Basic Terms in Psychological Warfare

In the West, psychological warfare is linked to controversial issues such as propaganda, brainwashing, and demagogy, all of which tend to evoke strong antagonism. These concepts clash with the value systems of a democratic government, values that can be traced back to the French Revolution. Mass persuasion, for example, generally arouses mixed feelings in Western countries (including Israel). There are different expressions for "psychological warfare": psywar, propaganda, public relations, public diplomacy, *hasbara* (Hebrew), political warfare, and psychological operations (psyops).

Evolution of Terms in the Twentieth Century

The word "propaganda" was coined in the seventeenth century from the *Congregatio de Propaganda Fide* (Congregation for Propagation of the Faith), the Catholic Church's worldwide organization whose goal was to bring new believers into the fold. In South America, for example, the organization was responsible for proselytizing millions of native people, and, in this part of the world, propaganda still means "publicity" without a negative connotation.[2]

Great Britain entered World War I with an extremely limited propaganda machine. Prime Minister Herbert Asquith set up a mechanism known as the British War Propaganda Bureau whose goals were to win public support for the war, undermine the enemy's morale, and convince the neutral states—especially the United States—to enter the war on Britain's side. Asquith appointed a close associate, Foreign Minister Charles Masterman, an accomplished official, to head the bureau. Masterman believed that such a mechanism should operate far from the public eye and therefore set up the bureau in an unassuming office building known as Wellington House, a name that has since become synonymous with Britain's central propaganda machine.

After a change of government during the war, the British propaganda bodies reorganized, and novelist John Buchan was appointed head of the organization. His tasks included tracking enemy propaganda and producing films and newsreels. Another change soon followed—Lloyd George, the new prime minister, established the Ministry of War Information and appointed Harold Beaverbrook, a British newspaper tycoon, as director of the new ministry. Lord Northcliffe, another press baron and owner of the prestigious *Times*, headed the Department of Enemy Propaganda Affairs and served as Beaverbrook's subordinate (although the two men preferred to conceal the exact nature of the hierarchy).[3] In this way the British prime minister gained the support of the press, as well as a vast reservoir of creative thinking, foreign policy expertise, and the means to convey messages rapidly.

Twenty years later, with the rise of Joseph Goebbels' Nazi propaganda machine, the term "propaganda" took on a categorically negative connotation that continues till today. The British realized the crucial role that information played in attaining victory. Therefore, at the outbreak of World War II, they set up an effective mechanism but were careful to eschew the term "propaganda," preferring "political warfare" instead. During preparations for the invasion of Normandy (June 1943–June 1944), the Americans and British established a joint command and coined a new term: "psychological warfare." This term is still used when referring to activities that promote military interests in wartime.[4]

During World War II, the differences between the democratic and totalitarian regimes' application of psywar were readily apparent. In democratic regimes, founded on freedom of ideas and choice, citizens opposed centralized thought control and looked upon government attempts to influence their thinking as unethical. People in totalitarian regimes, in contrast, viewed propaganda as an inseparable part of government organization, where it was applied extensively for domestic and foreign needs.

With the advent of the Cold War, the United States had to face the problem of employing propaganda against the Soviet Union and Communist Bloc. Since the West associated "propaganda" with totalitarian regimes, the term had to be avoided at all costs, even if its advantages in the superpower struggle were unarguable. The semantic solution was to find a term with a positive connotation—such as "diplomacy"—while the organizational solution was to transfer the propaganda machinery to the area of clandestine activities. It was duly put under the Central Intelligence Agency (CIA) established in 1947 directly responsible to the president. In the same year, President Truman approved the creation of a new body—the United States Information Agency (USIA)—whose goal was to spread information overseas. This name was chosen in order to emphasize that, unlike the Soviet Union, the United States did not engage in "propaganda" but in conveying "information" to the target audience.

At the same time, the term "psychological warfare" began to go out of use. During the Korean War of the early 1950s, it referred to conventional military activity. Toward the end of the war, the US Army looked for a new term, one without a negative connotation, and decided that battlefield propaganda would henceforth be called "psychological operations" or "psyops." The army apparently believed that the word "operations" brought to mind a series of brief, local actions. The term "perception management" was considered but was dropped. Thus, the term "psychological operations" or "psyops" remained in use while the army continued to look for a better one. This is how applied anthropological skills are used to constantly update doctrines and manuals so as to communicate better with non-Western audiences ("human terrain" in army jargon). Interestingly, the latest development in US military doctrine reflects the ever-existing democracy's ambiguous attitude toward propaganda. The current usage dictated by the

Pentagon is MISO (Military Information Support Operations).[5] Officers in the field have expressed their displeasure with this vague terminology that leaves them unsure of which supports which. The term, they say, should have remained on Japanese restaurant menus.

Terms in Israel and the Arab Countries

In the years following Israel's independence, a debate raged over the official names of the nation's propaganda bodies. Aversion toward the appellation "propaganda" was strong because of the new state's democratic principles and the Jewish peoples' still-fresh memory of the Nazi use of the term. Nevertheless, given the vital role of information dissemination in foreign policy, the state agencies that engaged in "propaganda" fought bitter turf wars over authority and resources.[6] Finally a compromise was reached: the state would engage in public information and the secret agencies would deal with the clandestine areas of psyops (similar to the United States after World War II). Psychological warfare in military affairs was transferred to a small unit in Military Intelligence; the Mossad (Israel's equivalent of the CIA) was given charge of special tasks and the covert areas of information spreading; the Ministry of Foreign Affairs (MFA) was given responsibility for propaganda (*hasbara* in Hebrew)[7] in foreign countries and international organizations; the Jewish Agency dealt with *hasbara* in the Jewish world; and a new body, the Hasbara Administration (later, Merkaz Ha-hasbara), was charged with propaganda dissemination among Israel's citizens.[8] The name of this last body—the Hasbara Administration—reflects the stormy evolution of the term. Toward the end of the War of Independence, internal memos of the Israeli Defense Forces (IDF) still employed the term *ta'amula* (propaganda), as in "propaganda for the recruit," but, by early 1949, *hasbara* appeared as an alternative.

Interestingly, no term comparable to *hasbara* exists in other languages. Israel felt that the best way to enhance its image in the international arena was to "explain" its unique situation: rising from the ashes of the Holocaust, catapulted headlong into a bitter political and military struggle against Britain's Mandatory Regime, and then fighting for its life, or rather, birth, in a war of independence with the Arabs. In effect, Israel forced the term *hasbara* on the Jewish world and on everyone it came into diplomatic contact with. The MFA's information desk was named the Hasbara Department—a title that was kept until the 1987 Intifada. Since then it has undergone several organizational reshufflings, and today *hasbara* is a full-fledged directorate within the ministry and renamed Public Diplomacy. The World Zionist Organization, too, had a division called the Hasbara Department, but this was disbanded after a decade. *Hasbara* became a basic term in the Zionist lexicon, along with other terms such as *shaliach* (envoy) and *aliya* (immigration).

The Arab military lexicon contains a number of terms related to information. *Wizrat al-A'lam* refers to the Ministry of Information. In many Arab countries this ministry is part of the state machinery. The term *harb al-nafsia* is used in Arab armies to refer to psychological warfare. In the 1960s, the Palestinians embarked upon a methodical study of wars of liberation in countries such as Algeria, Vietnam, and Cuba, with the intention of applying some of the lessons to their own struggle. They termed this style of fighting *harb al-asabat* (guerrilla warfare). Even at an early stage in their struggle against Israel, the Palestinians seem to have tried to exploit the advantages inherent in psychological warfare.[9]

American Concept of Information Use in War

In the last decades of the twentieth century, the US Army made an impressive, systematic effort to develop a detailed, state-of-the-art combat doctrine. According to the new doctrine, psywar is part of information warfare, and is applied in conjunction with deception, electronic warfare, and cyberwarfare. The doctrine calls for an integrated system among all official bodies—civilian and military—that deal with information so that they operate in full coordination according to predefined objectives and in a way that serves the national interest. In order to work toward the same goal, the following bodies must operate along identical guidelines: the White House press officers, government officials, CIA, USIA,[10] psychological warfare units, and the untold number of public affairs officers in military units and agencies responsible for disseminating American culture around the world.

The principal document in this area is the US Army field manual *FM 3-13* that emphasizes the importance of information in modern warfare, and lays the ideological groundwork for its implementation within US strategy. The main aim of *FM 3-13* is information superiority through various activities, each of which has its own operational doctrine: psychological warfare, deception, electronic warfare, cyberwarfare (the defense, attack, and exploitation of information networks), and indirect activities that influence the military's relations with the media.

A second manual deals with the doctrine of applied psychological warfare.[11] The Americans are currently working overtime on producing an updated version of this manual to include the lessons learned in the Second Gulf War (2003). The manual sees American goals on four levels:

The strategic level: deals with the international arena. This is the responsibility of the president, the State Department, and other official bodies.

The operative level: prepares the target population for military action that only a superpower with international interests is capable of. The army is sent to areas of conflict and, as the 1992–1993 Somalia experience has taught, must prepare the local population for the US military presence so it will not be interpreted in a way that proves detrimental to the mission. Information is generally circulated by the senior military and political levels.

The tactical level: deals with standard psychological warfare on the battlefield, down to the individual unit level.

The consolidation level: prepares the civilian population in an occupied territory for the new reality.[12]

The US Army also published a doctrinal field manual, *FM 46-1 Public Affairs*, that details the rules the army must observe in contact with the media, based on lessons learned during the Vietnam War. The manual is predicated on two yardsticks: First, the media is not the enemy; on the contrary, it should be seen as the prime agent serving the interests of the American people and the army should assist the media in obtaining information rather than exploit it for propaganda dissemination. Second, the army has a key interest in providing accurate, credible information to soldiers' families and the American public as long as operational security is not compromised. The manual also defines the professional soldiers who are responsible for this public relations system. The public affairs officer (PAO) determines the guidelines for professional training and the rules for briefing commanders who appear before the press.

Commanders must be aware of the limitations and pitfalls of employing psychological warfare. First, updated, accessible "anthropological data" on the enemy's society and culture is absolutely necessary for identifying exploitable cultural and psychological codes that could bring the enemy or one of its groups to surrender. This type of intelligence also aids in identifying battle fatigue, general exhaustion from fighting effort, or tension between groups (for example, between junior and senior officers or between officers and civilians). Second, psywar's effective application requires special skills that are the product of professional training and experience. Third, ethical, ideological, and psychological obstacles in the West prevent peacetime use of psychological warfare because it is perceived as an unethical weapon of overwhelming influence that the government can wield to convey brief, hard-hitting messages to the enemy or its own citizens. Furthermore, Western democracies associate psychological warfare with controversial subjects such as propaganda, brainwashing, and demagoguery. Finally, the preference for physical combat and the public's ignorance of the effectiveness of psychological warfare give it low priority in both peace- and wartime.

Psywar messages can be categorized according to their source or signature: "white propaganda" refers to a source of information that is the same as its signature; "black propaganda" refers to the source of a message that assumes a false identity; and "gray propaganda" refers to the source of the information that is intentionally dissembled although its identity may be inferred.

The twentieth century witnessed dramatic advances in telecommunications for wartime message delivery. During World War I, the press was the main means of conveying psychological warfare messages to the home audience (and indirectly to the enemy). Messages reached the enemy on the battlefield via printed leaflets; in World War II, psywar messages were also transmitted by radio and newsreels; in the Vietnam War, on the television screen; in the War in Lebanon, via satellite; during the Intifada, by fax; and in the Second Gulf War (2003), by satellite telecommunications (satcom). The Palestinians have employed all of these media at one time or another (especially visual means), often through manipulation of the international media. In 2009, in Gaza, they took full advantage of digital social networking.

The main principles of psywar, as applied in the two world wars, are still relevant in the twenty-first century. The first principle is to make sure that the message is accurate. If the enemy discovers the message is false, it can demolish the entire lengthy and costly effort invested in credibility building. Therefore, the first and guiding principle is: keep to the truth, though not necessarily all of the truth. The second principle calls for quick, smart exploitation of opportunities, whether chance events or carefully planned initiated ones. The rule is to overwhelm the enemy with messages, just as massive firepower is used in conventional warfare, and not give it a chance to "raise its head" or deploy operationally, thus rendering the enemy incapable of response. The third principle is to employ methods designed to spark the interest of the enemy target audience through public relations gimmicks, such as stories allegedly based on the enemy's own reports; this is especially effective when accompanied with visuals. The fourth principle is to make maximum use of media technology such as the Internet, telephone, and satcom for message conveying, together with traditional vehicles such as leaflets and radio transmissions.

Unlike regular military systems, psyops can succeed if given the necessary logistical support. Herein lies the difficulty: psywar needs skilled academics and civilians in wartime much more than in peacetime, but recruitment is difficult because secrecy must be maintained and also because of unwillingness to allow new people into the exclusive club. Psychological warfare's involvement in political issues adds to the reluctance to engage in it, since armies prefer—at least on the declarative level—to steer clear of political affairs.

Resources have to be channeled into developing an operational doctrine, selecting and training professional manpower, and designing conduits for conveying messages to target audiences. But this is easier said than done. Developing a psychological warfare doctrine requires tough decisions on very serious issues: the nature of civil-military relations in the era of LIC, where traditional limitations and the familiar terrain of conventional wars are blurred; a high degree of cooperation among intelligence services and military and civilian secret agencies, where competition over prestige, turf, and resources tends to be keen; the establishment of television stations for transmitting messages to the enemy that raises the government's fear of losing its ability to control information transfer, which could undermine its own existence.

Basic changes have recently occurred in two vital areas of psywar. First, the nature of warfare: the era of massive battles has given way to the era of LICs and the war against global terrorist organizations. Second, mind-boggling technological advances have taken place in information dissemination, and psychological warfare, too, has to change if it wants to provide effective solutions to current and future challenges.

Dealing with the political elements of psychological warfare is especially vexing when it is waged by small organizations, such as radical Islamic groups, that lie beyond the reach of any state. These groups operate according to one basic rule: the lower the intensity of the conflict, the greater the need to convince the enemy audience that its chances of winning are nil. These groups' use of psychological warfare exhibits a profound understanding of Western media and culture in their extensive and clever ways of delivering messages. Ambitious, extremely innovative members of terrorist organizations operate at their full creative capacity, unhampered by bureaucratic restrictions, to apply psychological warfare to its maximum extent as an inexpensive, accessible, highly effective weapon. In contrast, organized states, bogged down by bureaucratic and other constraints, are hard-pressed to employ psywar effectively, despite their military and technological superiority.

Organized states must improve their mechanisms for waging psywar if they hope to deal with the dramatic changes in information dissemination. Low-cost, available technologies enable small groups with a handful of computers in the cellar to spread tendentious information on a global scale. Today's technologies have reached the stage where information can be accessed in real time from the very spot where it is happening. The downside of modern technology is that it facilitates the hostile takeover of communications channels through cyber invasion or invasive broadcasting via standard radio and television frequencies, which can then be used to convey inimical messages.

The main themes of US Army instruction manuals are the demand for and free dissemination of information—in both war- and peacetime—to the military and civilian population. This includes the need to keep the public informed of the war's progress. The best proof of this principle is the fact that all of the manuals are in the public domain on the Internet. There still remains a wide berth for maneuvering between the public's thirst for information and information manipulation for advancing military and political goals.

In the early 1980s, the US Army developed an ambitious and sophisticated mobile unit for analyzing and formulating information and producing and circulating messages. The unit, currently based at Special Forces Headquarters, Fort Bragg, North Carolina, is equipped with mobile, airborne printing facilities, a radio studio, and a television station, and can be rapidly deployed anywhere in the world. Its personnel are trained in photography, editing, broadcasting, graphic design, and printing in field conditions. The unit's job, which is to support combat units as the need arises, has previously operated in Panama, the two Gulf Wars, and Haiti, to mention but a few instances.

Until the First Gulf War (1991) many commanders were skeptical about the psywar unit's capabilities. When forced to allocate valuable assets, such as aircraft, for its application, they questioned its operational benefits. Solid proof was lacking that it actually induced the enemy's demoralization: no single determining factor had been isolated as the prime reason for the enemy's enervation during war, and no one could say whether this was due to psychological means such as messages, or military means such as heavy bombing. Uncertainty over psywar's effectiveness radically changed in the First Gulf War when nearly seventy thousand Iraqi troops surrendered to the coalition forces waving leaflets entitled "safe passage" that the Americans had circulated and which guaranteed protection to every soldier who gave himself up. The Iraqi troops surrendered even though their commanders prohibited possession of these leaflets and threatened heavy punishment if they were caught.

Since 1991, commanders in many armies have become increasingly aware of the need for the large-scale deployment of psywar units on the battlefield alongside the traditional fighting branches. The British, Italian, and German armies, to name a few, currently maintain large psychological warfare units. The US Army is still in the forefront of training and doctrinal development, and NATO countries as well as others are following suit.

CHAPTER 2

Principles of Psychological Warfare Management

The three basic elements in psychological warfare are the target audiences, the messages, and the means of delivery.

The Target Audiences

The three target audiences, in order of importance, are the home audience, the enemy audience, and the neutral audience.

The home audience is of prime importance because the state has to mobilize its resources in a conventional war and persuade its citizens of their duty to enlist in the armed forces and sacrifice their lives for their country. History shows that victory is unobtainable in a state that fails to convince its soldiers of the justification of the war's aims. Obviously then, the state needs to make an enormous effort in explaining to its citizens the life-or-death situation facing them and the ultimate sacrifice it justifies. Delivering these messages to the home audience is relatively easy since society is generally united in wartime (especially if attacked).

The enemy audience is made up of the army and the citizenry. Psywar operators seek to undermine the enemy troops' psychological base by convincing them of the futility of the struggle, and that the sooner the war is over the sooner conditions for them and their country will improve. The goal is to force the enemy to consider the dangers and wastefulness involved in pursuing a lost cause. To do this, the stronger party has to present facts and figures on the balance of military and technological power and combat experience between the two sides and their respective allies. The weaker party stresses its human assets, determination, and readiness for self-sacrifice as the deciding factors in the struggle. The former has to convince the latter of the pointlessness of the war, the ineffectiveness of a military solution, and the advantages of negotiating while asserting that only the wealthy profit and that the "average citizen" pays a terrible price when loved ones are lost or maimed and property destroyed. Enemy civilians can also be told that the army has failed in its responsibility to the troops (emphasizing, for example, that the officer cadre has acted irresponsibly or the troops were issued antiquated weapons). The aim is to drive a wedge between the civilians and the army that creates alienation and frustration, and eventually leads to a retreat from the goals first presented. In wartime, information receives wider dissemination than in peacetime because of the large number of rumors rampant on the front and even greater number circulating in the rear. Rumors are a key means of spreading information because they satisfy the insatiable hunger for news. They are also the byproduct of official censorship on information spreading.

One of the most common mistakes is speaking to the enemy target audience disparagingly or in threatening tones. Conveying a message effectively demands a profound understanding of the target state's social fabric and culture. In wartime many psychological factors are at play, such as irrationalism and emotionalism (anger at the physical damage to the state or sorrow at the loss of life). Therefore strategies that employ coarse, blustery threats are counterproductive and must be avoided. Delivering a convincing message to the enemy during wartime is also a challenge because soldiers tend to shun hostile information and the upper echelons take measures to block circulation of subversive information. In totalitarian regimes soldiers are threatened with severe punishment if found with enemy propaganda.

The effective delivery of messages calls for diligent intelligence gathering. Unlike traditional military intelligence (the enemy's size, location, weapons, combat proficiency, and intentions), psywar intelligence seeks out the enemy's psychological strengths and weaknesses, fears and motivations, which enable skilled psywar units to manipulate enemy behavior and response.

The reason for courting a neutral target audience not directly involved in the conflict is to win its support or at least prevent it from supporting the enemy. This is achievable if sufficient resources are invested. Psychological warfare perceives neutral parties as crucial target audiences and the world media as one of the main conduits for conveying messages to them. Therefore every state is interested in maintaining good relations with foreign journalists and editors—especially in wartime—in order to enhance its image. Later in the book, especially in the chapter on the Intifada, Israel will be shown to still retain an ambivalent attitude toward the "Gentiles." On the one hand, it regards them with apprehension and suspicion; on the other, it harbors an increasing desire to be close to them. This dualistic approach, combined with the fear of the media's power, has created in Israel a conscious disregard of and obtuseness toward the foreign media. The result is a perpetual state of organizational chaos, the clearest expression of which is the Government Press Office's low status in the eyes of foreign journalists.

The Messages

The standard, albeit erroneous, view is that propaganda deals with lies. However, the first lesson that the use of propaganda in the twentieth century teaches is the need to maintain credibility. Many propaganda agents have followed this rule by keeping as close to the truth as possible, though not necessarily presenting all of the truth. And truth, as is known, can be presented from various angles without flagrantly distorting it.

The themes conveyed by propaganda agents to the target audiences can be classified according to types. Some themes are universal, such as hatred of the enemy or "we have nothing against you, only against your leaders"; others are local, based on the dynamics of the battlefield or political arena. For example, the radical change in German-Soviet relations at the start of World War II after the signing of the Molotov-Ribbentrop Pact. Themes, too, can be classified: preplanned themes and those that develop in the course of the fighting, such as the "*Lusitania* Affair" (see below). In these cases meta-messages are conveyed to the target audiences. Themes to the home audience include: demonization of the enemy (the devil incarnate); defining and justifying the war aims; confidence-building in the ability of the government, nation, and armed forces to achieve the war's goals. To the enemy audience: driving a wedge between the leadership and citizens, and between the citizens and the army; inducing demoralization; undermining the legitimacy of the struggle; implanting guilt feelings in the soldiers; driving home the futility of the war. To the neutral audience: arguments for the justice and morality of the war; and, as stated, efforts to win its support, or at least prevent it from siding with the enemy.[1]

Another reason for targeting enemy soldiers is to cause them to surrender, desert, or at least hesitate before carrying out an order. Psyop operatives must approach the enemy with respect for their courage and willingness to sacrifice themselves, but at the same time point out the hopelessness of their situation. The message has to relate to the soldier's anxiety regarding their own life and the fate of their family if they are killed, badly wounded, or captured. A common argument is: "We have nothing against you, only against your traitorous leaders. Help us topple them and end the damned war."

The "safe conduct pass" is still the most common message delivered to enemy troops. First employed in World War I, the message was designed to convince the enemy combatant to surrender in an orderly way. The natural distrust that it generates is offset by printing leaflets that resemble official documents issued by senior commanders. To strengthen the leaflets' credibility, surrender instructions are written in both the soldiers' language and the language of the army circulating them (troops receiving the surrendering enemy will be able to read the message). Even if the leaflets do not cause mass desertion, they nevertheless contribute to the enemy's demoralization.

The primary goal of psywar operators is to get the enemy troops to read the message. A number of methods have been devised to achieve this: leaflets dropped on Japan in World War II were eagerly collected because they gave detailed information on scheduled bombing areas. Japanese leaflets to the Allies carried a pornographic picture on one side to entice the enemy to pick them up and in so doing be forced to read the message on the other side. Propaganda leaflets in the Vietnam War were printed to look like paper currency.

Psychological warfare's primary message is the iniquity of war. Since war involves the taking of life, various methods have been developed throughout history to overcome the natural aversion to shedding blood and turning peaceful humans into killers who obey a leader or cause: for example, by training soldiers to act on instinct rather than think things out for themselves.[2] Psychological warfare tries to sabotage the psychological state of the enemy soldiers, and cause them to rethink their conduct in the war and their existential situation in general (life's goals, debilitating wounds, captivity, and death). Psywar often employs meta-messages aimed at instilling guilt feelings. This type of message proved highly effective in the Vietnam War, where moral thinking and guilt pangs interfered with the American soldier's capacity to kill or maim, in effect neutralizing him. The messages must not demonize the enemy combatants or extend beyond their training (responding automatically in combat); instead, they must force them to weigh their conduct and view their counterpart as human beings like themselves.

In conventional wars, messages that elicit guilt feelings are hard to convey since civilian casualties are accepted as an unfortunate concomitant of large-scale battles. Also, in the technological age, heavy destruction rains down from afar (aerial bombings, artillery fire, and precision-guided weapons). In low-intensity conflicts, where battles are often a drawn-out series of brief encounters in close enemy contact, a guilt message is more applicable. Showing the enemy that an attack could have taken place elsewhere, far removed from peace-loving noncombatants, can expose them to human values such as not injuring civilians.

The main drawback in analyzing psywar messages is that, unlike in advertising, focus groups cannot be established in the first stages of the war. A focus group examines a message's effect on a target audience. In wartime this is done by checking the messages' impact on prisoners of war (POW) and collaborators. In the first stages of the fighting, all that can be done is to seek the advice and experience of academic experts, expatriates, or tourists.

Means of Delivery

Various means are used to convey messages to the target audiences. The home audience receives messages mainly from the media: (radio, television, and the press), lectures, music, and public advertising. The neutral audience, lacking an official position on the issues, is less accessible, and becomes the target of public relations gimmicks, such as roundups of foreign news in the local media and advertisements that put diplomatic, commercial, and cultural ties with the combatant state in a positive light. The enemy audience is the hardest to penetrate since it instinctively feels that every message beamed at it from the enemy is intended to erode the war effort. Therefore an effort is made to block the messages from reaching the army and civilians.

Delivery methods employed in World War I are still used: dropping leaflets from planes or dirigibles, and delivering them with artillery shells. As for aircraft, psywar operators and the air force seem fated to be locked in a perpetual struggle. Psyop officers want to scatter the leaflets over the widest possible area; the air force perceives the risk to its aircrews from anti-aircraft fire and enemy planes, and wants to be certain that the operation attains maximum effectiveness and justifies the danger. In World War II, the US Army partially solved this problem by means of a semantic ploy: the psywar units termed the leaflets "paper bullets" so that pilots could identify more easily with the mission. In the Vietnam War the US Air Force allotted special planes for this task. In the First Gulf War the effectiveness of psywar messages was no longer in doubt as proven by the surrender of tens of thousands of Iraqi soldiers who absorbed the messages on the air-dropped leaflets.

Nowadays Unmanned Aircraft Vehicles (UAV) can solve the problem once weapon carrying UAVs are transformed to carry leaflets.

Another conduit of dissemination is the international media, which is perceived as objective, credible, and persuasive. However, this method of message delivery depends on the enemy troops' and civilians' exposure to the foreign media, which is possible when journalists and editors believe in the legitimacy of the side delivering the messages and use their influence to slant surveys and editorials in its favor (claiming, of course, that their work is factual and impartial).[3] Since the end of the twentieth century, the global news channels and Internet have become powerful means for conveying messages to the enemy.

Another way of getting messages across to the enemy is through collaborators who oppose the regime or by creating the impression that the messages come from anti-government elements within the state. For example, during World War II the British intelligence department beamed radio broadcasts into Germany as though they were being read by a German officer from the back of a truck inside Germany who was explaining the catastrophic implications of Hitler's grandiose schemes and illusions. In reality, the announcer was a British citizen broadcasting from Britain. In another case, a German radio station disguised itself as a French station. During the First Intifada the Palestinians accused Israel of spreading leaflets in Arabic supposedly written by Palestinians and aimed at intensifying the internal debates. This method is called "black propaganda."[4]

Black propaganda is risky business since it is liable to damage credibility—the all-important asset of every message delivery system. Once credibility is blown, all the effort spent on information dissemination will have been wasted since the message will no longer be taken seriously. This is one of the strongest arguments against black propaganda. However, in extraordinary cases, when successfully applied, it can reap a windfall, and its use is reconsidered. Alternatively, a third party can be used for this type of psyops, and if a credibility gap between the source and the propagators is discovered, any links to the message can be immediately denied. In many cases black propaganda attracts psyops operators into using it because it demands a high level of skill and imagination. When talented, ambitious operators are keen on proving themselves, the lure of this type of propaganda increases.

Two other modus operandi are "initiating events" and "exploiting events." Initiating events means creating an event from scratch, such as staging a massacre. The Germans staged an attack by the Polish army which gave them the pretext to invade Poland in September 1939 and launch World

War II. A more recent example is the Hamas initiative to launch the "Turkish Flotilla." The attempt to break the Israeli naval blockade of the Gaza Strip was based on an attempt in the First Intifada to have hundreds of Palestinian deportees sail from Greece to Israel, thus simulating the voyage of the illegal Jewish immigrant ship *Exodus* from France to British mandate Palestine in 1947. The advantage of this method is that all of the elements are controlled by the initiator of the event. The disadvantages of discovery are credibility loss and the enormous effort wasted in a failed operation.

Exploiting events is an easier method. Events that are identified as having a strong persuasive potential can, with a slight twist, be effectively used in psychological warfare. In 1915 A patriotic German civilian minted a victory medal honoring the German U-boat sinking of the *Lusitania*, a passenger vessel that sailed the Great Britain-US line. The British re-struck the coin, minting hundreds of thousands of copies that demonized the Germans, picturing them as predatory beasts. The event and its skillful manipulation went far in getting the United States to join Britain's side in the war. Other examples are Israel's exploitation of opportunities to demonize the Palestinian public[5] after two of its reservists were lynched in Ramallah in October 2000; and Israel's publication of a picture of the baby Shalhevet Fass, who was shot by a Palestinian sniper in Hebron in March 2001. The initiative in the last case came from the settlers, and was later adopted by the government agencies.

During the twentieth century, psyop departments in intelligence branches waged a bitter struggle for power and prestige. All intelligence bodies—including the IDF's—implicitly believe that they alone know how to market their messages. Reality has proven otherwise. Not every skilled psywar officer understands that psywar demands methodical training and experience. Psywar officers must be blessed with perspicacity, imagination, creativity, organizational skills, persuasive power, and, above all, they must be profoundly knowledgeable in and sensitive to the enemy's culture. These skills, innate and acquired, will enable them to do their job efficiently.

CHAPTER 3

Psychological Warfare against the British in Prestate Israel (the Yishuv)

During the British Mandate in Palestine, the Yishuv waged psychological warfare against the British and Arabs. People intimately familiar with the enemy were in demand, and fortunately such individuals existed in large supply. The leaders of the Yishuv and paramilitary underground movements—David Ben-Gurion, Menachem Begin, and Avraham Stern—were well acquainted with European culture and the cultural codes of His Majesty's Government. The combination of effective persuasion tactics, military activity, and intimate knowledge of the Arabic and British cultures had a powerful impact on target audiences.

The Yishuv's Struggle against the British (1945–1948)

After World War II the British government refused to change its policy of enforcing severe restrictions against Jewish immigration to Palestine. HMG intended to continue the mandatory rule until an independent state with a large Arab majority was established.

There were three underground movements in the Yishuv. The largest, the Hagana, submitted to the authority of the Yishuv's elected institutions. The other two, Etzel (National Military Organization) and Lehi (Fighters for the Freedom of Israel, nicknamed "The Stern Gang by the British after its leader Avraham Stern), were smaller organizations that generally shunned the authority of the Jewish Agency (the prestate Jewish government) and for this reason were termed "dissenters." Etzel and Lehi adopted a radical policy against the mandatory government that was carrying out Britain's anti-Zionist policy. The dissenters proved to the British government and the people that the continuation of mandatory rule meant British political and economic loss and heavy toll on the lives of British troops and police officers.

Thus, the underground organizations escalated the military struggle. Some operations were carried out jointly by all three groups, as when they united during the Resistance Movement. The paramilitary movements blew up coastal radar stations, railroad tracks, and bridges, and attacked military installations and police stations across the country. In response, the British reinforced their troops, bringing the total number to ninety thousand. But the casualty rate continued to climb. The cost of maintaining military personnel became an increasingly heavy burden on His Majesty's treasury, especially during the severe postwar economic crisis. In effect, the underground movements practiced the revolutionary principle "from asset to liability," demonstrating that the cost of maintaining British rule in Palestine was greater than its benefit. At the same time the Yishuv intensified and radicalized its propaganda campaign. The British, who were considered "the liberators of the Nazi concentration camps in Germany," were now called "British Nazis."

The underground movements displayed considerable skill in the use of psychological warfare. Etzel was a small, underground movement whose headquarters was staffed with a few dozen fully employed members backed by a few thousand volunteer reservists, but the organization gave the impression of being widely supported by the Jewish public through the huge number of notices it posted on billboards and its intense propaganda campaign overseas. One of the leading *hasbara* activists was Shmuel Katz from South Africa. In a one-room Tel Aviv flat, Katz single-handedly set up a news service—the Irgun Press—that posted daily news updates on Etzel activity. English-, German-, French-, and Italian-language reports were aimed at foreign correspondents and news agencies.

The underground's other propaganda goal was to underscore Britain's inhumanity, while bringing home to Britain and America the Yishuv's determination to fight for independence. This was best expressed in illegal immigration to Palestine. This effort intensified at the end of the war, with Yishuv propaganda emphasizing the soul-felt yearning of the Holocaust survivors—some of whom were languishing in British- and American-run displaced persons (DP) camps in Germany and Austria—to reach Palestine and only Palestine. The illegal immigration struggle was accompanied by mass demonstrations and wide-scale public campaigns that had a powerful appeal to the media. For example, when underground pipelines announced the arrival of an illegal immigrant ship, hoards of Jewish citizens came to the beachfront and intermingled with the new arrivals, thus stymieing police efforts to apprehend and expel the newly arrived illegals.

One of the most tragic events in this period was the Hagana's sabotage of the deportation ship *Patria* in the Port of Haifa on November 25, 1940. The ship was assigned to transport illegal immigrants to a detention camp on the island of Mauritius in the Indian Ocean. The Hagana attached a mine powerful enough to sabotage the voyage by blowing a small hole in the hull that would delay deportation. However, since the vessel was barely seaworthy the charge ripped open a gaping hole that sank the *Patria* in minutes. Over 200 of the 1,800 illegals drowned. The Yishuv leadership lost no time in exploiting the event for propaganda gain. Even as the British were checking the explosive charge and circumstances surrounding the tragedy, the Hagana hastened to inform the media that the British had in fact sabotaged the ship.

Another incident that attracted world attention was the ship *Exodus 1947*. Yishuv leaders employed various tactics to embarrass the British and force them to alter their anti-immigration policy. The Zionist propaganda network exploited Britain's mistakes in the treatment of the refugees. The British seized the ship as it approached the shores of Palestine loaded with 4,500 illegals, but instead of deporting them to Cyprus—as they had done in the past—they returned them to Southern France, to their port of embarkation. The refugees refused to get off the ship, and the British responded rashly—either out of ignorance or unaware of the effect their action might have on world public opinion—and transferred the Holocaust survivors to DP camps in Germany, towing the vessel there by force. The Yishuv catered to the media's interest and exploited the event to the hilt. The Zionists claimed that the British had decided to finish what the Nazis had failed to do, stressing the Holocaust survivors' will-power and resolve to rebuild their lives in Palestine. The Yishuv's overarching message was that the Jews intended to establish their own state so that they would never again be victims of genocide.

When the "Biria Incidents" erupted, Yishuv propagandists aimed their messages at the domestic audience. Situated north of the mixed Arab-Jewish city of Safed in the north of Israel, the small Jewish settlement of Biria had been established in 1945 by religious soldiers from the Palmach (the Hagana's assault force). After the British discovered illegal weapons there, they proceeded to destroy the settlement. Thousands of youth from the pioneering movements reached the ruins and rebuilt the settlement three times despite the troops' repeated attempts to obstruct them. Eventually the British realized that their efforts were useless against the Yishuv's firmness of purpose and that the Zionists would never allow one of their settlements to be dismantled for political reasons. Since its inception the Zionist Movement has presented Jewish settlement on the Land of Israel as a basic principle that morally justified Jewish rule in the country and outlined the borders of the future state.

Etzel's and Lehi's attacks against British official agencies and military installations reverberated throughout Palestine and Britain. Especially troublesome was the Acco Prison breakout in May 1947, when Etzel succeeded in liberating twenty-seven out of forty prisoners from the most heavily guarded fortress in Palestine. In October 1946, Etzel also carried out an attack on the British Embassy in Rome, which succeeded even if it caused no damage, since it forced the British into taking stricter security measures at their overseas representations.

One of the primary tools that the three underground paramilitary movements employed for disseminating their messages was radio broadcasts. Each organization operated independently, but frequent searches made it incumbent on Etzel and Lehi to regularly move the transmitters to different hideouts. The broadcasts relayed their version and interpretation of events, inspirited the listeners, and urged them to join the underground ranks. Since it was assumed that British Military Intelligence (MI) was listening to the transmissions to glean information, it too became a part of the target audience, and portions of the messages were aimed at the British military and the political level in the country and abroad.

Billboards also served as a battleground between the Hagana and Etzel, and between the two movements and the British.

[explanation next to one placard said the following]

The Etzel placard: "Think about it!" was aimed at the hearts and minds of the British soldiers, explaining the futility of Britain's struggle in Palestine and the dangers to their own lives. British intelligence had beamed an identical message at German soldiers in World War II; the Vietcong did the same to South Vietnamese troops twenty years later. (The Jabotinsky Institute in Israel).

[explanation beneath a leaflet said the following]

An Etzel leaflet read: "Illegal Immigration and War"—a struggle for the soul of the Yishuv. The message on the lower right undoubtedly gave British intelligence room for concern.

[translation of a leaflet said the following]
"Illegal Immigration and War"

The arrival of the ship *Ben Hecht* with six hundred illegal immigrants of all political shades has put an end to the despicable acts of those boasting to be the ruler of this nation.

We, the organizers of illegal immigration that others [in the Yishuv] branded "anarchy," will continue our work. Unlike the do-nothings, we will not feed the nation an opiate of slogans: "Illegal immigrants will reach a safe haven because the truth is this that they may be illegal but they are not new immigrants. They are being forcibly deported by the oppressor to remote islands, and from there transported group by group according to the cursed Bevin-quota.

Illegal immigration—no matter who organizes it—is a historical vision that reflects the indomitable yearning of the nation's masses for their homeland. It also paves the way for the liberating forces who, when the day comes, will invade the shores of the homeland, battle-ready, in support of the forces fighting on the domestic front. But we must not lead the nation astray. In the present situation free immigration is banned, and the defenseless illegals lack the power to storm the gates.

The gates will be taken and the homeland liberated in a war that combines the Return to Zion, Combat, and Nation Building. The illegal immigrants will arrive = the troops will fight. This is our way.

The National Military Organization in Eretz-Israel
April 1947

Shmuel is waiting for a consignment of goods—victory is near

In its effort to win the attention and support of local and foreign readers, the Yishuv gave the widest possible coverage—with the help of sympathetic foreign journalists, most of whom were Jewish—to the destruction wreaked by British troops during weapons searches. Heartrending stories, accompanied by scores of pictures, had a powerful effect and hurt the British, who accused the Jews of exaggerating the extent of the damage.

In the struggle for legitimacy, the courts became a political battleground. The British brought the underground members to criminal courts for civilian felonies. The underground members, however, claimed that they were freedom fighters and should be tried in military tribunals where the punishment was indeed harsher, but where the court's status gave their struggle an aura of legitimacy. The trials provided scores of journalists with human-interest stories—the staple of every newspaper. Etzel and Lehi members waiting for the hearing argued that the courts lacked the moral and legal authority to try them for activity perpetrated against an occupation government. They sang Etzel national songs and belted out the *Hatikva* (Israel's national anthem) at every opportunity, especially when the verdict was being read.

In the United States, Hillel Kook, also known as Peter Bergson, a prominent Etzel leader, set up an extended network of front organizations that fought British rule in Palestine, collected donations, and drummed up Zionist political support from writers, journalists, and Hollywood personalities. Decades later, the Palestinians would adopt the same techniques, applying them on a much wider scale.

CHAPTER 4

Psychological Warfare in the Arab-Israeli Wars (1948–1982)

The War of Independence (1948–1949) witnessed little psywar activity. Both sides—the Arabs and the Israelis—were too busy fighting on the battlefield and incurring heavy losses (proportionally, the Yishuv paid a heavier price), and psywar seemed a relatively unimportant area of activity.[1] During ceasefires, the IDF concentrated on force building (establishing new units and absorbing equipment).

One event of singular psychological impact was the "Deir Yassin massacre"—about one month before Israel's declaration of independence. Even though Deir Yassin was neither planned nor designed to have a lasting psychological influence, what transpired was exploited to the hilt and became a turning point and major factor in the Palestinian Arabs' mass flight to neighboring countries. The incident occurred when Etzel forces tried to capture the village. After the fighting, many dead villagers—including noncombatants—were discovered. The Arabs claimed that the Jews killed 240 innocents; Israel avowed that the number was exaggerated, and in any case, many of them were undoubtedly killed in the heat of battle, caught in the crossfire. Reports of the number of casualties spread quickly, as did rumors that the Jewish forces were rapidly growing in strength. The cross-border flight that mostly the Arab middle- and upper classes had precipitated a few months earlier now engulfed Arab villagers and the urban lower class. The rumors were fanned by Hagana intelligence officers and Arabic-language radio broadcasts and ballyhooed the Yishuv's military might.

Once the IDF was officially established (late May 1948) a small psychological warfare unit was set up in the intelligence branch.

During the war the IDF circulated leaflets calling on Arab troops to return home, to cease fighting in a war that was not theirs. "Why die on foreign soil?" the leaflets asked. Other leaflets were dropped over Lebanon, the route that Iraqi and Syrian volunteers took on the way to the battlefields. One of its improvised operations was to play phonograph records at enemy troops. Phonographs were circulated in firing positions on the Jerusalem front. Israeli troops were warned about the enemy's likely response to the transmissions. Given the volume of Jordanian fire, the Israeli commander reported that the messages had struck home.

At first the psychological warfare unit caused something of an uproar in the army. One psywar officer complained that the material he had prepared failed to reach its target, and that leaflets being printed had to be cancelled because an air force officer claimed that fifty kilos of TNT was more effective than reams of paper.[2] In late 1948 the psywar unit's commander (with the rank of captain) wrote to Lieutenant Colonel Vivian (Haim) Herzog of the intelligence branch stating that he considered submitting his resignation because "they" were not letting him do his job.[3]

Another device that had not been intended for psywar but that produced a powerful psychological effect was the "Davidka" mortar, invented and manufactured by the fledgling Israel Military Industries. Davidka shells were shot off with a deafening bang and screech that petrified the Arabs. One Hagana commander in Jerusalem reported that he fired the contraption by transporting it all around the city (in the family car) to intensify the psychological effect.

The Arab armies carried out some psywar operations as well. The Egyptian army (probably recalling British army operations in World War II) dropped leaflets on a number of kibbutzim (collective farms) in the northern Negev (Nir Am and Yad Mordechai), urging the settlers to surrender and promising them safety and fair treatment. In addition to the linguistic grotesqueries, the authors were flagrantly ignorant of the target audience's culture. The starting point of the propaganda sheets was religious Islam: exhorting the settlers to lay down arms in the name of Allah. The target audience—hardcore socialist kibbutzniks reinforced with tough Palmachniks (assault troops)—was light-years away from a religious-based message, especially the religion of the enemy in wartime. Furthermore, ninety-six Jewish fighters who surrendered to the Jordanians at Kfar Etzion (south of Jerusalem) a few weeks earlier had been collectively shot after being called to stage a group photograph, an undoubtedly powerful psychological barrier against giving such a message a second glance.

The Syrians dispatched a similar leaflet in three languages—Hebrew, Arabic, and German—before their attack on Kibbutz Sha'ar Hagolan (south of the Sea of Galilee), apparently to the new immigrants on the kibbutz who came from Germany. It said the following.

> In the holy words of the Koran, I address the settlers and pledge responsibility to act according to these holy words. Our goal is to restore quiet, on condition that you act peacefully and surrender your lives, property and children.
>
> It was not our intention to start the war. Any resistance on your part will be in vain and will not last, and only if you try to destroy your food and supplies [sic].
>
> I entreat all of the inhabitants: lay down your weapons peacefully, hang out the white flag, and surrender your ammunition, mines and war equipment. Collect everything in one place, without destroying anything.
>
> Please obey these orders within one hour from the time you receive this leaflet.
>
> After that, anyone who has not obeyed will be considered a combatant.
>
> God says: "When attacked—respond with an attack—and you should know that God is on the side of the righteous." (Koran)
>
> The Great God Who Speaks the Truth

Propaganda Organizing in Israel

After Israel gained statehood, it continued broadcasting Arabic-language programs aimed at audiences in the neighboring countries. The programs gave Israel's version of security incidents which, in many cases, was very different from the reports in the Arab media. The Israeli broadcasts also conveyed various *hasbara* messages. The programs of the Arabic-speakers Eliyahu Nawi and Salman Dabi greatly influenced the development of psychological warfare in Israel. A look at the backgrounds of the two men is instructive in understanding the period.

Nawi was born in Iraq and, as a child, immigrated to Jerusalem with his family during the British Mandate period. In the 1940s he hosted an Arabic-language program on the Hagana radio station called *Sawt al Hagana* (Voice of the Hagana) in which he retold popular allegories and folk tales, and assumed the alias *Daud Abu Natur* (Daud the Guard) which stuck with him for the rest of his life.[4]

Dabi had been a police officer in Iraq, and in this capacity visited many places around the country. After reaching Israel he joined Voice of Israel's

Arabic-language division; and in the 1950s and 1960s broadcast a regular radio program called "*Ibn el rafidyn*" (The Son of Mesopotamia). The familiar, well-loved stories that he told had political messages attached to them. The show became a hit in the Arab world. Dabi reviewed the Arabs' defeat in 1948, the grievous mistake they would be making if they attempted a second round, and the attitude of Israel's Arabs and the Arab countries toward the Israeli government. Dabi used the indirect approach in presenting the "facts," telling well-known parables and yarns and letting his listeners draw their own conclusions. Nawi's strategy was to go, straight to the point, explicitly stating his messages. Both announcers were relegated to the sidelines as the Voice of Israel's Arabic-language division declined. This downswing was the result of the growing unimportance attributed to psychological warfare, whose material expressions were budget cutbacks, lower standards, and diminished resources.[5]

The structure of the Israeli intelligence community already crystallized into its present shape in the early 1950s. Various organizations fought tooth and nail in a turf war over areas of responsibility and budgetary allocations. Also at stake was the question of who was in charge of the Israeli image. The compromise that was reached had the Ministry of Foreign Affairs dealing with *hasbara* around the globe—the Jewish Agency handling it in the Jewish world, military intelligence engaging in psywar with the Arab armies, and the Mossad pursuing psywar through clandestine operations.[6] Information on IDF activity in psychological warfare is fragmentary, though it is known that courses and advanced studies were held in the 1950s. Declassified IDF documents include a translation of the popular book by the American propaganda expert Paul Linebarger (published in 1954) that was internally circulated to psywar military officers.[7] The Hebrew translated book, naturally, was classified "secret."

After numerous changes, a military unit known as "Hatzav" was finally assigned responsibility for keeping track of the Arab media (press, radio, and television). Until the mid-1970s Hatzav published a regular survey, *Propaganda Lines*, that analyzed the Arab media's views on Israel. After the Six-Day War, Israeli and Jordanian military intelligence reached an arrangement whereby each side transferred its respective newspapers to the other on a daily basis rather than going through the complex process of obtaining the other's editions. Thus, every day a surreal ceremony took place at the Allenby Bridge as both sides exchanged packages of newspapers. Data on the Arab world was collected for conventional intelligence needs, but produced very little designated intelligence for psychological warfare.

The Six-Day War

The Six-Day War was too brief for the use of psywar layouts. In the weeks leading up to the war, Voice of Israel broadcast Arabic-language "listener friendly" programs to Egyptian soldiers stationed in Sinai. Israeli doctors provided truthful professional advice on the treatment of snake and scorpion bites and other maladies endemic to the desert. The programs were designed to instill fear and heighten the stress in the Egyptian troops waiting for the eruption of hostilities.

A classic psywar move was Israel's handling of a conversation between President Nasser and King Hussein. On June 6 the two leaders discussed Egyptian-Jordanian coordination in a joint statement that said American warplanes had attacked their airfields. These reports created a major crisis between the Arab countries and the United States, and the Egyptians turned to the Soviet Union because of the alleged American intervention. The conversation was picked up by an Israeli eavesdropping unit but the head of MI, General Aharon Yariv, decided not to exploit it lest Israel's intelligence capability and modus operandi be exposed. Defense Minister Moshe Dayan disagreed, claiming that the importance of revealing the conspiracy and the fear that the Egyptians would indeed drag the Soviet Union into the war overrode all other considerations and therefore ordered the conversation publicized. This exposé had powerful repercussions, given the immensity of the intrigue and the prestige accorded to the Israeli intelligence community for its standout intelligence gathering. This was a textbook case of exploiting intelligence material for propaganda purposes.

After the war Israeli MI set up a special psywar infrastructure in the newly acquired territories. The members of the units organized tours for village elders (*mukhtars*) and other leaders to Israeli industrial plants and IDF installations, allowing them to gain their own impression of Israel's strength. This was the "golden period" in Israel's relations with the foreign media. The air force issued films of dogfights that showed enemy aircraft being shot down. The films were flown directly to the United States and broadcast on primetime over the major television networks. This was also the case for photographs and articles by journalists who accompanied the fighting forces.

The Egyptians broadcast Hebrew-language radio programs during the war, aware of their tremendous propaganda value. However the broadcasts were far from professional. The programs on Voice of Thunder from Cairo contained linguistic incongruities that sounded ludicrous to the Israeli listeners. The reports reflected wishful thinking more than reality. Once the audience—whether Egyptian or Israeli—realized that the vaunted victories were fictitious, they ceased taking the broadcasts seriously.

The Yom Kippur War (1973)

In the opening days of the Yom Kippur War the IDF spokesman reported that Israel had succeeded in blocking Arab forces, but made no mention of the enemy's surprise advances. This was the first time that official Israeli reports were so far removed from the reality on the ground—a style that until then had been attributed to the Arab media. When the mistake was finally revealed, the IDF spokesperson's credibility was seriously tarnished. Many foreign and local journalists criticized the IDF spokesman and his superiors for the damage they caused military-media relations. After the war, the parties responsible confessed to the inaccuracy of the reports. They stated in their defense that this had been done to instill high morale and confidence in the public and army, especially in the initial days of the war, given Egyptian and Syrian military successes. Such excuses convinced no one; irreparable damage had been done to IDF credibility. Some scholars claim that it has still not been restored.

During the war Voice of Israel announced that a Syrian officer of Druze background was summarily executed because of poor performance under fire on the Golan Heights. The truth was that a Druze officer had been killed in the battle. The IDF applied a psywar mechanism to drive an ethnic-religious wedge into the enemy camp—in this case between the Druze minority and Muslim majority serving in the Syrian army. This is a classic example of exploiting an opportunity. Some observers believe that an IDF eavesdropping unit picked up reports that a Druze officer had been killed and the Israeli psywar officer immediately realized the psychological implications of such information.[8]

The Egyptians corrected their mistakes in the Six-Day War by improving the Hebrew-language radio programs. During the 1973 war, scores of Israeli soldiers were taken prisoner. Egyptian announcers integrated top-quality pop music with letters allegedly written by the POWs. Israelis were mesmerized by these programs, in the hope of catching a glimmer of information regarding their loved ones.[9] This successful campaign had a major role in the mood of national depression in Israel; social unrest, topple of the government and the basis for an unending misjudgment of the "catastrophic defeat".

Operation "Peace for Galilee" (1982)

After a long period of tension in the north of Israel, which culminated in the attempted assassination of the Israeli ambassador in London by Palestinian terrorists, Israel launched Operation "Peace for Galilee" (later known as the First Lebanon War). The assassination attempt was the *casus belli* that Israel had been seeking for months to expel the Palestinian terrorists from Lebanon and establish a Christian pro-Israeli government—Israel's grand design to solve its problems in the north.

Psychological warfare was also taken into account in the general preparations. The Ministry of Foreign Affairs prepared information kits for correspondents and set up a mechanism of reservist escort officers to give briefings and provide information. Despite this, there was no serious place in IDF plans for psychological warfare per se. A successful tactical move was the distribution of leaflets from aircraft calling civilians to move away from the residence which indeed cleared the roads for IDF vehicles. However, military intelligence emphasized the importance of operational data collection on Palestinian terrorists and the Syrian army, but not the application of psywar against them.

The main players on the psywar front were the Palestinians, who took full advantage of the IDF commanders' insensitivity and the absence of information. After gaining control of Beirut, IDF commanders permitted Christian militiamen to enter the Palestinian refugee camps of Sabra and Shatila to search for terrorists. The operation quickly turned into a massacre of civilians and the IDF commanders reacted slowly to reports of Christian Phalange score settling. Valuable time was to pass until they took steps to halt the carnage. The Palestinians charged that Israel was responsible for the massacre, and in a successful media campaign they swayed public opinion in the West, and even in Israel, to believe that the guilty party was not the Christian militiamen who perpetrated the massacre but obtuse IDF officers along with Defense Minister Ariel Sharon.[10] Foreign correspondents posted to Lebanon in the 1970s and early 1980s led the criticism against Israel.

Israel fell asleep on the watch in the Lebanon War and missed the development of a major process. The Palestinian Liberation Organization (PLO) had progressed far in enhancing its media capabilities and establishing a multi-branched network of contacts with the Western media in Lebanon.[11] The Palestinians reaped the harvest of their close ties with the media in the coming years, especially during the First Intifada in 1987, and the international media became the main conduit in the PLO's psywar campaign to convey their messages to the target audiences.

CHAPTER 5

The War between Israel and Hezbollah in Southern Lebanon (1985–2000)

The struggle between Israel and Hezbollah (the Party of God) between 1985 and 2000 was characterized by asymmetry: Israel was a regional superpower; Hezbollah could field five hundred fighters on the ground, backed by three thousand more on the home front. The power gap narrowed as Iran pumped massive technological and organizational aid into Southern Lebanon and Hezbollah applied increasingly sophisticated psychological warfare. During the decade and a half campaign, the Shiite organization combined guerilla activity with psywar and succeeded in creating a political climate suited to its interests: getting the IDF to withdraw from Lebanon and destroying the Israeli-supported South Lebanese Army (SLA). This was a textbook case of applied psychological warfare in a low-intensity war.

Historical Background

Lebanon, independent since 1941, is a multi-ethnic, multi-religious country whose population is made up primarily of Shiite and Sunni Muslims and Maronite Christians. In 1926 the three major communities agreed on a tripartite government when they signed a "National Pact" that allotted the post of prime minister to a Maronite Christian, the presidency to a Sunni, and chairmanship of parliament to a Shiite. The last group, concentrated in the south, was for many years relatively neglected in the distribution of government assets and budgets.

When Ayatollah Khomeini came to power in early 1979, Iran openly intervened in Lebanese affairs by sending Shiite clerics to the south. This involvement was preceded by grassroots preparation under the guidance of Sheikh Musa Sadr, a cleric who had been educated in Iran and who went to Lebanon in the 1950s. Sadr united the fractured Shiites and established a political infrastructure in 1975, the "Amal" (Hope) Movement, which evolved from a military arm to a political group that facilitated the Shiites' integration into government. Sadr's decision to turn to politics came from his sober realization of the Shiites' military inferiority vis-à-vis the Christian phalanges, witnessed during the Lebanese Civil War.[1] Sheikh Sadr disappeared under mysterious circumstances during a visit to Libya in 1978.

In response to the shelling of Israeli settlements, the IDF attacked Southern Lebanon. The largest military action, Operation "Litani," took place in March 1978. When the IDF withdrew, it left a few border enclaves under the command of local Christian militiamen. Four years later, following a long spate of rocket and mortar fire, the IDF launched Operation "Peace for Galilee" whose aim was to oust the Palestinian terrorist organizations from Southern Lebanon. In 1983 the IDF drew back from Beirut to an area south of the Awali River, and in 1985 withdrew to Israel, leaving a security strip in Southern Lebanon that the SLA (three thousand soldiers under the command of Christian officers) was responsibility for. Israel equipped its allies, trained them, and paid their salaries. The main source of SLA manpower was the Christian population of Southern Lebanon, which joined the ranks out of political, security, and economic interests. Some Shiites also volunteered—a small number that grew over the years and admittedly some were coerced as well. One of the basic problems with some SLA Shiites was their loyalty, which ranged from passive approval to active support of Hezbollah.

The first group in the south to resist Israel's occupation of Lebanon was Amal that had ballooned into a large force under the patronage of Iran and Syria. Amal was followed by Hezbollah, the umbrella organization of the religious Shiites that submitted to the religious authority of Khomeini. With the help of the Iranian government, the Lebanese Shiite ideological factions and military organizations united in 1982[2] into the Iranian branch of the Islamic Revolution, which was part of a worldwide endeavor. The Islamic revolutionaries perceived the struggle against Israel (the "Little Satan") as the initial stage in the larger struggle against the United States (the "Great Satan"), and a key link in the Islamic struggle for world hegemony. Aided by Iranian military instructors, veterans of the

Revolutionary Guards, Hezbollah crystallized into an extremely capable guerilla force. The organization proved itself highly proficient in applying guerilla principles, exploiting its intimate knowledge of the area, and maximizing local support.

In the 1990s Hezbollah intensified its attacks against the IDF and SLA troops. The high rate of losses and damage that it afflicted boosted its fighters' self-confidence and induced them to undertake increasingly audacious strikes. In parallel with this, Iran escalated its involvement in the region, transferring sophisticated military equipment to Hezbollah via Damascus. Hezbollah displayed impressive cognitive flexibility in planning and carrying out operations and devising solutions to whittle down the IDF's technological superiority. For example, to counteract Israel's state-of-the-art night vision devices based on thermal sensors, Hezbollah fighters donned scuba wetsuits.

Hezbollah's answer to Israel's military might came from its ability to obtain quality intelligence—military, political, or psychological—by exploiting family ties among the Shiites serving in the SLA, applying pressure—blackmail and threats—and making them and their families pay dearly if they failed to cooperate.[3] In addition, the organization recruited agents inside Israel, including Bedouin trackers serving in the IDF who were often recompensed with generous amounts of drugs.

Hezbollah's Psychological Warfare

Methods

Hezbollah applied two principles of guerilla warfare in ejecting Israeli forces from Southern Lebanon. The first, "from asset to liability," made Israel realize that the high price of the ongoing occupation was disproportional to the advantages of remaining in Lebanon. Hezbollah struck in three areas: in the military sphere—killing and wounding soldiers, destroying equipment, upsetting the training schedule and IDF war preparations, demoralizing the army, eroding Israel's self-confidence, and chipping away at deterrence; in the psychological sphere—undermining the Israelis' self-image; and in the main sphere, the political arena—marring Israel's image in the world and diminishing the government's and army's image in the eyes of its citizens.

The second principle that guided Hezbollah was winning hearts and minds; that is, gaining the trust and support of the population of Southern Lebanon by addressing their basic needs in security, employment, and social services. The natural growth and urbanization of the Shiite population created unemployment hubs that were ideal breeding grounds for recruitment into the resistance organization. In this way, Hezbollah picked up new members in the south by offering higher salaries than Israel did for serving in the SLA. In addition, it set up health, education, and welfare systems for all the inhabitants of Southern Lebanon regardless of religious, ethnic, or political background, and repaired homes damaged by Israeli military activity.

The aim of Hezbollah activity was to impose on Israel a different military agenda. Indeed, following a string of successful guerilla actions against the IDF and SLA, the Shiite organization forced Israel to beef up its military deployment, invest huge sums in defensive strongholds, and increase its involvement in Southern Lebanon, which, according to the original plan, was supposed to be the SLA's job. Hezbollah applied one of the cardinal rules of guerilla doctrine: instead of capturing (in this case, reclaiming) territory, the focus was on killing and maiming enemy troops (which was especially effective given Israel's acute sensitivity to losses and the enormous psychological effect it produced). For every society the death of a soldier is a painful event, but in a small, closely knit state like Israel its impact was much greater.

One of Hezbollah's most effective tactics was its attempts—occasionally successful—to kidnap soldiers. The organization realized that the redemption of prisoners of war was deeply engrained in Jewish tradition and Israeli culture,[4] and it exploited this emotionally charged issue to the hilt. Thus, negotiations over the release of Adi Avitan, Benny Avraham, and Omar Sawaid, three IDF soldiers abducted on Mt. Dov in 2000 became an effective tool for applying massive psychological pressure on Israeli society. Up until the last minute Hezbollah withheld any information of the soldiers' fate, and in this way it played its bargaining chips for all they were worth.[5]

Exploiting abductees was not a new ploy for Hezbollah. It had experience in wielding this trump card since the 1980s. The exhaustive efforts invested in attempting to release the Israeli airman, Ron Arad, who was captured when his aircraft went down over Lebanon in 1986, is an example of the political profit that can be reaped from such activity. Since then Israel has been trying in vain, using all its public and covert connections, to gain a scrap of information as to the airman's fate. By causing Israel such consternation and expenditure, a relatively small Islamic revolutionary organization has gained top billing on the world stage.

Another guerilla tactic that Hezbollah improved upon was to subordinate the fighting to the visual medium; in other words, it adopted a policy of "no photo—no victory." The Shiite organization proved that it could reap a windfall with the effective use of creative imagination and simple gadgets, the camcorder being the main tool. Assault units that embarked on a mission were accompanied by a photographer who recorded the operation up close. The jagged movement in the filming due to the terrain was of minor importance compared to the drama and realism of the documented life-and-death struggle. In retrospect, Goebbels, the Nazi minister of propaganda, was the first to send photographers to the front lines as an integral part of the war-fighting doctrine. Hezbollah's innovation was that in many cases the filming itself, rather than the military outcome, was the goal of the mission.

The material was brought directly from the battlefield to *al-Manar*—Hezbollah's television station—and screened along with commentary and victory music. The camcorder is used to capture reality in a selective fashion, which is why Hezbollah attributed enormous symbolic significance to these operations. For example, in the attack on the Rotem Stronghold in Southern Lebanon in May 2000, Hezbollah fighters succeeded in briefly planting the organization's green and yellow flag on the roof of the fortress before being repelled. Symbolically and propagandistically, broadcasting the image of the Shiite flag waving on top of an IDF stronghold repeatedly reaped great benefit, though the raid ended with Hezbollah's withdrawal. The organization's close ties with the media enabled it to make immediate contact with the purveyors of Middle East news after the attack and gain media coverage in a series of interviews in which the organization's leaders conveyed their triumphant message to the public. Hezbollah is fully aware of the media's appetite for battlefield images, and when such material is unavailable it has no qualms about reprocessing old or staged material.

Target Audience

Home Audience. The goal of propaganda is to gain as much public support as possible and convince the home audience that today's suffering is only temporary and worth the price of victory. Hezbollah acted on this principle, merging religious motifs into the speeches it addressed, first and foremost, to the underprivileged Shiite public of Southern Lebanon. But it also directed its message to the Christians and Sunnis in the area, promising that Israel's presence in Southern Lebanon would be short-lived and that Hezbollah was the force they could count on. This persuasion campaign was backed by brutal acts of terror (death threats and assassinations) against political opponents and SLA supporters. Moreover, as stated, Hezbollah set up health, education, welfare, and religious institutions, intensive activities designed to chalk up political and propaganda points for the organization and create a mechanism to supplant the Israeli institutions that had replaced the Lebanese ones. Hezbollah showcased its military strength in parades through the districts it controlled in Beirut and the Beqaa Valley. It adopted the interpretation that Iranian Islamic clerics had bestowed on the Shiite religious ceremony—the *Ashura*. In the original ceremony, Lebanese Shiites mourned the death of Hussein ibn Ali (Muhammad's grandson and successor designate) and identified with his anguish by symbolic blood-letting, whereas the Iranian religious leaders whipped the masses into Iranian-style frenzy in an ecstatic ceremony of public self-flagellation and blood-flowing in the street. Hezbollah institutionalized this version of the rite endowing it with a deterrent message: "We are fanatics, ready to sacrifice our lives for our goals. Don't tangle with us!"

SLA Soldiers. Hezbollah identified the SLA's weak points: factionalism, enlistment due to economic constraints rather than ideological motivation, and, occasionally, even forced conscription. It opted for psychological warfare in order to deepen the soldiers' doubts and concerns. The organization's intelligence mechanism was assisted by the local population, which furnished it with valuable tactical data, and even recruited spies within the ranks of the SLA. Hezbollah instilled in the inhabitants of Southern Lebanon the sense that it knew everything that was happening in the region. This went far in demoralizing the SLA. For example, it publicized the names of SLA officers and threatened them with severe punishment if they did not defect. It identified and exploited the apathy and dissatisfaction in the SLA for its own needs by announcing that SLA deserters would receive clemency and generous financial compensation. It also published the names of the deserters, which further dispirited those who remained. When opposition mounted in Israel to pull out of Lebanon, Hezbollah enhanced its messages in Southern Lebanon with excerpts from interviews with Israeli politicians who supported the withdrawal. Added to this, the organization relentlessly assailed SLA troops with the message that they were "traitors to Lebanon" and that Hezbollah was acting in conjunction with the Lebanese government in putting many former SLA soldiers on trial for treason in military courts. The accused were sentenced in absentia. The main message that Hezbollah drove home was that Israel would eventually withdraw and abandon the SLA. To substantiate its claim it asked its audience to recall the IDF's evacuation of Palestinian territories following the Oslo Accords that left Arab collaborators on their own.

The Enemy Target Audience. Hezbollah's strategic goal was to convince Israel's decision-makers through indirect pressure to quit the security zone in Southern Lebanon. It tried persuading different elements in Israeli society with messages that answered the expected counter-arguments. The bitter debate in Israel over its presence in Judea and Samaria (the West Bank territories captured in the Six-Day War from Jordan) made it easy for Hezbollah to market arguments against Israel's presence in Southern Lebanon to those groups that opposed Jewish control of Arab populations. At the same time, Hezbollah waged a guerilla war against the IDF and SLA that was geared to the psywar campaign by inflicting heavy losses and demonstrating Israel's inability to supply an effective military response. Hezbollah's goal was to ingrain in IDF soldiers and officers the sense of futility in persisting in a campaign against a small, well-trained, tenacious enemy. The organization knew that Israeli reservists were the Achilles heel of the IDF and that inflicting casualties among them would have the strongest repercussion in Israeli society. The IDF, too, was aware of this and in the late 1990s sent only conscript units for operational duty in Southern Lebanon. Hezbollah's main tactic was to single out officers and it made a supreme effort in intelligence gathering to attain this goal. Its success rate in officer killing—the first victim (March 1999) was Brigadier General Erez Gerstein, the commander of the IDF Liaison Unit in Lebanon in charge of the security zone—implanted in the target audience the sense that Hezbollah—and not Israel—had control of the area.

The Neutral Target Audience. This effort was aimed at Western countries like the United States and Arab states that were not directly involved in the conflict, but that had a fluctuating degree of influence on it. Hezbollah devoted its least amount of attention to this audience.[6]

The Messages[7]

Hezbollah addressed the diverse audiences with messages that integrated Iran-inspired Islamic motifs and secular-revolutionary elements (taken from the ideological lexicon of twentieth-century national liberation movements).[8]

Internally Directed Messages

Unity against a Common Enemy. The aim of the message was to calm the population's concern over Iranian meddling in Southern Lebanon's social and political affairs after Israel's withdrawal. Hezbollah presented its own leadership as the standard bearer of the national struggle against Israel and the representative of all Lebanese ethnic and religious groups whose goal was to expel Israel from Lebanon. The most effective way to inculcate its message was to downplay its real political aim—the establishment of a Lebanese Islamic Republic; therefore, it guaranteed the people of Lebanon the freedom to elect their regime without any foreign interference.

Jerusalem. Jerusalem was a unifying theme because of its importance in Islam (the third holiest city after Mecca and Medina and, according to the Muslim tradition, the site from which Muhammad ascended to heaven), though it is not mentioned in the Koran. Jerusalem's sanctity grew with the intensification of the Arab-Israeli conflict. In 1980, in order to remember that Jews still occupy the Holy City, Khomeini pronounced "Jerusalem Day" to be held on a key religious date—the last Friday of the fast of Ramadan.

Justification of the Cause. The justification was that the struggle (against Israel) was just and, therefore, the Hezbollah would emerge victorious and Islam would defeat the infidels.

"A Promising Future." This theme was a corollary of the previous one and underscored the idea that suffering in the present was a small price to pay for attaining the sublime ideal of an Islamic Republic and free Lebanon.

The Long-Term Struggle. The explanation for a long-term struggle was that though they may be weak compared to the enemy, one day the Hezbollah would emerge victorious. Until then the population would have to be patient and put its trust in the leadership.

Demonization. Hezbollah conveyed the message that Israel was linked to Satan on two levels. On the ideological level, in anti-Semitic motifs, the Jew was a treacherous, blood-sucking leach; and on the moral level, that Israel brutalized innocent people. For proof it presented television viewers and Internet surfers with uncensored pictures of Lebanese civilians horribly wounded by Israeli bombings. The audiences were shown mangled limbs and dead babies.[9]

Victory is the Will of God. The message from the leadership read: "At the end of the struggle we will expel the Israelis from Southern Lebanon, and in the second stage enter Jerusalem as the victors. This is the will of Allah." Be this as it may, the organization downplayed the second part of the message—the dream of retaking Jerusalem—so as not to strengthen the voices in Israel that opposed unilateral withdrawal.

Messages to the Enemy

Willingness to Sacrifice. The willingness to sacrifice their lives and property until the final goal was attained was the main theme of Hassan Nasrallah, the leader of Hezbollah, whose son Hadi was killed while fighting in Southern Lebanon in September 1997. The suicide bombing campaign and the videotapes of the martyrs before they set out on their final mission heightened the sense of Hezbollah determination.[10]

A Protracted Struggle. The power gap with Israel is undoubtedly large, but because of the will to make long-range sacrifices Hezbollah will emerge victorious. Just as Moslems triumphed over the Crusaders and Mongols, so will Israel go down in defeat.[11] This message was also aimed at the home audience.

The Futility of Defense. Hezbollah's main theme was that the IDF's efforts—no matter how technologically advanced—would prove futile in protecting its troops. This theme, reinforced by numerous military actions (in which Hezbollah introduced significant changes in its methods of attack and ambush, and choice of targets and weapons), was followed by the IDF's intensified efforts to improve the defense of its strongholds and troop movement.

A Defined Political Goal. "Leave Lebanon, we demand nothing else of you"—this was a rational political slogan intended to give ammunition to those enemy's supporters advocating a pullout. In order to strengthen its main principle that "the war is only about liberating Lebanon from the yoke of occupation," Hezbollah temporarily put its declared goal of retaking Jerusalem on the back burner. As Israel's withdrawal date approached, the Shiite organization kept its artillery fire in the north of Israel to a minimum.[12]

Accusation. From a historical point of view this was the most effective means. Its goal was to plant guilty feelings in the enemy that would plague its conscience with second thoughts before every operation and delay the natural response of the soldiers. These feelings were exacerbated by televised pictures of civilians severely injured by Israeli shelling.

"The Lebanese Mud." was an effective metaphor that captured the imagination with its idea that: "Since you will eventually be leaving Lebanon, why prolong the senseless agony." The message's historical roots were naturally exploited—every foreign conqueror in Lebanon had been defeated.

Hizballah's Messages to the Neutral Audience[13]

Human Rights Violations. Israel has violated basic human rights by its occupation of Southern Lebanon and its operations against civilians. As an example, Hezbollah pointed to the el-Hiam prison where Lebanese prisoners were held without trial.

Hizballah's Means of Dissemination

Conveying messages to the various target audiences grew steadily more sophisticated. The primary means of the revolutionary groups in Lebanon (beginning in the mid-1980s) were periodicals aimed solely at Lebanese citizens (Hezbollah lacked an English-language newspaper). The organization also set up three radio stations: the most popular was al-Nur (The Light), followed by The Voice of Islam and The Voice of the Oppressed. The key media vehicles were the two Lebanese television stations, al-Manar (The Lighthouse) and al-Fajar (The Dawn),[14] that were beamed in Arabic to the home audience, and the monthly journal *Kabdat Allah* (The Fist of God). Beginning in the mid-1990s Hebrew-language programs were also aired and aimed at the troops in the strongholds.

Psywar's weak point is that it cannot force the target audiences, especially the enemy, to listen to the messages. To overcome this obstacle Hezbollah did what armies have learned to do ever since World War I: broadcast programs that the enemy is naturally drawn to. Hezbollah captured the Israeli public's interest by combining pop music with information on the course of the fighting in programs that were replayed at frequent intervals. Israeli Military Intelligence was the main consumer of these messages, followed by the Israeli media and military journalists, especially correspondents for the territories and Arab affairs. For its home audience, Hezbollah conveyed information that concentrated on events in Lebanon.

Hezbollah's reliable reportage of its successful operations against the IDF posed a serious dilemma for the Israeli media, as the credibility of its own correspondents was called into question (the American media experienced the same problem in the Vietnam War in the 1960s, a dilemma that climaxed in the First Gulf War). News reporters deliberated over what was more important—loyalty to the state or viewer rating. Other issues that suddenly surfaced were: the media's limitations, who determines them, and whether the nation's morale in wartime be maintained at all costs. The rivalry between Israel's television stations also found its way into the debate for a brief period when, for the sake of ratings, the networks decided to telecast Hezbollah's previously televised pictures. Although the pictures were of low quality they ensured a high rating because they were the only uncensored material being shown. The Israelis watched them with a mingling of abhorrence and fascination: soldiers stumbling into an ambush, an IDF vehicle being blown up by an improvised explosive device (IED), or a stronghold being overrun by masked Hezbollah fighters. The video clips were aired continuously and created a cumulative psychological impression in the Israeli public that Hezbollah was unbeatable; the organization could not have asked for more.

Another channel for disseminating messages was the Internet. The image of Hezbollah as a band of illiterate Shiite villagers was proven false by the high quality of its Internet sites. Israelis who browsed these sites were treated to gory videos of military operations. Israeli and Lebanese Internet surfers soon confronted each other in cyberspace and tried to sabotage each other's sites. The clash ended when the speaker of the Knesset, Dan Tichon, called on Israeli surfers to cease their cyber attacks.

Israel's Psychological Warfare

Target Audiences

There were four types of audiences, each of which had different messages addressed to it.

The Enemy Audience. Israel wanted to convey messages to different enemy audiences: Hezbollah's supporters—to convince them to stop supporting the organization; Hezbollah activists—to warn them of the dire consequences if they persisted in attacking Israel; and the rest of the inhabitants of Southern Lebanon—to make it clear that Israel was a powerful and stable pillar in the region that intended to remain in Lebanon for a long time and help them, and had no intention of abandoning them to their fate.

The Home Audience. The government had to convince its own citizenry that the price being paid for Israel's presence in Southern Lebanon—the loss of life and the tarnishing of Israel's image at home and abroad—was justified; these were key issues in the public debate. The government defended its Lebanese policy by insisting that it was the most effective way of protecting the Galilee from Hezbollah attack.

The Neutral Audience (the United States and Western Europe). Israel gave little thought to *hasbara* in these countries, and rebutting the information that Hezbollah conveyed. A major incident was Israel's shelling of the Lebanese village of Kafr Qana in 1996 and the loss of civilian lives. This tragedy sparked great interest in the foreign media, forcing Israel to terminate a large-scale military operation.

SLA Members and Potential Supporters. The messages to this group were that Israel was a trustworthy ally, that it had a blood pact with SLA troops who were putting their lives on the line to protect the northern cities, that Israel was committed to the long-term support of the SLA; and that its special relationship with SLA was based on mutual security interest rather than on cultural or voluntary interests.

Means of Dissemination

A sovereign state finds it relatively easy to convey messages because its access to the media is unlimited and its citizens generally take the information to be credible. The Arab states complained that Israel's Arabic-language television functioned as a propaganda tool. But, until the establishment of the Palestinian Authority (PA) in 1994–1995 and the inauguration of Arab satellite transmissions, the Israeli broadcasts had a high rating among the Arabs living in Israel, as also among the Arabs in the territories and neighboring countries (including Lebanon). This was proven by the mounds of letters and answers to quizzes that reached the station. The extreme anger that Syrian Defense Minister Mustafa Tlass expressed in his book, *The Israeli Invasion of Lebanon*, testifies to the Syrians' acknowledgment of the powerful influence of the Arabic-language "Voice of Israel."[15]

In addition to its TV programs, Israel, like all of the rival factions, also used an alleged Lebanese radio station, Voice of the South, to get its messages across. Another means of dissemination was leaflets, a tried and tested system for addressing the enemy audience, especially as thousands of copies could be printed quickly and dropped on the target audience (Israel had absolute air supremacy). Israel's good relations with the inhabitants of Southern Lebanon enabled the leaflet makers to integrate the latest themes and slang into the messages, which facilitated their absorption. But the main drawback of this method was that the target audience could not be forced to read the message.

An example of a successful message was the film taken by an Israeli attack helicopter of the targeted assassination of a senior Hezbollah figure traveling in his car. Although the operation failed, Israel still scored high propaganda points. The film was screened on Israeli television and had all the elements of a spellbinding thriller movie-computer game: a helicopter swooping through valleys and gorges, zeroing in on a vehicle wending its way through village paths, then the helicopter stabilizes, launches a missile that hits the vehicle but the driver jumps out and flees. The message was clear: Israel has the technological know-how and determination to find and destroy its enemies.

The Reasons for Israel's Failure

The Organizational Factor

The reasons for Israel's failure in the psychological warfare campaign can be traced back to structural problems in government and society that are not unique to its struggle in Lebanon. While Israeli politicians made full use of the media to advance their political agendas, they attributed little importance to a psywar campaign's potential in foreign affairs and security matters. The only civilian mechanism dealing with psywar was the Ministry of Foreign Affairs, which lacked the training and resources for waging this kind of a struggle against Hezbollah.[16]

Another reason for Israel's failure in psychological warfare was its bureaucratic mechanisms compared to the Hezbollah organization—a compact, relatively young, still-developing political-military body capable of improvising and acting fast and flexibly. Victory in psywar demands dynamic energy, immediate adaptation to change, and unlimited creativity, all of which were areas suited to the mentality of young people or experienced professionals. It was easy for Hezbollah to revise its psywar strategy whenever necessary. In addition, as a revolutionary religious organization it enjoyed ideological unity and obedience. Moreover, political thinking in Israel was wracked by turf wars, political survival, and organizational interests. The rivalry between two of the country's most important intelligence organizations—the General Security Service (Hebrew acronym, Shabak, Israel's FBI) and Military Intelligence—severely hampered the effort to gather information and disseminate it in a psywar campaign.[17] The IDF was hard pressed to adapt quickly to rapidly changing situations compared to Hezbollah and the Palestinian organizations, which overcame their shortage of manpower and technological inferiority through improvisation and effective implementation.

Another factor that benefited Hezbollah stemmed from the human tendency to identify with the weak side.[18] The Yishuv had exploited this principle to the fullest in its struggle against the British Empire, but after winning independence it gradually dispensed with the rubric of "a small state surrounded by enemies," and completely abandoned it in the Six-Day War.

Another major reason for Israel's failure in psychological warfare was the limited number of people in the political system closely acquainted with Arab culture and Shiite religious society. Knowledge of the enemy's culture was essential for getting persuasive messages across. A good example of this was the speech of the former Israeli foreign minister, David Levy, in February 2000. Levy used graphic language to warn Hezbollah about firing Katyusha missiles over the border, lest there "be blood for blood, a child for a child." The Moroccan-born foreign minister was intimately familiar with Arab cultural codes and knew how to reach the Shiites' soul. For years the home page of Hezbollah's Internet site carried a videotape of Levy's speech spliced with pictures of Hitler.

The combination of disdain toward *psywar* campaigns, inter-agency rivalry, paucity of knowledge, shortage of resources, confusion, and ignorance in the application of information for advancing political and military goals culminated in organizational chaos in the field. The chaos was also the result of short-lived governments that brought leaders to power whose strategic perceptions sharply diverged from their predecessors' outlook, and the fear that experienced, senior officials harbored that whoever controlled the psywar arena might exploit it for domestic political purposes.

The Professional Element

Israel waged a low-keyed psywar in Southern Lebanon. The defense establishment seems to have ignored the crucial importance of exploiting the vast storehouse of knowledge available in academia and the intelligence bodies, and their familiarity with the local population's thinking. In retrospect, a number of themes come to light that could have provided the basis of effective propaganda activity:

- Applying proven covert or overt tactics to create fissures in the enemy's solidarity and force it to divert valuable resources to repair the damage caused by disruption. For example, Israel could have exploited its knowledge of Shiite stratification in Lebanon: in the north (Beirut and its vicinity) dwelt an urban Shiite population, some of it middle class, the majority working class; in the south were indigent farmers, a small middle class (storeowners), and a handful of wealthy land owners whose roots trace back to the Ottoman period. Israel could have applied its data on these socioeconomic gaps to undermine religious differences and social and political loyalties.

- Israel could have taken advantage of the bitter rivalry between the two Shiite organizations—Hezbollah and Amal—to win hearts and minds. On occasion this rivalry escalated to physical violence that left many dead on both sides in its wake (whose number Hezbollah downplayed unlike the figures of losses in fighting with Israel). Israel did take some initiatives in this area. For example, it exposed the financial and moral turpitude of military activists in both organizations, but failed to go far enough in getting the information across. Another issue that could have been tactically criticized was the short-term marriages (*mut'a*) that gave religious sanction to women who engaged in sexual relations with suicide bombers before they set out on their fatal mission. The Shiites are divided over this custom, and some denounce it as institutionalized prostitution. Israel could have attacked Hezbollah for its infraction of Islamic Shiite morality.
- In a concerted effort to stem the flow of the Iranian assistance to Hezbollah, Israel could have addressed the Iranian people,[19] stressing the immense quantity of resources that the cash-strapped Iranian people were expending on a futile struggle in Lebanon.
- Israel could have exploited the incarceration of the Hezbollah leaders Abd al-Karim Obeid and Mustafa Dirani in Israeli prison for psychological gain. It went to great lengths, operationally and in intelligence gathering, to kidnap them but it made no attempt to follow up with a propaganda blitz (for example, publishing statements by them in which they plead for freedom), excluding a few interviews with Obeid.
- Israel could have clarified to the neutral audience the close ties between Hezbollah and Iran. The political atmosphere in the United States in this period was strongly anti-Iran. The crisis had begun with the Islamist students' takeover of the US Embassy in Tehran in 1979 and holding fifty-two Americans hostage for 444 days. Tension escalated with the Hezbollah suicide bombing of the US marine compound in Beirut in October 1983 that left 241 servicemen dead. A few minutes later, Hezbollah blew up a French military barracks in the same city, killing fifty-eight French paratroopers. Here too, Israel could have influenced French public opinion and eroded France's traditional

pro-Arab support, had it consistently reminded the French people and government of the results of Hezbollah terrorist activity.

- Israel could have made a much greater effort in publicizing Hezbollah's rabidly anti-Semitic messages—"Jews drink children's blood"—and its even cruder anti-Western sloganeering, such as "Jews and Americans are the enemies of Allah and Islam" and "the United States is the 'Great Satan.'" Israel could have emphasized Hezbollah's barbarity by describing its observance of the *Ashura* ceremonies and linking them to the attacks on the American and French troops in 1983.

Following its usual pattern of response, Israel launched a tepid information campaign after the Kafr Qana incident, which Hezbollah exploited to the hilt for political points. During Operation "Grapes of Wrath" in April 1996 an IDF artillery shell accidentally hit civilians in the village of Kafr Qana in Southern Lebanon. The event aroused worldwide condemnation. But Israel's second mistake was in not examining Hezbollah's figures of the number killed (102), a figure that became universally accepted even though it was unverified by other sources. Moreover, the information center that the IDF set up during the operation failed to provide the foreign media with convincing answers and was soon shut down.

Operationally, Hezbollah succeeded in recruiting agents from the SLA, who collected information used in targeting SLA and IDF officers. The organization succeeded beyond all measure in instilling the impression of its hegemony and victory in Southern Lebanon.

* * *

In 2000 the Ehud Barak-led government decided to withdraw unilaterally from Lebanon, a decision that precipitated the SLA's demise and IDF's abrupt, chaotic pullout. Hezbollah's dynamic psywar campaign and Israel's meager information efforts both had a decidedly powerful impact on the protest movement in Israel that demanded immediate withdrawal.

CHAPTER 6

The Arab-Israeli Conflict and the First Intifada (1948–1989)

Historical Background—The Arab-Israeli Conflict (1948–1987)

The Arab-Israeli conflict is a complex clash of historical, cultural, social, religious, and strategic interests. Small wonder that so many writers, especially journalists, have failed to make a comprehensive study of all its details, a fact that helps the interested parties in presenting the picture according to their needs.[1] Disagreement abounds in every aspect of the conflict, even in its roots. The Israelis begin their history in the biblical period and regard Zionism as beginning with the waves of immigration to the Land of Israel in the late nineteenth century, and Palestinian history as starting in the 1930s. However, Palestinians see the Phoenician period as the first stage in their history, and the early twentieth century as a later stage. According to the Palestinians, Zionism is an imperialist movement and Zionist history starts with the 1917 Balfour Declaration.

Some scholars have noted that both peoples see national destruction as a central theme in their historical narrative: in Israel it is the Holocaust of the European Jewry in World War II, while for the Palestinians it is their defeat in the 1948 War, which they term "al-naqba" (the catastrophe).[2] Israeli and Palestinian societies are both characterized by diversity, the result of having been formed by waves of immigration. Each group relates differently to the country's conquerors—from the Turks to Napoleon, Muhammad Ali, the British, and culminating with the Zionist state.

Israel's War of Independence was a transformational event in the conflict. The Palestinians see it as the cause of a double catastrophe: first, the State of Israel came into being and the Palestinian state did not; second, the majority of the country's Arab inhabitants went into exile and became refugees (Palestinians in the south fled to the Gaza Strip, those in the center to Jordan, and those in the north to Syria and Lebanon). The reason for the Palestinians' flight to neighboring states is one major topic in the propaganda of both sides. On the one hand, the Israelis claim that the local leadership and Arab countries that invaded in May 1948 exhorted the people to flee the battle zone, and return home after the fighting when they could loot the Jews' property.[3] The Palestinians, on the other hand, charge that they were forcibly ousted from their homes, and that various events, such as the Dir Yassin case, induced the mass flight of the Arab population. The Six-Day War generated another wave of refugees who fled the West Bank into Jordan. Those who remained came under Israeli rule.

After the war, Israel set up a military government in the areas captured from Jordan and Egypt. This was replaced by a civilian administration that was subordinate to the defense minister and that coordinated its activity with the army. The government immediately announced an "open bridges" policy with Jordan that permitted commercial ties (agricultural and industrial products) between Israel, Jordan, and the territories, and allowed family visits between West Bank residents and Jordanian citizens and vice versa. Israel annexed East Jerusalem a few months after the war but restored responsibility for the administration of the Temple Mount (Haram al-Sharif) to the Muslim religious establishment (excluding security arrangements, which remained in Israel's hands).

Organized activity against Israel began with the founding of Fatah in the 1950s by a group of young Palestinian nationalists led by Yasser Arafat, Faruq Qaddumi, and Khalil al-Wazir (Abu Jihad). They set up their organization in the University of Cairo, and transferred to Kuwait in 1953 when the Egyptian regime kept too close a watch on their operations. In 1964 the Arab League (an organization founded by Britain in 1945 comprising all the Arab countries) backed Nasser's initiative to establish the PLO—an umbrella organization of all Palestinian groups. Ahmad Shuqeiri, a lawyer of Lebanese origin who was appointed chairman of the PLO, drafted a charter whose main principles were the determination of Palestinian identity, nonrecognition of Israel, and armed struggle against Israel.

After the Arabs' 1967 debacle, Yasser Arafat, the head of Fatah, the largest group, and other Palestinian organizations gained control of the PLO and removed it from Egypt's hegemony. They amended the charter and paved the way for a guerilla war against Israel from bases in Jordan, the West Bank, and the Gaza Strip. Israel thwarted their moves by integrating intelligence activity, military force, and a sophisticated fence with electronic sensors and mines along the Jordanian border. When PLO's guerilla strategy[4] failed in 1969 it adopted the strategy of global terror in order to gain international recognition of the Palestinian problem (its most outrageous acts were the skyjacking of commercial airplanes and murder of eleven Israeli athletes in the Munich Olympics in 1972). Not only did the PLO's international terror campaign fail, but the September 1970 attempt to overthrow the Hashemite regime in Jordan and establish "East Palestine" in its place proved its undoing. After the PLO was mercilessly crushed by King Hussein's army, most of the survivors found refuge in Lebanon.

There the PLO tried to set up an operations base from which they could attack Israel and immediately withdraw, according to Mao Zedong's guerilla doctrine. Israel responded aggressively by hitting terrorist targets in Lebanon and launched a ground invasion on two occasions: the first in 1978 (Operation "Litani") when it occupied Southern Lebanon and quickly withdrew; the second in 1982 when it gained control of South and Central Lebanon (the First Lebanon War) and forced the PLO to remove itself from the country and transfer its headquarters to Tunisia. This move hurt the organization by effectively cutting it off from the West Bank and the Gaza Strip and marring its prestige.

On December 7, 1987 a road accident occurred on the outskirts of Gaza. An Israeli driver lost control of his truck and slammed into a Palestinian car, killing four workers returning home from their jobs in Israel. Within hours rumors spread that the accident was intentional and had been perpetrated in response to the previous day's murder of an Israeli shopper in Gaza. An angry outburst followed. The small unit of soldiers stationed in the area was unprepared to deal with the volatile crowd and opened fire when they felt their lives threatened. More Palestinians were killed and wounded, which in turn unleashed an unprecedented storm of rage in the strip. This was the background of the outbreak of the First Intifada.[5]

Although there was nothing new in mass demonstrations or attacks against IDF troops or Israeli civilians, the dimension and intensity of the December 1987 outbursts awakened in the Palestinian public the sense that this was a new stage in the struggle. Within twenty-four hours, rioting spread to the West Bank and East Jerusalem and the number of dead and wounded Palestinians mounted, which in turn further fueled the demonstrations. These developed into a campaign of protests, hunger strikes, commercial and school shutdowns, and strikes by day laborers who worked in

Israel. After several weeks of protests Arafat's PLO gained control of the events and made maximum use of the organizational infrastructure to galvanize the popular uprising and offer an alternative to Israeli rule. The PLO leader realized the significance of the events in the territories and tried to exploit them for political gains. Thus, in its first announcement it attempted to create the impression that all of the events had been planned by the "external PLO" (the headquarters in Tunisia) as opposed to the "internal PLO" (the leadership in the territories).

Scholars cite a number of reasons for the rapid spread of the Intifada: the Arab states' indifference to the Palestinian problem at the Amman Summit Conference in October of that year (which threw the Palestinians into a deep state of despair), increasing economic depression, the policy of Prime Minister Yitzhak Shamir's Likud Government that launched a building spree of Jewish settlements in the territories, and the IDF's unilateral withdrawal from Southern Lebanon in 1985.

The Intifada lasted three years,[6] until the Gulf War (early 1991). In retrospect it was a milestone on the road to political negotiations between Israel and the Palestinians, when the PLO changed its strategy from being a popular uprising to seeking political negotiations within the framework of an international conference, namely, the American-initiated Madrid Conference convened in October 1991 where, as a gesture to the Israelis, Palestinian representatives were admitted only as part of the Jordanian delegation.

Definitions of the Palestinian Uprising

One of the Palestinians' major accomplishments was keeping their problem on the world agenda for so long a time. Proof of this was the universal adoption of the Arabic term "intifada" (awakening) not only by the Palestinians but also by the Israeli and international media, and the rejection of the alternative term—riots or disturbances—that the Israelis proposed. The Palestinians were fully aware of the importance of the struggle's name, especially in the foreign news agencies, since the Arabic title immediately associated the events with the Arab-Israeli conflict, whereas the term "riots" was bland and neutral and could refer to events anywhere. Be this as it may, affixing a positive title to a political (or any other) psywar campaign is a major asset since it helps the readers and audience focus on the subject.[7]

Another area that both sides invested great effort in was the name of the struggle itself. The Palestinians finally came up with the "Israeli-Palestinian conflict," which emphasized that the struggle was separate from the

Arab-Israeli conflict. The Israelis saw it as another chapter in the ongoing conflict. The "right" title grants legitimacy to a campaign in the eyes of the neutral target audience, and herein lies its importance. The Palestinians claimed that a solution to the problem of the Occupied Territories would end the entire Middle East conflict. This was a vision that convinced the Americans and the Europeans to apply pressure on Israel to make a greater effort in solving the Palestinian problem. Israel, however, argued that the conflict was not only with the Palestinians but with the entire Arab world; therefore, any arrangement with the Palestinians would be to Israel's detriment (since it entailed transferring the territories to Palestinians) and would not solve the problems in the Middle East. Over the years the Israeli Ministry of Foreign Affairs has constantly updated the published list of violent conflicts between Arab states in the region in order to prove that they were totally unrelated to Israel. The events of what has been ironically known as the "Arab Spring" render all these efforts obsolete.

Palestinian Leadership during the Intifada

One of the main features of the Intifada was the identity and modus operandi of the leadership. The Intifada's degree of success was unexpected, and many elements in Palestinian society hopped on the bandwagon to bask in the glory. The rule was simple: as long as the struggle centered on gaining independence, the status of the leaders engaged in it strengthened. The Palestinian leadership was one of the most important factors in the Intifada's success. For the first time the Palestinians felt they had leaders who knew how to lead. This feeling convinced many people to take an active part in the struggle. A new type of leadership gradually developed. At first it had been an informal organization of highly motivated individuals, most of whom had little or no experience in political activity and were therefore unknown to Israel's security forces—which made it difficult to keep track of them. When one leader was arrested his place was immediately filled by another with similar talents. This enabled effective and continuous activity. Later, the leadership became institutionalized according to the PLO's organizational division.

The leaders maintained contact with the people through leaflets that contained instructions, inspirational slogans, and political announcements. In the first months of the Intifada, the Palestinians loyally followed the leaflets' instructions out of a sense of patriotism and solidarity. Later on, an organized structure employing diverse methods of persuasion forced obedience to the PLO. Leaflets, pirate radio stations, and graffiti announced important dates and events and encouraged the population to persist in the struggle. Alternative communications pipelines—leaflets and graffiti—that were used in the territories since the beginning of Israel's occupation of Gaza had been adopted by Palestinian leaders, borrowed from the popular resistance movements in Algeria and Vietnam.

The leaflets were signed by the Unified National Leadership, which was made up of activists in all of the main political networks (Fatah, the Popular Front, and the Islamic groups). The name of the committee, the Unified National Leadership, signified two fundamental aspirations in Palestinian society—unity (as opposed to divisional and internal contentions that had characterized Palestinian society until then) and secularism. The PLO's phenomenal success in the early stages of the Intifada was attributed to its ability to present a united front to the world. This front included both the leaders and support for them from Palestinians of all classes.[8]

The PLO directed the Intifada and determined, to a great extent, the level of resistance. Having gained control of the Unified National Leadership it was in the position to make major decisions that generally obligated the rest of the Palestinian organizations. The PLO owed its hegemony in the general public to three elements: Fatah's youth movement "Shabiba" (established in 1981 in preparation for a popular uprising); the alternative mechanism to Israeli Civil Administration; and the sectorial organizations (workers, farmers, journalists, academics, etc.) and popular committees.

The popular committees that were set up in every village, neighborhood, and refugee camp in the first months of the Intifada performed many functions in the administration of daily life, and were part of the professional committees that dealt with commerce, medical aid, agriculture, charity, and so forth. The strength of these committees came from their large membership of people who had never taken part in the national struggle or political activity before the Intifada and who were not identified with any political group. This situation changed in the weeks after the PLO gained complete control of the popular committees (with the help of the violent Shabiba). The nature of the Intifada shifted from a popular uprising to an organized revolt. At this stage public enthusiasm diminished but was coordination between the different bodies strengthened.

After the initial months of the Intifada, an ideological struggle surfaced between the secular and Islamic organizations (Hamas and Islamic Jihad). The breach widened when the Islamic organizations began issuing their own leaflets and deciding independently on the dates for strikes as well as exploiting the media after witnessing the success of the secular Unified National Leadership. After the first weeks of the uprising the population had to return to its daily routine, and the political factions had time to reassess the situation and plan their next moves.

Another factor that left visible cracks in Palestinian unity was the manner of directing the struggle. The Intifada was autocratically forced upon the Palestinian public by the informal organizations that Arafat had established a few months before its eruption. These groups operated within the framework of the "popular committees" or "shock committees" that challenged IDF troops, executed collaborators, and exacted boycotts and strikes on the public.

Israel's Reaction

When the Intifada broke out, Israel's presence in the territories consisted of the Civil Administration, headed by the coordinator of government activities in the territories who answered directly to the defense minister. The Civil Administration employed approximately fifteen thousand Palestinians and five hundred Israelis. Its budget derived from taxes that the Palestinians paid (in the mid-1980s this came to US$120 million annually). The start of the Intifada was marked by an incongruous situation: Israel administered the territories through the Civil Administration, and the Palestinians sought to sabotage its activities and thus damage the services intended for their benefit, such as schools and municipal utilities. Israel adopted a carrot and stick policy, for example, at the public economic level: developing and raising the standard of living and on the personal level: easing procurement of travel and building permits. The stick came in the form of detention and withholding of permits.

The bodies that maintained law and order in the territories were the army (until the outbreak of the Intifada two brigades were stationed in Judea and Samaria, and one in the Gaza Strip), the police, and Shabak. Nevertheless, the Civil Administration and security bodies had different territorial and organizational turf struggles and in most cases operated separately. This naturally resulted in organizational chaos. Inter-organization coordination took place at a lower level and was generally carried out on a personal basis, according to trial and error—a surefire recipe for disaster for Israel's interests, especially in light of the Shabak's decision to give lower priority to tracking the Palestinians' political activity than to preempting terrorist strikes. Had there been better cooperation between the IDF and

Shabak, with advisors on Arab affairs from the Civil Administration, Israel probably could have foreseen the outbreak of the First Intifada.

The Intifada caught Israel by surprise and the IDF unprepared. The small military contingent stationed in the Gaza Strip was untrained in dispersing large, violent crowds and lost its nerve when faced with raging masses. At first the IDF believed it could talk sense into the Palestinians as it had done in the past, and bring in more troops to calm the storm. But after a few weeks the authorities realized that they had something new on their hands, and in January 1988 Yitzhak Rabin, then defense minister, formulated a new policy, announced publicly, of exerting physical force against the protestors. The policy was based on the assumption that beating the demonstrators was preferable to killing them. IDF units were ordered to avoid bloodshed by using truncheons instead of live ammunition. The Palestinians exploited this policy as a means of harming Israel by presenting the beatings as another expression of Israel's cruelty and brutality toward the Palestinian people. The policy came under bitter criticism, especially after the international media broadcast photos of four IDF soldiers pummeling two Palestinian children with a rock and helmet (late February 1988). The wide-scale exposure forced the Israeli government to rescind the policy. This was a case of effective psywar succeeding in changing the enemy's modus operandi and evoking internal debate. A number of soldiers were put on trial for excessive use of force in an incident that ended with the deaths of four Palestinians. Afterwards, whenever soldiers clashed with demonstrators they made doubly sure not to overdo their use of force, which enabled Palestinian activists to chalk up a victory on many occasions.

Israel took additional steps, such as mass arrests, fines, administrative detention of senior organizers, exposing the plans of the Unified National Committee, sealing up or demolishing houses, enforcing lengthy closures and curfews, and, in extreme cases, expelling activists from the territories. The IDF adapted the game rules to the new tasks of policing and enforcing law and order. Furthermore, cooperation improved between Israel's security services—the army, police, Civil Administration, and Shabak. Shabak provided the IDF with information it obtained from interrogating collaborators and detainees. The IDF purchased or developed crowd dispersal tools such as water cannons, tear gas, gravel-firing vehicles (*hatzatziot*), and nonlethal anti-personnel weapons such as plastic and rubber bullets.

Most of the IDF soldiers who served in the territories in the Intifada period were reservists—some infantrymen, mostly tankists and artillerymen. They were adults who had been trained in modern mechanized combat, not in running after Palestinian youth in alleyways and across boulder-strewn hills. The Palestinians had another advantage: familiarity with the terrain. Also, in the first months of the Intifada the IDF kept to rigid fighting methods, such as full combat gear, unsuited to the conditions. The local youth successfully exploited this shortcoming. The IDF's main problem stemmed from the nature of the reservists' service. When a unit finally became experienced in its sector and the Palestinians' methods of operation, its tour of duty was up and had been replaced by a new reservist unit. Although the IDF was aware of the problem, it made no effort to solve it. Partial, short-term solutions included updating the IDF units operating in the territories on the new tactics for dealing with the Intifada, improving the briefing to commanders at all levels at the outset of reservist duty, deploying border police units to the territories (that were better trained for quelling demonstrations and that had a large number of Arabic-speaking Druze soldiers and officers), using conscript troops whose entire military service was in the territories, and employing counter-intelligence units disguised as Arabs.

CHAPTER 7

Applying Psywar Themes in the Intifada

In psychological warfare the term "theme" refers to the justifications, argumentations, and emotional elements used in a military-political conflict to elicit hatred, fear, and second thoughts within the target audience. The themes are conveyed through speeches, books, newspapers, magazines, leaflets, electronic and digital networks, and street graffiti. The choice of theme is crucial because its effectiveness depends largely on an intimate familiarity with the target audience's culture and mentality.

Arab and Israeli intelligence services assemble a cultural profile of their enemies by obtaining material from the media and academic research institutes. In the Israeli-Palestinian conflict the quality of the picture they formed of one another was asymmetrical: the Palestinians' superior knowledge and understanding of the enemy culture added immensely to the effectiveness of their messages. They set up research centers that focused on Israeli culture and psychology[1] as early as 1968 (which testifies to their awareness of the latent potential in this field). Palestinian prisoners organized Hebrew language study groups where they read Israeli newspapers and listened to Hebrew radio stations. East Jerusalem Palestinians with Israeli citizenship attended Israeli universities and acquired profound insight into Israeli culture. Palestinians in low economic fields worked in Israel and picked up a working knowledge of Hebrew.

Israel, too, collected a vast amount of material on the enemy through military intelligence (such as the Hatzav Unit that translates open-source information from the Arab media) and the Shabak, but the material was designed for operational purposes rather than for psywar. The Shabak was responsible for collecting intelligence to preempt terrorist attacks but, it will be recalled, it gradually withdrew from overseeing the political uprising.

Until the Intifada broke out the Shabak had been considered practically omniscient, now it had to admit that its intelligence was "only" intended to stave off terrorist strikes. Military intelligence was responsible for "psychological warfare" but lacked many basic tools for applying it. The upshot was that at the start of the Intifada Israel failed to analyze the target audiences and their messages. Nonetheless, when the parties responsible realized that the uprising was going to be a drawn-out affair they quickly prepared a comprehensive analysis of its causes, directions, and the ways of quelling it.

Israel's Themes[2]

"Educational" Themes

These themes provided target audiences with Israel's view of the Middle East reality and the Israeli-Palestinian conflict.

The Lack of Historical Context. This theme claims that criticism of Israel stems from the lack of historical information given to the neutral audience and the deliberate ambiguity of the Arabs and Palestinians. If foreign countries are given enough factual background, their criticism of Israeli policy will change. The Ministry of Foreign Affairs' first publication on the Intifada was entitled *The Riots in the Territories—Remembering the Context.* The theme reflects a *hasbara* approach.

Israel Is a Democratic Country. Living in the only democracy in the Middle East, Israeli citizens enjoy freedom of speech, freedom of movement, and free access to information; therefore, Israel does not need to prevent the media from photographing events or prohibit people from participation in nonviolent demonstrations. Security forces intervene only when the protests turn violent.[3]

A number of spinoff themes were derived from this.

Israel Acts Legally. This was an important theme for Western consumption, and the Palestinians disputed it from the start. The two sides battled over the legitimacy of Israel's punitive steps in the territories, which included administrative detention, the demolition of homes, and, most infuriating for the Palestinians, deportation. The legal arguments revolved around the interpretation of two historical documents in international law: The Hague Convention of 1907 and the Fourth Geneva Convention of 1949. The Palestinians claimed that Israel's conduct in the territories violated these conventions. Israel counterclaimed—and the Supreme Court upheld the argument—that the Geneva Convention of 1949 had to be understood against the background of World War II and its intention to prevent

s deportations, but it said nothing about acts
ıse of Palestinians in the territories.

In the late 1970s and 1980s the Palestinians
ıd South Africa. The goal of this charge was to
st and the apartheid regimes by showing their
:he ruling group and dominated population,
)rers prohibited from remaining overnight in
ections in the territories, discrimination in the
for Palestinians and Israelis, the demolition of
s' unions, deportations, torture of Palestinian
onditions, and wage gaps. Israel took the indi-
se charges. First, it attacked the Arab regimes, accusing them of hypocrisy since they themselves maintained secret ties with South Africa; second, it described Israeli development and commercial projects in Africa; and third, Israel invited South African leaders to visit the country and personally refute the comparison.[4]

Israel's Good Side. A basic theme that has been used for decades (and still is), presents Israel's technological, cultural, and social achievements, especially in comparison to the track record of the Arab states. Israel publicized its success in economic and agricultural development in third world countries in Asia and Africa.

Israel has Introduced Progress into the Territories. This complemented the previous theme and was aimed chiefly at the home and neutral audiences (but proved ineffective with the Palestinians despite the dramatic rise in their standard of living in the decade following the Six-Day War). Israel also used this theme to answer the US State Department's queries regarding human rights abuse in the territories.

Attack Themes

The PLO's Double Standard. This theme was in vogue in the early 1970s when the PLO began operating through diplomatic channels. The idea was to expose the PLO's true intentions, namely, to use diplomacy as a means of destroying Israel. Israel published the speeches of senior PLO members (Yasser Arafat in particular) to illustrate the blatant differences in their messages when addressed to Western audiences (political steps to be taken against Israel) and Arab audiences (the promise to annihilate Israel).[5]

The PLO As a Terrorist Organization. The PLO carried out murderous attacks against Israel from across the Lebanese border and in Europe, including skyjackings. Israel's aim in publishing their details was the same as the PLO's in presenting the Palestinians' casualty rate in the Intifada.

The Use of Legitimate Institutions for Terror Infrastructures. Israel sought to reveal the gaps between reality and the way Palestinian activists presented it to the media. Israel accused the Palestinians of converting hospitals into operations bases and the wide-scale use of mosques for political and military purposes—such as training grounds, arms caches, and headquarters for disseminating inflammatory material against Israel. Although the input accumulated weekly, Israel rarely made it public in order to protect the informers and avoid arousing hostility in the West where the Palestinians had enlisted a sympathetic audience to their cause. Figures such as Dr. Sari Nusseibah, Dr. Hanan Ashrawi, and Hanna Siniora labored for years in shaping their image as concerned Palestinians who became politically and socially active only when their suffering reached breaking point. Israel had no means of countering this image without jeopardizing its sources of information and embarking on a long-term image remake. The same was true of the International Red Cross whose prestigious symbol the Palestinians appropriated to cover up their militant activities. A decade and a half later, when the Palestinians shifted from civil disobedience to active violence, Israel at last publicized their use of Red Cross ambulances for transporting weapons and combatants.

Israel's attack on a "different level" was directed against the Palestinians' impressive success in co-opting the Holocaust and converting it into a Palestinian term—*al-nakba* (the catastrophe)—a reference to Israel's birth in 1948 and the subsequent suffering of the Palestinians. Israel countered that the annihilation of European Jewry was an unprecedented event, the first time in history that a state engaged in the systematic effort to exterminate an entire nation.

Blaming the Media. This was one of the Ministry's main *hasbara* lines that gained considerable attention in academia and the media. In the First Lebanon War, especially after the Sabra and Shatila affair, Israel criticized the foreign press for the way it presented the Arab-Israeli conflict. During the Intifada, Israel attacked the press in even sharper terms. The public response in Israel spanned the extremes—from accusing journalists of anti-Semitism to justifying their integrity and ethical standards.[6] In the first weeks of the Intifada the government did not believe that the foreign media was involved in a world conspiracy against Israel. On the contrary, it understood that superficial presentation of events by the press lay in the nature of the media and the pressure to convey bite-sized messages in real time.

The official Israeli view held that the main reason that events in the territories were portrayed to the Palestinians' advantage was that the Palestinians had cleverly adapted themselves to the media's demands and exploited their working relationship with the journalists better than Israel had. Israel also claimed that the world-wide criticism against it stemmed from its democratic society, which allowed the foreign media to roam the territories freely (excluding cases where their presence was liable to spark violence). Whatever the case, after a few months the *hasbara* line of "understanding the media's limitations" changed.[7] A good example of the new approach was the publication of a Ministry booklet in January 1989 written by Eliyahu Tal—a pioneer in the field of advertising in Israel and a citizen deeply concerned about Israel's world image. The publication, titled *Israel in Medialand*, brazenly accused the media of slanting the news against Israel, and contained caricatures, headlines, and statistical figures on the media's presentation of major world events. It compared the broad, dramatic press coverage of Palestinian demonstrations and the Intifada with its low-keyed coverage of terrorist events in other parts of the world, attacks that had caused thousands of deaths. This appraisal of the foreign media was also aimed at the home audience. The IDF took immediate steps to inculcate this approach in its military units, especially where soldiers and officers had arbitrarily interfered with reportage by journalists in the field.

The Palestinian Themes[8]

Themes Aimed at the Palestinian Home Audience

Recruitment to the Cause. The main problem that revolutionary movements face is how to expand their circle of supporters. The chief obstacle generally lies with the middle and upper classes that oppose revolutionary activity against their interests. The Intifada leaders wanted passive supporters to take a more active part in the struggle. They conveyed the idea that the occupation could be ended only through the active involvement of the masses. The following themes were designed to motivate Palestinian society to confront Israel's security forces.

Unity. This would prove that rival political and social groups were amalgamated in the common struggle.

Popular Support for the PLO and Its Leader Yasser Arafat. This theme had been around since the PLO was established, and read: "the sole legitimate representative of the Palestinian people". The slogans chanted by demonstrators after the PLO wrested control of the Intifada in January 1988 had been scrupulously planned, and included classic Palestinian battle cries, such as "in blood and spirit we will redeem you Filastin" (the phraseology was slightly changed at funerals—"in blood and spirit we will redeem you, O holy martyr") or expressed Islam's glorious past—"O Khaybar, Khaybar Jews, Muhammad's army will return."[9]

Islam. Beginning in January 1988 the leaflets opened with the religious blessing "In the name of Allah." This was the result of collaboration between the PLO and Islamic organizations. However, even after the two camps split and distributed separate leaflets, the Islam-oriented heading remained on the PLO's leaflets, which shows that the National Unified Leadership was aware of Islam's hold on the public.

Excoriating Cooperation with Israel. The Palestinians' goal was to sever economic and security dependency on Israel.

Attacking IDF Troops. From the outset, the leaflets described IDF troops as heinous, merciless, and, sometimes, ludicrous creatures. The aim was to reduce the fearsome image of the Israeli soldier and embolden the population to engage them.

Victory Is Inevitable. This is the major theme of revolutionary movements and the Palestinians employed it on a permanent basis. It was used directly—"Palestinian victory and Israel's downfall are imminent," and indirectly—"all of the colonial powers (and Israel is the last of the lot) eventually collapsed." Other messages were that Israel's moral corruption would ultimately lead to ruin and that the Palestinians' resolve and tenacity would emerge victorious ("determination" became official policy and one of the PLO branches was called *sumud*—steadfast perseverance). The message on the leaflets stated that the path to victory required tremendous effort and self-sacrifice. Most of them opened with the sentence "no voice can overcome the cry of the uprising—[signed] the Palestinian People." The Islamic leaflets made it clear that victory was incontestable because "it is the will of Allah."

Jerusalem has the greatest emotional and symbolical appeal for all Arabs. It provided the religious and historical link to contemporary politics, and reflected the glorious past and strife-torn present in which the Al-Aqsa Mosque was being controlled by the infidels.[10]

In Praise of Women. Women were extolled for their courage and involvement in the uprising. The PLO enlisted educated women to prove to neutral target audiences that Muslim society had undergone a profound transformation. When beamed at the Palestinian population, the message was different: women were urged to break the fetters of tradition and convince their menfolk to let them participate in the struggle.[11]

Christianity. The Unified National Leadership reached out to Palestinian Christians to partake in the struggle. They could serve as media assets since they were positioned to win the hearts and minds of the Western world, and they were living proof of the unity in Palestinian society during the Intifada (Christians and Muslims had a long history of turbulent relations in the Holy Land). Since the economic situation of Christian Arabs in the territories was better than that of the Muslims, and Christian Arabs made up a greater proportion of the upper and middle classes, Intifada activists sought financial backing by mobilizing their Christian neighbors to the struggle.

Themes of Self-Sacrifice

These themes sought to win support by enhancing the Palestinians' pride and their sense of national unity.

Sumud: Steadfast Perseverance. According to PLO philosophy and policy, every Palestinian in the territories had to take an active part in the struggle, regardless of the hardships involved, or at least resist the occupation passively. During the Intifada *sumud* inspired the Palestinians to persevere in the face of Israel's relentless pressure to quash the uprising.

Shahada (Sacrificing One's Life for Islam). According to Islam tradition a *shahid* is someone killed in a *jihad* (holy war against nonbelievers). Such a martyr is guaranteed a place in the Garden of Eden. Political and religious leaders in the territories proclaimed that every Palestinian killed by the Israelis was a martyr for Islam. The goal of the theme was to ease the Palestinians' pain at losing loved ones by giving meaning to their deaths and consolation to their families in the knowledge that the victims had gained eternal reward in heaven.[12] Intifada activists presented the uprising as a religious war (in addition to a political struggle) in order to win the backing of Islamic groups.

Sacrifice. This theme was repeated throughout the Intifada. Its aim was to hearten the soul of all Palestinians and guarantee that the fruits of the struggle were theirs. The theme was also targeted at Israel by reiterating the Palestinians' determination to wage their struggle to the bitter end and ingraining in the Israeli consciousness the fact that Palestinian zeal and self-sacrifice—rather than military and technological superiority—would determine the outcome of the Intifada. Stated differently, all of Israel's efforts at quashing the Intifada were in vain since the Palestinians were willing to die for their cause.[13]

Heritage. This theme was designed to answer Israel's allegations that a Palestinian state had never existed. Therefore the Palestinians constructed a Palestinian historical narrative that refuted the Zionist historical perspective by negating the Jewish connection to the land. To do this they devised a separate Palestinian cultural identity and set up a number of organizations (dealing in history, literature, archeology, folklore, etc.) under the direction of the PLO's cultural department and activists from the territories and abroad. Political messages were frequently integrated into traditional cultural activities, such as needlework, folk dancing, and cooking. During the Intifada the heritage theme was stressed in order to stiffen resistance by instilling in the Palestinians respect for their historical and cultural legacy.

Themes of Hatred

The PLO transmitted emotional (nonrational) themes that inflamed the Palestinians to execute attacks on IDF personnel.

Nazism. The purpose of this theme was to offset the Holocaust in Israeli-Zionist identity and implant feelings of guilt in Israeli soldiers (and society), thus lessening the army's effectiveness. The Nazism theme claimed that by an ironic twist of fate Israel was doing to the Palestinians exactly what the Nazis had done to the Jews. This was a most serious charge that struck at the heart of the average Israeli. Even Israeli spokespersons were so enraged by the comparison that they were incapable of dealing with it rationally. The theme became popular with the Palestinian audience, who accepted it matter-of-factly, without giving second thought to an in-depth assessment or historical analysis.

Satan. This theme was used to deprecate Israel. Hamas frequently employed it, especially with reference to the United States ("the Great Satan"), which it viewed as its foremost ideological enemy. The PLO, however, avoided the term when alluding to the United States, as it was engaged in secret contacts with the Americans in the months preceding the PLO's announcement of its recognition of Israel (November 1988).

The Deliberate Prevention of Education. The Palestinians regarded the closure of its schools as extreme punishment and portrayed it as Israel's deliberate policy to foster ignorance in the population. They also conveyed the theme to the neutral audience.

The political themes changed according to political circumstances. For example, the PLO inveighed against Secretary of State George Schultz's initiative in February 1988,[14] alleging that it was slanted in Israel's favor.

From its headquarters in the territories, the PLO launched wide-scale violent demonstrations against the American initiative and castigated its futility in a series of interviews.

Themes Aimed at the Neutral Audience

These themes expressed Western values and, as such, aspired to scourge Israel in the West.

Themes of Aspersion

The Jewish Lobby in the United States. The Palestinians exploited international publications that the American Israel Public Affairs Committee (AIPAC), the Jewish lobby in the United States, had a top-heavy influence on the US government and that the number of American Jews in the media was extravagantly high. In this light the Palestinians decried "Jewish omnipotence in the United States." The Arab lobby took up the theme, accusing the Reagan Administration of unfair treatment toward them, a charge that gained prominence in the early 1980s following the First Lebanon War.[15]

Nuclear Israel. This theme served two goals. The first was to disparage Israel in the eyes of opponents of nuclear weapons; the second was to use it in the following argument: if Israel possessed atomic weapons, it had nothing to fear from a puny Palestinian state.[16]

Israel Oppresses Christians. The Palestinians tried to exploit the religious and cultural affinity between Arabs and Christians in the territories and Christians living in the United States. Therefore, they played on Israel's control of Christian holy sites. They organized demonstrations at holy places—the Church of the Nativity in Bethlehem and Church of the Holy Sepulcher in East Jerusalem—and scored many points from photographs of IDF troops lobbing tear gas grenades at the demonstrators with the holy sites in the background.

The Unscrupulous Mossad. The PLO's aim was to undermine Israel's positive image in the world by bitterly attacking one of its most prestigious intelligence agencies (regardless of the fact that the Mossad does not operate in the territories). Criticism of the state's intelligence services was often effective because such organizations usually refrain from responding, and the Mossad was no exception. During the Intifada it generally managed to keep its activities and methods of operation under wraps. The secrecy, combined with an untold number of successful operations, created the image of an invincible organization but, at the same time, rendered it vulnerable to political attack.

Israel's Unwarranted Conduct in the Territories. In leaflets, interviews, and press conferences the Palestinians charged that Israel systematically tortured Palestinian detainees and prisoners.[17] When Israeli troops fired tear gas on violent protestors, the Palestinians defined this means of crowd dispersal as morally reprehensible. They always used the word "gas" rather than "tear gas" to create the impression that Israel employed internationally prohibited toxic materials, implying mustard gas or nerve gas. These accusations proved highly effective because they called to mind the Nazis' use of Zyklon B to liquidate the Jews. The Palestinians gave the media detailed information on the number of people killed in the territories as a result of Israeli operations, and especially noted cases where children and old people were among the casualties.

Apartheid. The Palestinians tried to link Israeli activity to the ostracized regime in South Africa by comparing Israel's dealing with the Palestinians in the territories and its treatment of Israeli Arabs as second-class citizens with that of the apartheid state. The Palestinians found other points of similarity, such as both countries' nuclear capability and isolation in the international arena. This theme gained prominence and was used to exert political and economic pressure on Israel to change its policy.

Themes of Justice

Human Rights. The Palestinians were keenly aware of the importance of this theme in Western tradition and tried to make maximum use of it to create a positive image for their cause. By pointing to the inherent inconsistency between Israeli occupation and Palestinian human rights, they portrayed Israel as a nondemocratic superpower that was tyrannizing and oppressing the Palestinian people.

International Law. Like the previous theme, violation of international law provided the Palestinians with an argument to interpret the territories' unique legal status to their advantage and wage a successful campaign. International law was a springboard to the media and enabled the Palestinians to employ ostensibly legal arguments to support their demands. They created the impression that Israel was operating in violation of international law and exploiting the fact that only a few understood the complexities and nuances of international jurisprudence. They raised several issues, such as the legal basis for Israel's presence in the territories, the destruction of houses, land confiscation, and expulsions. Eventually this theme succeeded in remaking their image in the Western media from that of terrorists in the 1970s to a downtrodden people struggling for their ancestral homeland. The PLO's diplomatic activity in the UN also contributed to the organization's newly gained aura of respectability.[18]

Searching for Canaanite Roots. Since the mid-1970s the Palestinians have alleged that they are the rightful heirs of the country because they are the direct offspring of the Phoenicians whereas the Jewish people are invading tribes who conquered the land.[19] Addressing a Christian audience Arafat defined Jesus as "the first Palestinian martyr."[20] The Palestinians often claimed that their historical ties to the land are at least as strong as that of the Jews because, according to their reading of history, the events in the Bible occurred on the Arabian Peninsula and not in Palestine! They tried to sever the Jewish people's historical link to the land and prove that the Jews are a religion and not a nation. Therefore the Jews have no right to demand territory.

The Palestinian Holocaust. The Palestinians endeavored to present themselves as the victims in the conflict; therefore, they adopted Holocaust terminology with an added Palestinian exegesis: the War of 1948 was the *nakba* (the catastrophe); the words "deportees" and "uprooted" were frequently employed; Israel's Kitzeot detention facility in the Western Negev was referred to as a "concentration camp"; prodigious use was made of the term "Nazi" with reference to Israeli soldiers; tear gas was described simply as "gas"—"Israel uses 'gas' in the territories"—the analogy being self-understood.

An Appeal to the Conscience. The Palestinians were extremely successful in appealing to the world's conscience, petitioning foreign governments, political groups, and VIPs to rescue them from Israel's choking grip. This theme was based on extremely critical reports of Israel's policy that were circulated in the West (written mainly by international organizations and delegations on study tours of the territories, and journalists whose visits were initiated and organized by the PLO).

Women. The Palestinians made a two-pronged use of this theme. The first was to present the traditional, submissive Palestinian woman who could no longer endure Israel's conduct in the territories. This image was enhanced by televising Palestinian women pleading with IDF troops to free their children from arrest. The second was to enlist prominent Palestinian women (most of whom were Christians) to address the Western media, especially since their clothing and demeanor were decidedly more Western than that of their Muslim counterparts.[21] In scores of interviews they described the Palestinian woman's awakening and cry for equal rights. The Palestinians exploited academe's growing interest in the modernization of the Palestinian woman by inviting foreign scholars to the territories, granting interviews, and organizing discussion groups.

Political Themes—Short- and Long-Term Goals

Political themes were designed for both the neutral audience and the home audience, that is, they were advanced and discarded according to political exigencies. Some were stock themes dating back to when the PLO embarked upon its diplomatic campaign in 1973; others were devised according to the need of the hour.

The Right to Self-Determination. This theme comes from the lexicon of international law following World War I and postwar anti-colonial struggles, and refers to the right of nations to establish independent states. The wording was phrased in a nonthreatening manner, which facilitated the theme's widespread circulation since no party wanted to be perceived as denying the natural rights of a nation.

The Right of Return. Innocuous at first glance, its goal was to win support based on the American principle of fair play. In the mid-1970s, at the height of the Soviet Jews' struggle to immigrate to Israel, the biblical aphorism "Let my people go," was often heard. The PLO co-opted the injunction and added its own twist: "Let my people return." What the theme really meant was that the Palestinian refugees and their offspring should be granted the right to return to their previous homes in Israel. Every Israeli government has regarded this theme as a trigger phrase to destroy the state, and has therefore rejected it point blank.

A Secular Democratic State. The Palestinians invented this slogan for Western consumption in order to distinguish themselves from the stereotype of corrupt, religiously orthodox, male-dominated Arab regimes. As the Islamic organizations grew during the Intifada, the PLO's secular façade became increasingly attractive to Western audiences.

American Aid to Israel. The real motives behind the use of this theme are not clear. Did the PLO really believe it could limit American financial aid to Israel? Did it want to attack Israel on every possible front, or exert political pressure so it would be forced to change its policy in the territories? Whatever the reason, the organization worked in various directions, such as publishing figures of American economic assistance to Israel and lobbying Congress to limit the sum intended.

Soviet Jewry. The Palestinians and their supporters based their belief in victory, inter alia, on demographics. In the early 1980s they estimated that in less than twenty years the number of Palestinians between the Jordan River and Mediterranean Sea would equal the number of Israelis. The Israeli Left used this figure to demand a partition between the two nations (the codename for establishing a Palestinian state). The PLO addressed its home audience with the theme "the fighting womb," which implied that a high birthrate would deliver the victory. The Palestinian response to the influx of one million Jews to Israel, following the collapse of the Soviet Union in 1989, was to denounce this wave of immigration via leaflets, the Arab press, and the international media.[22]

An International Conference. Until 1971 this was the Palestinians' short-term political goal and was conveyed in interviews, and through PLO newspapers and leaflets. Arafat expected to be the first leader whom Israeli leaders would recognize as being of equal status with them. His dream was partially realized at the Madrid Conference in 1991, when the PLO was accorded official seating (though only as part of the Jordanian delegation). Fully independent participation in discussions with Israel was attained three years later during the Oslo negotiations.

Themes Aimed at the Enemy

The following themes were planned solely for Israel—its civilians and soldiers.[23]

Themes of Justice

Oppression. During the Intifada the main theme of all Palestinian organizations was "Israeli oppression." The goal was to ingrain feelings of guilt in the Israeli public by focusing on the suffering caused by the occupation and the corrupting effect it had on Israelis themselves. The message contained detailed information on the Palestinians who were killed or wounded—names, addresses, and ages, thereby transforming the victims from just a statistic to human beings that the Israeli public could identify with.

Peace. The Palestinians claimed that their main objective was peace. They realized that the war option was unrealistic, given the asymmetry in the balance of forces and Israel's political situation since the establishment of the unity government in 1984.[24] The following themes were designed to reinforce the theme of peace.

Palestinian Weakness. The aim of this theme was to bring the Israeli public to gradually accept the idea of a small Palestinian state alongside Israel. For the theme to succeed it had to overcome decades of suspicion and hostility in successive Israeli governments that could be summed up as: An independent Palestinian state will lead to the destruction of Israel. Therefore the theme stressed Israel's overwhelming power (recall the nuclear theme) and that Israel had nothing to fear from a small, weak, demilitarized state next to it. The PLO pointed out that in an age of surface-to-surface missiles the concept that territory guarantees security is passé.

Morality. This theme had two goals: one, to imbue feelings of guilt in the Israeli public regarding its conduct in the territories, defining it as immoral, illegal, and ultimately self-defeating; and the corollary, that the shameless acts its soldiers were daily committing would boomerang back on Israeli society.

Democracy. Like the previous theme, this message claimed that Israel was forfeiting the democratic nature that it cherished so dearly and was descending into a dictatorship unless it agreed to a political solution to the Palestinian problem.

Attack Themes. The Palestinians identified major stumbling blocks on their path to achieving political goals. These obstacles became targets of attack.

Prime Minister Yitzhak Shamir. He was portrayed as a rigid nationalist indifferent to suffering and the Palestinians attributed this to his advanced age (in his seventies during the Intifada) and background as a senior Lehi commander (a hard-line underground organization during the British Mandate).

The Settlers too were a major obstacle on the road to establishing an independent Palestinian state. The Israeli settlements in the West Bank and Gaza Strip posed a serious threat in two areas. First and foremost, the settler's ideology, which was based on legal-historical claims to the land according to Scripture (this was a powerful belief system that competed with that of the Palestinians). The second was their government-backed physical presence that strengthened Israeli rule in the territories by means of land-acquisition and subsequent settlement expansion. The settlers represented an immediate danger because of their single-mindedness to realize classic Zionism, that is, Israel's borders being determined by the presence of Jewish settlements. Therefore, most of the messages directed at the Israeli public included bitter condemnation of the settlers for their cruelty and "Nazi-like" ways. The Palestinian strategy was designed to alienate the settlers from the Israeli mainstream by a gradual process of delegitimization. This began before the Intifada and gathered momentum after it erupted. The Palestinians succeeded in dissociating the settlers from the general Israeli public, and casting settlement activity in a negative light to Israeli and foreign eyes. The target audience was the Israeli public within the 1967 borders, as the Palestinians realized that appealing directly to the settlers that the creation of a Palestinian state would ruin everything they believed in and struggled for was useless.

The Fate of the Territories. The Palestinians managed to stir up a potpourri of opinions in Israel over this issue. After the capture of Judea and Samaria in the Six-Day War most Israelis felt that the newly won lands were Israel's rightful fruits of victory. However, during the Intifada some twenty years later, a sea change took place in public opinion toward the territories, and the balance of supporters and opponents about leveled off. During the Intifada there were a few instances where soldiers—conscript as well as reservist—refused to serve in the territories. However, the number never reached proportions that endangered Israel's control, and social solidarity remained intact.

Druze Soldiers. The Palestinians sought to undermine the military proficiency and loyalty of Druze soldiers serving in the territories. Many Druze served in the Israel Border Police, a branch better trained in crowd dispersal than regular IDF units. Since the Druze are culturally and linguistically close to the Palestinian population, the Palestinians employed the age-old technique of driving a wedge: They played up the cultural and linguistic commonality between Druze and Arab and underscored the Israeli government's discrimination toward the Druze (despite their military service). This effort generally failed. The Druze remained loyal to the state and continued to serve as outstanding soldiers. Nevertheless, in one notable case a Druze delegation visited Nablus with food and medicine, an act that was intended, as they stated, to change the image of the Druze as anti-Palestinian. Although the Druze continue to support Israel politically, since the First Lebanon War there have been differences of opinion among them regarding the territories, and a small number of Druze have refused to join the IDF.

CHAPTER 8

The Palestinian Information Mechanism

The Palestinian Information Mechanism

The PLO attributed great importance to its two-pronged tactic: information dissemination coupled with wide-scale terrorism. This was especially true during the 1970s when it initiated media events, exploited opportunities for propaganda points, conveyed information efficiently, and built strong ties with the international media. These activities were the outcome of the leadership's rational, systematic analysis of the balance of power between Israel and the Palestinians. Funds would have to be channeled to psychological warfare if the Palestinians hoped to attain their political goals (the establishment of an independent Palestinian state adjacent to or in place of Israel) since military means alone were unfeasible.

The Palestinians were adept at maximizing their assets: their diaspora and those of them who held high social standing developed extended business ties and were intimately familiar with cultural sensitivities. Inter-Palestinian coordination took place through diplomatic consulates established in the decade preceding the Intifada. The PLO set great store by the promulgation of messages, as testified by the large number of communications channels it created: spokespersons for all its bureaus and organizations (PLO, Fatah, Arafat himself, etc.); a newspaper or journal for each PLO faction; radio stations—Al-Quds Radio in Damascus, the mouthpiece of Ahmed Jibril, leader of the Popular Front for the Liberation of Palestine (PFLP)—General Command; and Radio PLO that broadcast from Baghdad. In addition, Arafat was readily accessible to the media, and granted countless interviews.[1]

The Palestinians' open sources of information on the application of psywar came from academic libraries and archives around the world offering professional advice and historical background on a wide range of subjects, such as defining target audiences, preparing credible messages, and evaluating the messages' impact on various armies. They gleaned a great deal of information from the national liberation struggles of Algeria and Vietnam where psychological warfare was used extensively.

Arab scholars, too, investigated psychological operations (literature on this field exists in Arabic). Arabic dictionaries include words such as "psychological warfare" and "leaflets." The presence of the British army in Arab states before World War II also contributed to the knowledge in this field.[2]

During the 1970s the Soviets trained the PLO in different types of warfare, such as guerilla fighting, conventional warfare, and propaganda operations (that the Soviets termed "active measures"). The PLO's official newspaper *Filastin al-Thaura* (Revolutionary Palestine) contained reports on members of the organization who underwent training in communications skills, such as public speaking, journalistic photography, and cinema.[3]

The Printed Press

Most of the Palestinian newspapers were published in Cyprus and East Jerusalem for many reasons: the relatively easy flow of information; greater freedom of movement for Palestinians living in East Jerusalem than for Palestinians in the territories under IDF control; ready access to information from government and nongovernment organizations in Israel, and financial pipelines from abroad, since East Jerusalem was annexed to Israel shortly after the Six-Day War and its residents received Israeli identity cards; and proximity to the foreign media, foreign consulates, and offices of international organizations, as this allowed demonstrations to be held and petitions submitted with relative ease. In addition, East Jerusalem is close to the Palestinian population centers and political events that are the fodder of the foreign media.

Israel tried to clamp down on the East Jerusalem press by strictly enforcing the censorship laws (fines and closures of newspapers) and confiscating issues at roadblocks outside the city. The Palestinians fought against the censorship, frequently turning to international organizations and the Israeli audience, and by smuggling small numbers of copies into the territories. Such "contraband" was passed from hand to hand, reaching scores of readers.

Many Arabic-language newspapers and journals were printed in Cyprus.[4] The editorial boards moved to Cyprus in the 1970s because it was a neutral site, geographically closest to the confrontational states in the Arab-Israeli conflict, and because the Cypriot government allowed freedom of publication and circulation, which existed neither in Israel nor in the Arab countries. Cyprus replaced Beirut as the newspaper hub of the Arab world and became a major source of information on events in Syria and Lebanon.[5] The reason for this was that during the Lebanese Civil War of 1976 and the intervention of Syrian troops, Arab and foreign journalists and editors became targets for putting pressure on the fighting sides that, in extreme cases, led to death threats, kidnapping, and murder.

The PLO leadership viewed the Palestinian press as a tool (or weapon) in the national liberation struggle and not merely as a means of conveying information. Every faction was affiliated with a particular newspaper whose publication was vital both economically and politically. Survival conditions for the Palestinian press were harsh. Besides the strict enforcement of Israeli censorship and security laws there was also an economic problem: since the supply of the newspapers and news organs was great and most people purchased them according to their ideological affiliation, the quality of the product often left much to be desired. When the standard of living declined in the wake of the Intifada, the papers became increasingly difficult to sell and their survival depended on outside financial support (from Jordan or Saudi Arabia, for example). This dependency limited the papers' autonomy. The Palestinians attributed so much importance to the written word that sometimes acts of violence erupted between rival journalists that reflected the political struggle between factions. Therefore, in order to survive, each newspaper had to receive political backing from the organization it represented.

Radio

During the Intifada the PLO leadership outside the territories circumvented the physical isolation that Israel imposed. It maintained fluid communication links with the Palestinians in the territories through its radio stations. The main stations that influenced the supervision of the psywar were Radio PLO (from Baghdad), Al-Quds Radio (from Damascus), and Radio Monte

Carlo (from Paris). The first two inspired hope and encouragement in the Palestinians for they relayed coded instructions to the activists, broadcast speeches and slogans, played national music, and reported political progress. The stations also transmitted indirect messages to Western decision-makers via Western diplomats and intelligence agencies translating the leading stories.

Radio PLO, the official PLO station in Baghdad, under the aegis of Saddam Hussein, began operating in the mid-1980s when the PLO was forced to leave Lebanon en bloc. In exchange, Arafat supported Iraqi policy, as was conspicuously seen in the First Gulf War. When the Intifada broke out, the PLO station broadcast messages of encouragement to the Palestinians, creating the impression that it had control of the situation. A few weeks later, when the PLO finally began to dominate events, the station transmitted slogans and instructions from the Unified National Leadership, which, for the first time, had Arafat's endorsement.

Al-Quds Radio was operated by the Ahmed Jibril faction, the PFLP – General Command, that was opposed to Arafat and acted under Syria's protection. Its transmissions were beamed directly into the territories. During the Intifada the station relayed messages from the rejectionist front calling for a violent activist line and urging the Palestinian population to undertake an armed struggle to eradicate the Israeli occupation. The station broadcast national songs, bulletins, and messages from the Unified National Leadership. According to Israeli intelligence's Hatzav Unit, a number of messages came very close to black propaganda in that they were intended to create the impression that their source was clandestine underground operations. This type of activity was probably adapted from World War II literature on radio transmissions or it may have come from the training that PFLP members received in the Soviet Union.[6] Israel jammed the Al-Quds Radio broadcasts for several months in 1988 (because of the programs' influence on the Palestinians), but lifted the obstruction due to political and technical difficulties.

Radio Monte Carlo went through a number of owners: In the 1960s it operated as a commercial pop station; in 1971 it was purchased by the French government in order to spread French influence in the Arab world; and at the end of the decade it was sold to private bodies. Israeli sources reported that the PLO was directly involved in the transmissions through commercial ties and close personal contacts. The station had a wide network of journalists in Arab capitals and its credibility was widely accepted in the Arab world.

The Palestinians' Information Policy

The Palestinians realized that their issues and demands had to remain in the forefront of the international agenda. Despite Israel's efforts to limit their effect, the Palestinians displayed creativity in advancing new issues from unexpected directions, such as land expropriation, Israel's "iron fist" policy, and revelations of brutality, trampling of justice, moral turpitude, and unlawfulness that violated civil rights and that were presented as problems that could be solved politically by the establishment of an independent Palestinian state.

Lacking a television station, the Palestinians' ability to deliver messages fell far short of Israel's. Still, they managed to churn out volumes of visual material that portrayed them in the best possible light. Jordan TV, transmitting from the territories and conveying graphic images of Palestinian suffering and valor, was a Palestinian station for all practical purposes. The station's news broadcasts in Hebrew and English transmitted pictures, most of which were not shown on Israeli TV, but were readily picked up in Israeli and Palestinian homes. The success of Jordanian television roused considerable anger in Israel, and the foreign media was criticized from both the Israeli Right and Left.

When images from the Intifada made the headlines in the American news, the Palestinian activists realized the immense power they wielded and, from that point on, endeavored to assist the foreign media to the best of their ability. They employed Palestinian stringers (part-time journalists or liaisons between foreign representatives and Palestinian activists in the field), the local populace, Palestinian journalists, and front organizations established in the mid-1980s that extended aid to the foreign press and networks. This was a relatively simple affair as the American networks looked for dramatic material and the Palestinian activists—who knew when and where an opportune story was about to break—transported the TV crews to the locale. This activity became somewhat complicated when the IDF adopted the policy of closing the territories, but the networks solved the dilemma by handing out camcorders to taxi drivers and local activists. After four months, the spontaneous stage of the uprising drew to an end, and the photos became stale, at which point there were two developments. First, the attitude toward the media became an issue in its own right: articles appeared describing the IDF's attempts to seal off the territories or Israeli soldiers' violence toward journalists. Second, the Palestinians' contacts with the foreign media grew even closer in the wake of new stories. Thus, correspondents and photographers were brought to areas declared "liberated from Israel's presence" in order to witness nighttime marches of armed Palestinian groups or hold underground interviews with Palestinians on Israel's wanted list.

Coverage of Intifada events was a cushy assignment: it afforded war zone image ops that played well on the visual media and human interest stories that found an eager audience in the printed press; Palestinians fluent in foreign languages willingly consented to interviews; reliable technical services processed the collected material; the theater of events was an hour's drive from the journalists' luxury hotel (in Tel Aviv or Jerusalem); and, the demonstrations erupted conveniently before Christmas—a dry spell for the Western news media. Moreover, foreign journalists were accorded generous help from the Palestinians who made every effort to assist them and supply them with newsworthy stories. The IDF was less keen on helping the media, but from its point of view the media crews and individuals who sought out the stories were in no immediate danger, and military censorship was rarely enforced even though all journalists in Israel were formally under its jurisdiction.[7]

The foreign media—American networks; international news agencies such as Reuters, AFP (Agence France-Press), and CNN; permanently assigned journalists from major papers and weeklies; and local correspondents who worked part-time for small- and middle-sized papers—was a formidable presence in Israel even before the Intifada broke out. Media people on assignment in Israel developed personal ties and received information from the Government Press Office, official spokespersons, universities, and social and political organizations. The Palestinians also developed information mechanisms before the Intifada. Each faction in the PLO had an information section in permanent contact with Israeli and foreign journalists. The foreign press displayed special interest in the Palestinian perspective of the events for the following reasons: the First Lebanon War (Operation Peace in the Galilee) and the great effort that the Palestinians invested in relations with the foreign newscasters and correspondents compared to the inefficiency of successive Israeli governments.

During the Intifada Palestinian activists effectively used the media to advance their political goals, assisted in the struggle by four key factors: first, the media's inherent limitations (strict deadlines, the demand for drama, and easily digestible stories), as a result of which news items had to be visual so they would be easily understood; second, the structure of the news industry restricted the journalists' ability to present in-depth programs on foreign affairs on distant lands, such as the Arab-Israeli conflict; third, the development of message-disseminating tools and information technology (faxes, PCs, camcorders, etc.) rendered the Israeli censorship irrelevant; and last, the Palestinians' expertise at nurturing cordial relations with the media.

The foreign media and news agencies tightened their links with the Palestinians and expanded their sources of information within Palestinian society and institutions because of the need for contacts and translators in preparing articles on the villages and refugee camps. Many unemployed Palestinian academics and former political prisoners opened media offices and offered their services to the foreign press. Some made the rounds of the hotels, while others set up media bureaus and advertised their services to foreign correspondents. Palestinian news services provided translation services and background material for interviews, and smuggled foreign journalists into areas declared off-limits by the IDF.

Since the Intifada was a spontaneous explosion, neither side was able to test the effectiveness of their messages in the media. Nevertheless, what happened in the northern West Bank city of Jenin four years before the Intifada may be seen as a dress rehearsal of what was to follow, and revealed each side's attitude toward the media. The event began when twelve Palestinian school girls suddenly felt nauseous because of foul odors emanating from a nearby sewer. The girls were taken to the hospital. The atmosphere quickly escalated to one of hysterics as more girls complained of similar symptoms. Rumors spread like wild fire that the girls' illness was intentional poisoning by Israel. The next day the rumor engulfed the entire West Bank. More girls claiming to be suffering from queasiness and headaches were hospitalized. The IDF was helpless in the face of the escalating protests and the foreign media's rapidly growing interest in the story. The number of hospitalized girls mushroomed, and Radio PLO announced that this was a nefarious scheme on Israel's part to cause infertility in Palestinian girls and thus defuse the Palestinian demographic bomb. The IDF was at a loss. Soldiers were helicoptered from Lebanon to the West Bank. The Civil Administration floundered in the face of outside pressure. After the Shabak investigated the incident (four days after it began)—it turned out that the events had been organized by a Fatah youth organization (the Shabiba). Its members had seized control of the hospitals, donned the uniforms of medical teams, and forced the real medical staff to follow their orders. They invited the media to witness the suffering schoolgirls and supplied them with pictures that showed rows of pupils lying on hospital beds, connected to infusions. The event proved the enormous potential in manipulating the international media and also revealed Israel's shortcomings. During the Intifada the Palestinians wielded all of these elements with impressive skill.

Shortly after the mass demonstrations, Palestinian leaders realized that opportunity was beckoning. Their first task was to penetrate their people, mostly those affiliated with PLO political factions or Islamic groups, into various areas of the foreign media.[8] This was an open secret among the foreign networks. When a senior correspondent was asked whether this was a breach of ethical standards, he rejoined that as long as they delivered the goods (exciting stories) the network would employ them.

Did the Palestinians' method of conveying information evolve gradually or was it dictated by senior leadership? The IDF believed the second hypothesis to be true. As proof, it noted that in the first week of the riots, rocks were thrown on foreign correspondents trying to cover events, but within a few days the situation reversed one hundred and eighty degrees and the Palestinians received the media with open arms. Other analysts held that the Palestinians' close relations with the foreign media did not begin with the Intifada but at least a decade earlier, and were cemented during the First Lebanon War. The rock throwing ceased because of the intervention of activists from all factions, who realized that the media's coverage could gain them lucrative returns.[9]

News networks set up shop in two East Jerusalem hotels—the American Colony and National Palace—where Palestinian organizations and private individuals maintained information offices. Journalists entering the territories quickly learned that these two hotels were their databanks. Guides, drivers, and translators offered their services, correspondents and news agencies were updated on a regular basis through a constant flow of reports from front organizations and Palestinian journalists (who identified with PLO factions). When the Intifada was already a few months old, media coverage became guided primarily by economic-commercial considerations. Prominent figures—Israelis and Palestinians—requested payment for their exposure time, and competition between the news networks grew fierce.[10]

The security establishment claimed that some Intifada events were planned solely for media coverage. The Shabak avowed that a price list existed for staged events from rock throwing to violent demonstrations. After the photojournalists paid the fee they were told when and where to stand in order to obtain the sharpest angle of the events. These allegations were utterly rejected, as expected, by the media and no proof for them was brought forth by the Israeli police or IDF Spokespersons Unit that investigated the accusations. A study revealed that foreign correspondents quickly caught on to the routine and knew, for example, that on Fridays clashes could be expected when the worshippers, primed and angry after a fiery sermon, exited the mosques. Other events received early warning publicity in leaflets. Teams of reporters congregated in spots where Palestinian-IDF confrontations were anticipated to record the breaking news. By the same token, the journalists tightened their working relationships with the local population to receive inside information on important events so they could themselves appear in prearranged areas.[11]

When IDF officers in the Gaza Strip spotted vehicles passing their base with journalists and photographers inside and the word *sahafa* (press in Arabic) on a large panel, they knew that riots would soon break out. Alternatively, if the media was absent, it was unlikely that violent demonstrations would take place and was a sure sign that the media was closely associated with the activists. A counter-argument is that the media did not initiate the events and the journalists were invited only as eye-witnesses. The media's presence seems to have exacerbated the events (with competition between media networks adding to the negative outcome), irrespective of the subsequent loss of life.

Techniques

From the time the Palestinians caught on to the rules of the game (in the third week of the riots) they determined the standards for netting maximum political profit from the events:

1. *Act in Conjunction with the Media*—Update the media on Palestinian casualties or events worthy of coverage. Both sides (the bereaved families and the media) were aware of the power of the positive image. Families who consented to the media's presence at the time of personal sorrow allowed photographers to wander around the funeral ceremony and interview the mourners. At first local activists helped the press get started. Later, when the political gains were made, the bereaved families no longer had to be persuaded to cooperate. However, the families of Israeli settlers denied the media entry to the funerals, and Israel forfeited "ammunition" in the image campaign. The Palestinians invested heavily in colorful, tantalizing stories, granting on-the-spot interviews, and depicting village life and exotic casbahs. Israel's claims

that the Palestinians fabricated events have never been proven, but the fact is that the media was invited to events that Palestinian activists organized, and the photographers' and journalists' presence contributed, as stated, to the exacerbation of violence.

2. *Attribute Importance to Terminology*—The choice of language plays a key role in a political struggle much more than commonly realized since it determines the agenda, gives meaning to the struggle, and captures the mind of the target audience. For example, the Palestinians described the events in the first year of the Intifada as "demonstrations" (rather than "riots") and, eventually, the media absorbed the term. Thus "demonstrations" entered the political discourse. It implied civil rights, fair play, and freedom of expression in a democratic society. The demonstrations turned violent when the security forces stepped in and forcibly dispersed them, which in turn served the organizers' goals since they were televised as the victims of a brutal regime. The Palestinians also adopted the word "stones," which connotated a little object that any child could throw. In reality, in many instances the Palestinians threw curbstones and heavy construction material from rooftops at the Israeli soldiers.[12]
3. *Score Propaganda Points*—Have the Western media present both sides of the conflict. After twenty years of working with the international media, the Palestinians realized the importance of giving a balanced picture; therefore, they interviewed Israelis who opposed the Likud government's right-wing positions (rather than interviewing government officials or party spokespersons). These were left-wing figures[13] who believed that Israel was stuck in an unjust and self-defeating policy (its rule in the territories) and that the Likud governments, beginning with Menachem Begin and followed by Yitzhak Shamir, had played a major role in the decline of Israel's moral and international standing since 1977. The Israeli oppositionists regarded the Intifada as an opportunity to amend government policy by the establishment of a Palestinian state alongside Israel. They expressed their positions with fervor, met with foreign delegations, and readily granted interviews to the media. However, most of the settlers interviewed by the media were of American background[14] and candidly admitted to entirely different views, such as the Jewish people's historical right to the land and implementing a transfer of the Arab population. As Western audiences' impression of the settlers was that they were merely a group of fanatics, these interviews had no impact on the audiences' positions.

CHAPTER 9

The Israeli Information Mechanism

The official Israeli bodies entrusted with information dissemination were the Government Press Office, Ministry of Foreign Affairs, IDF Spokesperson's Unit, and public relations units in the government ministries, especially the Prime Minister's Office and Defense Ministry. The secret services—Shabak, Mossad, and Military Intelligence (Aman)—also engaged in psychological warfare during the Intifada, but since the information on their activity comes from the Palestinian side, it should be taken with a grain of salt.[1] Other information-disseminating bodies can be added to the list.[2] Although not part of the mechanism in the MFA that shapes information, they are expected to carry out its instructions. However, in the period being discussed, they acted independently.

Joint activity among all these organizations was limited. While the three official bodies for information dissemination were supposed to work in tandem, cooperation was only partial as rivalry and discord characterized the relations between ministers. Foreign Minister Shimon Peres was Prime Minister Yitzhak Shamir's political rival and a challenger to Defense Minister Yitzhak Rabin, who had declared at the outset that the only solution to the Intifada was a political one. The prime minister was responsible for the Government Press Office and Shabak, whose personnel operated in the field but were not providing information that could refute the Palestinians' allegations.[3] Moreover, bureaucratic turf wars were a counterproductive feature common in many organizations and governments. In order to accrue power, authority, and resources, official agencies launched initiatives in areas outside their field of expertise, and the shoddy results were not long in coming. The third factor was the misguided approach to *hasbara* as expressed in the treatment of sensitive information. For example, the Intifada devolved into internecine assassinations after criminal elements joined the popular committees that were charged with police work and routine security measures. Criminals began carrying out arrests, interrogations, and executions of Palestinians who were sweepingly defined as collaborators. This presented Israel with a golden opportunity to publish pictures that could serve its image needs, but the idea was vetoed by the head of the defense minister's office who claimed that the images were too gruesome for viewing.[4]

The Government Press Office

Foreign journalists had the impression that the office was overburdened and, since it functioned as a pipeline for government messages, they attributed very low credibility to its announcements (government spokespersons are generally held in the same regard). A few weeks after the outbreak of the Intifada, an emergency *hasbara* team convened with representatives of the Government Press Office, the MFA and the IDF Spokesperson's Unit. The journalists felt that this team was more intent on blocking information than supplying it, therefore they used it only to gain Israel's opinion of their reports in order to create the impression of balanced coverage. The reporters' main complaint was the inordinate amount of time the emergency team needed to respond to their stories.

The office's chief task—holding "seminars on security, settlement, economics, society, and education"—illustrates the establishment's view of information dissemination as well as the gap between this view and the international media's expectation.[5] For Israel, security is of supreme importance—an outlook that reflects the bedrock belief of many Israelis that the world is acutely aware of their security needs ("a small country surrounded by enemies"). Be that as it may, foreign journalists attributed far more weight to Israel's disproportionate military strength vis-à-vis the Palestinians. And it was this perspective that was the source of the Israeli public's testiness, if not outrage, toward critical reports by the foreign media, especially on soldiers' actions in the territories. Another issue that the press office dealt with was Israeli settlements beyond the Green Line (land captured by Israel in the Six-Day War). Land settlement has always served security needs, and in many cases has determined the demarcation of the political border. The Likud government adopted a land settlement policy in Judea and Samaria after the Six-Day War. Foreign correspondents were perplexed by the connection between political borders and the number of new Israeli homes going up on a West Bank mountain top. The government's efforts to provide a convincing explanation of this nexus were too little and too wide of the mark. Another gap that the Government Press Office failed to bridge was the linkage between security and the economy. The office touted the message that Israeli citizens had to make heavy sacrifices in the form of exorbitant taxes in order to finance national security. The foreign reporters, however, who observed the high standard of living, especially in the urban centers where they worked, did not swallow the "personal sacrifice" line. Israel's efforts to close the conceptual gap were inadequate and unpersuasive.

The Ministry of Foreign Affairs (MFA)

The Hasbara Department is a branch of the MFA The original meaning of the Hebrew word *lehasbir* is to explain. In the political context it means making an organized effort to circulate information for political purposes. Israel preferred *hasbara* to "propaganda," which conjured up the term used by the Nazis. This feeling was reinforced by the Nazi-themed anti-Israel caricatures that appeared in the Arab press. Furthermore, Israeli culture is strongly influenced by Western values that regard propaganda as a crude, uncultured, heavy-handed, totalitarian vehicle, which may be one of the reasons for the absence of public discourse in Israel on propaganda's potential benefits.

In the 1980s the assistant director general of *hasbara* in the MFA mulled over this semantic issue at length. He explained, with more than a touch of irony, that *hasbara* meant disseminating information and presenting Israel's positions, whereas propaganda was the "skewered, mendacious information that Israel's enemies traffic in order to isolate Israel and strengthen international public opinion against it."[6] While the definition implies that *hasbara* is a positive endeavor, the artificial separation between propaganda and *hasbara* distorts the legitimate use of information for advancing political goals by implying that it is basically negative activity.

The 1989 Government Yearbook outlines the role and activities of the Hasbara Department in the first year of the Intifada. No changes were introduced in the department's structure in this period, excluding the formation of a production unit that was tasked with "dealing with media attacks, especially since the outbreak of events in Judea and Samaria, by gathering visual material, almost all of which came from Israeli television where the events were presented from Israel's viewpoint." The branch was ensconced in two small rooms in the basement of the Hasbara Department where it labored to publish leaflets and slides that depicted the "beautiful side of Israel" and supply TV producers with pro-Israel documentary material. The department's efforts to produce visual material boiled down to regurgitating Israeli television reportage rather than creating news films. A rare exception was the private production backed by American and Canadian Jews—the film "Searching for Solid Ground—the Intifada through Israeli Eyes." But this was a drop in the ocean.

According to the 1989 Government Yearbook:

> The Press Department witnessed a sharp rise in its activity. The spokesperson and department staff catered to hundreds of journalists this year . . . Through tours and briefings an effort was made to present the political-security facts and spur an interest in Israel's economic, social, scientific, and cultural achievements.[7]

These words reflect the Ministry's credo: It was prepared to engage only the written media. The staff assumed that if it explained Israel's daunting security concerns to the correspondents they would be convinced of the justice of Israel's cause.

The IDF and the Intifada[8]

Hasbara Aimed at the Home Audience

The IDF's Educational Branch published material in 1988 (the year the Intifada broke out) for *hasbara* purposes within the army. This material was the product of joint activity between the Behavioral Psychology Branch and Human Resources Departments, the IDF Spokesperson's Unit, and Military Intelligence. Cooperation was made possible probably because of the crisis atmosphere surrounding the stream of events. Much of the material dealt with the psychological aspect of military service in the territories. This came in response to complaints by soldiers of their ambiguous orders and shortened training schedules which had induced a general malaise and lack of motivation.

The soldiers' primary problem in the first year of the Intifada was how to respond to mass demonstrations that were deliberately designed to frustrate them. Whether the Palestinians preplanned this tactic or applied the lessons of violent events in past years when IDF troops were hard pressed to seize the rock-throwers is hard to say. Many Palestinians spoke Hebrew, having learned it from years of employment in Israel, and were aware of the soldiers' conflicts of conscience. They also gathered from the tone of the radio transmissions in the army vehicles and portable tactical radios that the IDF was not in control of the situation. The soldiers had to display self-restraint in the face of curses, rocks, and bags of urine or feces thrown at them by civilians. They had to wrestle with agonizing moral dilemmas that influenced their conduct in the territories. The troops were not trained in riot control of a civilian population, and when young Palestinians spat imprecations at them, the troops' reaction was often spontaneous and violent. As the cycle of hatred widened the number of Palestinians who actively supported the Intifada also grew. A byproduct of the soldiers' outbursts proved to be of great benefit to the Palestinians' battle in the media: the flare-ups provided graphic stories in the Palestinians' favor. Some were recorded on camcorders, relayed to the media outlets, and broadcast worldwide where they bolstered the negative image of Israel.

Until the outbreak of the Intifada, the IDF conceived of war as a short-term mechanized engagement in which the soldiers had to take the initiative and respond with lightning speed. The Intifada, however, called for police action over a long time stretch, and the troops had to maintain, inter alia, restraint and ensure that the daily civilian routine in the territories continued uninterrupted.

In order to halt the deteriorating situation the IDF briefed the troops and distributed brochures that analyzed the events and the way that they were liable to assist the enemy. Officers were instructed to speak candidly with their men in order to alleviate tension. In February 1988, two months after the eruption of the Intifada, the Chief of Staff sent a message to the troops exhorting them to display restraint and avoid the use of force as a form of punishment during a demonstration or after a mission was completed. In November 1988 the education corps published a brochure[9] that described how the exaggerated use of force conveyed to the Palestinians a message of Israeli weakness. The two documents indicate that the IDF correctly interpreted the political factors in the Palestinians' struggle.

In July 1988 the Field Psychology Unit in the Behavioral Sciences Branch published several instructional booklets for the units serving in the territories. These publications analyzed the psychological frustration stemming from violent clashes with a civilian population over an extended period of time and offered solutions for dealing effectively with the anguish. One technique that the military psychologists recommended was an accurate analysis of the Palestinians' situation, an analysis that presented the gaps between the information and stories relayed in the media and the real situation on the ground that had sparked an exaggerated response. In short, officers had to constantly remind their men of the importance of restraint. Another technique was to create a single formula in cases of uncertainty regarding the interpretation of an order (for example, the definition of a "life-threatening situation"). The goal was to prevent situations where every officer had a different interpretation of the steps to be taken in a given incident. But these instructions did not resolve the ambiguity that the soldiers felt in the absence of clear guidelines. In many interviews the soldiers told the same story: It was unrealistic to expect them to carry out assignments unless the rules of conduct in various situations were unequivocal. The army tried to come to grips with this complex issue by adopting legal principles. It drafted a short code of conduct (early 1988) in legal jargon that only caused the soldiers more frustration because of the impression that to act "properly" they would need a private attorney clipped to their webbed combat harness.[10]

Another factor that had an adverse effect on the soldiers' activity was the Israeli public's tendency to negatively stereotype Arabs, often expressed in apothegms such as "the only language an Arab understands is the use of force." An internal report of the Behavioral Sciences Branch in 1988 states:

> Devising stereotypes helps the individual deal with diverse behaviors in a hostile environment . . . since they provide a simpler picture of reality. In the case of service in the territories—where the easiest classification is to associate the local population with the enemy—a violent response towards the locals can easily lead to dehumanization . . . and to actions that overstep the orders for military conduct in a civilian environment.[11]

The method of coping with the negative stereotype was to furnish the troops with realistic information prior to and during a mission that explained the processes that Palestinian society was undergoing and the pressure it was under in each particular area that the soldiers were operating in.[12] The goal was to supply the troops with updated information on Palestinian society and the reasons for Palestinian pressure and aggression, so that they could perform their duties rationally instead of emotionally.

The material that the IDF circulated among the officers (from company commander up) in the first year of the Intifada reveals that the senior command was aware of the soldiers' difficulties, but stressed the importance of exercising maximum restraint against demonstrators, especially since the Intifada leaders wanted to escalate the violence in order to expand the cycle of hatred and gain greater press coverage. Therefore the IDF had to avoid being lured into the natural response of an armed force under attack.

Restraint in the face of taunting jibes, urine and excrement slinging, and hails of rocks was rooted in the IDF's ethical code. Senior officers had to define to the military's norms, educate and pacify young officers, and lower the tension in the units.

The first publication of the chief education officer came out in February 1988[13]—eight weeks after the Intifada erupted. The analysis explains the army's view of the situation at this relatively early stage. The brochure was intended to provide officers with the means for dealing with the army's most pressing issue—uncertainty on the part of conscripts and reservists regarding Israel's aim in maintaining control in the territories. The brochure addressed the questions that soldiers were most likely to ask. It also defined the IDF's two main objectives: first, to quell the riots because they endangered the soldiers and the local population, tainted Israel's image, and hurt its economy and resources; second, to rein in violent political elements who were bent on derailing the peace process and whose activities, if not curbed, would send a message of Israel's weakness to the Arab states and Arab radicals living in Israel. Accordingly, the IDF specifically ordered the troops to eschew as much as possible injuring the local population and representatives of the media. A unit's success was evaluated according to the speed with which it dispersed crowds, kept soldiers and civilians out of harm's way, and preserved Israel and the IDF's moral image.

The IDF and the Media

Conflict with the media emerged at the start of the Intifada. The IDF tried to resolve the differences, but just as it was caught by surprise by the intensity of the rioting, so was it unprepared for dealing with the media. Further exacerbating the situation was the soldiers' enmity—both conscripts and reservists—toward the media's coverage of events. If Israeli television broadcast an edited version of an incident, then Jordanian TV offered fuller coverage, and the weeklies such as *Time* and *Newsweek* sometimes described the incident in ways incredulously different from what the soldiers had experienced. The army tried to cope with its muddied relations with the local and foreign media by briefing conscripts and reservists at all echelons.

The Education Corps' 1988 brochure pointed out the impact of the foreign press on the demonstrations:

> The media was allowed into the territories only three weeks after the Intifada erupted. This was because of IDF officers' opposition to its presence. They had noted a direct link between the media's presence and the outbreak of riots. There is historical precedence to closure—during the Falkland War British authorities refused the media access to the battle zone.

This statement expresses the IDF's defensive attitude toward the foreign press and its inability to deal with the new reality or acknowledge it publicly. However, the media found its way into the territories. It did not have to wait three weeks for IDF permission; it received material from alternative sources. The IDF's use of the Falkland War to justify its off-limits policy (read: Israel is not the only democracy that forbids reporters access to areas in wartime) reflected the bitterness in the army. In effect it implied that Britain was not criticized as harshly as Israel was.

Another area rife with tension was the strict time frame within which the IDF public relations officer had to respond to articles in the media so that a balanced presentation in line with Western standards could be conveyed. During the Intifada the IDF Spokesperson tried to obtain a picture of events from the forces operating in the field. This entailed a lengthy process that fell far short of the media's demands for instant news bytes, with the result that many Western news outlets televised coverage based on minimal input (or none at all) from the Israeli side. This was also true of reports by Israeli and Palestinian human rights organizations.[14] Only after Israel exerted pressure did the organizations agree to extend the time frame so that the IDF Spokespersons' Unit could study and respond to the egregious charges being made against IDF units and individual soldiers.

The army tackled the situation in two ways: first, by issuing clear-cut instructions to senior officers regarding the criteria for declaring an area off-limits to the media, and second, by improving cooperation with the media via reservist liaison officers in a special unit subordinate to the IDF Spokesperson.[15] On May 30, 1988 the Government Press Office and IDF public relations branch distributed a document on the army's media policy, according to which: soldiers were forbidden to take part in interviews without express permission from the IDF Spokesperson or its representatives; incidents with reporters were forbidden, such as blocking photojournalists' camera lenses by hand; soldiers had to speak politely but assertively to journalists who refused to obey instructions (and only in extreme cases was the officer in charge allowed to apprehend a reporter and transfer him or her to the nearest police station); and requisitioning material was allowed only if there were grounds to suspect a serious security breach. The legal language of the orders seems to express the IDF's difficulty in balancing the journalists' needs with Israel's negative representation in their stories.[16]

The brochure distributed to units in June 1988[17] set forth two oft-repeated assumptions: the media, by its presence in the territories, encourages violence, and, the Palestinians are bent on portraying themselves as the downtrodden side waging a heroic struggle against a powerful brutal enemy. Therefore the IDF had to convey a counter-image that combined confident assertiveness with restraint, and firm action with a courteous, respectful demeanor; officers and soldiers could be interviewed only after obtaining permission from the IDF Spokesperson's Unit; all closed military areas were off limits to civilians and the media. This policy, which was formulated in the first months of the Intifada, remained essentially intact during the following years.[18] Tension with the media spiked when the soldiers discovered that Israeli citizens were on the technical teams working with the foreign press.[19]

On another level the IDF dealt with the situation by developing a special training program for all units assigned to the territories. Each training class included lectures, discussions, and an instructional film entitled "The Camera Sees It All" that was produced by the IDF's Spokespersons' Photography Branch. The film showed how reporters work and explained the principles behind their choice of a story. It also focused on problems stemming from the presence of TV crews in the territories and discussed the damage caused when the IDF refuses to cooperate with the press.

The brochure "Facing the Cameras in the Territories," written by the Chief of the Education Corps Headquarters/Hasbara Branch, and the IDF Spokesperson's Unit in June 1988, states that an officer has to explain two principles to his men: one relates to values: the media is the bastion of democracy; and the other relates to tactics: both sides in the conflict are striving to exploit the media for their own needs. According to the text, it took the IDF a year and a half to realize that the media's presence in the territories was a fact, and that Israel and the Palestinians were in aggressive competition for the media's attention. The authors of the brochure acknowledged that at the time the Intifada broke out, pressure was heaviest, and the regulations and methods of coping with it were still hazy, the IDF had committed unwarranted mistakes in its relations with the press, such as manhandling it and forbidding it entry to certain areas. The authors also noted that the organizers of demonstrations and street riots made clever use of the media to convey their feelings and positions. This admission was an indirect recognition of the army's failure, and the subtext was that amends could still be made and victory won in the battle for the media.

The brochure described at length the political war that Israel was engaged in and the crucial role the media played in it:

> The situation analysis makes it immediately clear that the clashes in the streets between [IDF] soldiers and local Palestinians were the means rather than the end . . . The goals are political . . . The overall objective toward which our efforts have to be directed is political. In this struggle we need the media's help.

However, at this point it seems that the leitmotif in the stories emanating from the territories could not be reversed since the media had settled into a routine of work patterns with its information sources. The headline describing events in the territories—Civilians against Soldiers—was far more eye-catching than any alternative the IDF could come up with. Moreover, the lower ranks in the army still failed to comprehend the Intifada's political agenda, so that even after the brochure was circulated some locations remained "closed-off military zones." At this stage the media no longer took these limitations seriously and found other ways of entering the area and getting a story.

The brochure adopted the reverse psychology approach. It tried to convince the soldiers to change their attitude toward the media by first listing the reasons why they should not cooperate with the media, and then refuting the reasons one after the other through logical argumentation. For example, it claimed that the territories could not be completely cordoned off since such an act would require an exorbitant investment in manpower. An argument like this fell on attentive ears because the reservists had begun to feel the onus of service in the territories. Or, even by partially shutting off the territories to the media, Israel would lose its credibility, especially in the Arab world which has great respect for Israel's Arabic-language radio and television programs, because the Arabs would understand that Israel had something to hide. But an even more cogent argument was that the Palestinians' trade in video cassettes documenting the events was booming, therefore recorded data could not possibly be kept from the media. With the wisdom of retrospect, this was the correct decision because, as stated, the foreign networks had supplied camcorders to the Palestinians and in return often obtained stories worthy of reportage—an undeniably lucrative investment for both sides. Although the films were not of the highest quality, they nevertheless revealed what Israel wanted to hide and offered viewers the requisite dramatic impact.

Still, the IDF kept its longstanding tradition of overseeing information. Its orders were that interviews would be granted only if the IDF or its representatives gave their approval. This strict procedure seems to reflect the army's awareness of the danger that information could have on Israel's position. Worse from the point of view of Israel's public relations, officers who gave interviews were unskilled in how to comport themselves in front of the media. A few years later, after the Intifada, the IDF changed its policy. In 1995 some senior officers were taught the basic do's and don'ts in television appearance, and a paper was published explaining how to present oneself in a TV interview. In August 1994 the IDF Public Relations Branch prepared a kit with lectures on the IDF's relations with the media. This came in answer to the increasingly negative attitude that the troops—conscripts as well as reservists—displayed toward the media. The kit—complete with slides, a video cassette, and guidelines—was designed for lecturers who spoke with soldiers before and during their service in the territories.

The document reveals the paradigm shift in IDF-media relations since the start of the Intifada. Three years after the rioting ended the IDF no longer harbored resentment toward the media or the Palestinians for the way they exploited it. The army realized that if it wanted the cooperation of certain correspondents it had to take necessary steps to gain it, such as providing the reporters with area access, allowing them to get their own impressions (rather than interpret for them what was happening), preparing the area convincingly so they would "buy" the story, and taking the Palestinians' reaction to these measures into account. In the new game rules the army should provide the correspondents with assistance so that they could do their work quickly and efficiently, so that the story—that has involved much time and energy—would not be lost. However the IDF must understand exactly what the reporters are interested in—this is the only way that victory can be won in the media war.

The document laid out the basic principles of the IDF's relationship with the media. Its purpose was to instruct the troops on the importance of allowing the media and their representatives a free hand in their work. The principles have become the IDF's standard in military-media relations: credibility must not be compromised under any condition; action must be quick—since whoever reports first wins the greater amount of sympathy and support; access to an event must be permitted, though security restrictions also have to be taken into consideration; gain the initiative—as in war; display professionalism—engage in a dialogue with the media, build a cooperative rapport with journalists; check the material, and assist the correspondents as much as possible.

The publication indicates the major volte-face in the IDF's approach to the media. The army realized that whatever information it blocked would eventually find its way to the media and be counterproductive to Israel's interests. In retrospect, this approach would have been far more beneficial had the IDF adopted it at the outset of the Intifada.

Be nice

CHAPTER 10

ing its Goals

PLO had control over the its media policy, hone its pments. In the first months e communists and Islamic al Leadership, creating an key principle in successful the tighter the centralized

d like combustible tinder in the lap of all the parties. Nevertheless, as it progressed, the layout and delivery of the messages became meticulously planned. The Palestinians exhibited superb skill in short-term planning—a matter of weeks—once the events came under the PLO's centralized control and the pattern of the struggle was determined. The leaflets of the Unified National Leadership contained weekly or monthly timetables for protest marches, confrontations, strikes, and demonstrations.

The Palestinians defined their long-term political goals in the clearest of terms: the end of the occupation and establishment of an independent Palestinian state. To realize these objectives they had to calm Israeli fears of a Palestinian state across the border and convey the image of a democratic organization. The PLO's intermediate-range political goal (defined several years before the Intifada) was to convene an international conference. Because the organization was certain of its goals, short-term steps were easier to plan: keep the Intifada burning, and graft it onto the world agenda for several years by staging a large number of media events.

A good example of event planning was the return of deported Palestinians to Israel on the ferry *Al-Awda* (The Return) in February 1988. The organizers wanted to excite the public's imagination by likening the sea voyage to the famous Jewish refugee ship *Exodus 1947*. To do this the PLO chartered a ferry and planned to transport hundreds of Palestinians who had been expelled from their homes during the last twenty years together with a large press corp. The operation testified not only to a profound understanding of the media's functioning, but also to a sophisticated level of organization. Over one hundred foreign journalists were invited to Athens; the PLO supplied all their needs and was especially generous in furnishing information. But, when a mysterious bomb destroyed the ferry in the port of departure in Cyprus, the Palestinians' plans for a political windfall from the media's coverage of a mega-event were thwarted.

The Israelis

A major factor influencing Israel's moves in the Intifada was that neither the IDF nor Shabak had any contingency plans for countering a large-scale Palestinian uprising. In fact, Israel's intelligence layout was caught totally by surprise. The military felt that this was the second time it had been strategically caught off-guard (the first time was the Egyptian-Syrian attack in the Yom Kippur War in 1973), even though the Palestinians had not planned the uprising and its political goals were limited. Despite the surprise, Israel had sufficient time to assess the situation and examine various courses of action. But, according to published material, the military establishment lacked long-range political and military solutions and did not take into account the consequences of its measures for quelling the uprising.

Israel immediately made two moves that proved its military response took priority over political considerations for long-term relations with the Palestinians or even with Israel's image in the international media. The first was in April 1988—the assassination in Tunisia of Khalil al-Wazir (Abu Jihad), the head of the PLO's armed military wing, the person in charge of organizing the Intifada's financial outlay and supervising events in the territories. (Israel has never admitted its part in the assassination.) The mission's success—which required an incredibly complex logistical effort in data-gathering 2,400 kilometers from Israel—had very little effect since the Intifada's modus operandi was already institutionalized and its channels of communications and funding functioned like a smoothly running machine. Israel's second step was the formation of two *mistaravim* units (undercover counter-terror units: Duvdevan and Shimshon) in the territories that were designed to curb the extent of the riots by arresting field activists who directed the Intifada from the sidelines. These units came at a very high political price because, as expected, the Palestinians lost no time in presenting them as assassination squads.

The main reason for the absence of clearly defined, long-range goals was the raucous public debate in Israel that polarized positions and hampered the formation of a national consensus on the future of the territories. This situation had a major impact on the soldiers' operational capability and the IDF's efforts to define its goals. In other words, the ambiguous wording handed down by official spokespersons in statements such as: "The IDF has to allow the political level to act in a position of strength by making sure the violence does not compel the government to make decisions under pressure," or "The IDF must reduce the level of violence so that the politicians can negotiate an arrangement," led the officers and men to ask themselves why they had to put up with so much suffering if a Palestinian state is eventually going to be established.[1] The main reasons for Israel's failure to wage psychological warfare were the lack of planning, lack of means, and especially the near indifference toward its vital importance despite evidence that the Palestinians were employing it most effectively. Israel limited itself to reacting to Palestinian initiatives and took no significant measures to counter them.

Target Audience

The Palestinian Side

Delegations. To win political support the Palestinians turned to foreign aid organizations, such as the Quakers (an American religious, pacifist movement) and various UN agencies. They also invited delegations on study programs and eye-witness tours in the territories. These delegations often represented professional sectors, such as trade unions, doctors, lawyers, and even pop singers and film stars. The itinerary always included a refugee camp, a meeting with a senior Palestinian figure (Dr. Sari Nusseibeh, Hanna Siniora, Dr. Hanan Ashrawi, and others) who presented the events from both the academic and personal perspective. Sometimes the members met with Israelis who spoke against the government's policy and supported an independent Palestinian state. Prominent among these figures were Major General (res.) Matti Peled; Uri Avneri, a leftwing journalist; and Dr. Meron

Benvenisti, a political scientist and deputy mayor of Jerusalem from 1971 to 1978. The culmination of the visit was the publication of a joint statement that criticized Israel and called for the creation of a Palestinian state and peaceful solution to the conflict.

Some of the delegations were organized by the American-Arab Anti-Discrimination Committee (ADC). As part of the Eyewitness Israel Project, fifty-four US congressmen and senators arrived on a fact-finding mission in 1988. In addition, the Palestinians organized group visits for clergymen, lawyers, and educators, in order to influence grassroot decision-makers. The delegates were expected, on their return home, to relate their impressions of the Palestinian plight in interviews, newspaper articles, and books.

Tourists. In the years preceding the Intifada, the East Jerusalem travel agencies enjoyed a surge in tourism, mostly pilgrims coming to the Holy Land. Efficient, low-priced package deals (hotels and tours) undoubtedly contributed to the boom. The travel agencies organized tours through the territories and Israel, led by tour guides who presented the Palestinian view out of personal conviction or patriotic motives that intensified after the First Lebanon War. The tourists were also swayed by the media, a field that Israel had all but abandoned. Tourists obtained information mainly from the radio—the BBC or Voice of Israel in English. Israel's *Jerusalem Post* was the most accessible local paper for English readers. Jordanian television had a daily English-language newscast, but Israeli TV was without an English-language news program until October 1990, when it was introduced as a result of public pressure.[2]

Key Communicators. Several years before the Intifada the Palestinians already identified a number of prominent Israelis who responded favorably to their ideas. These Israelis supported the establishment of a Palestinian state alongside Israel.[3] Certain Israeli groups and institutions maintained relations with the Palestinians, such as the Givat Haviva Center of Arab-Israeli Studies whose activities included seminars, Arabic-language courses, and meetings between Arabs and Jews. The largest leftwing movement, "Peace Now," had broad public support. Another group was the Committee for Solidarity with Bir Zeit University (a Palestinian university near Ramallah, north of Jerusalem, noted for its radical leftwing activism since its establishment in 1981). The Committee for Solidarity was one of the first groups with membership of significant size. In 1982, when the IDF entered Lebanon, the group's membership expanded. Two other radical groups, "Yesh Gvul" ("There's a Limit") and the "21st Hour," both opposed service in Lebanon.

Although the activists traveled between groups their numbers continued to grow. One of their activities was to travel to the territories and meet with Palestinians. These meetings were frequently held in refugee camps where the stark living conditions left a strong impression on the visitors. Israeli and Palestinian academics engaged in extended dialogues, and Palestinian experts were invited to learn and lecture in Israeli institutions.

Israeli journalists for Arab affairs were also an important target audience. Their contact with the Palestinians was a basic facet of their work and many of them made no effort to hide their criticism of the Likud government's policy (1977–1984). The Palestinians cultivated relations with Israeli commentators and correspondents who backed them, and passed on valuable information to them, but withheld it from unsupportive newsmen.

The Israeli Side

Delegations. The level of Palestinian-initiated visits to the territories jarred the MFA, responsible for activity in this area. Therefore the government withheld official assistance from delegations known to be hostile (in order to discredit their reports), but extended generous help to delegations that asked to learn the situation "properly." In response and as counterweight to the Palestinians' delegations, Israel arranged tours for Jewish and Zionist organizations from the United States and Europe. On their return home, members of these organizations published statements in leading American and European newspapers and journals expressing unqualified support for Israel.

Tourists. The number of tourists declined sharply after the Intifada erupted (excluding pilgrims), and following the First Gulf War (1991) the number dropped to an unprecedented low. Tourists were an audience to whom Israel could convey its positions and policy. The Hasbara Center, for years linked to the Prime Minister's Office, took Israelis on visits of historical areas to strengthen their ties to the national heritage and conducted fact-finding tours for overseas visitors to improve Israel's image.[4]

Means of Dissemination

The Palestinian Side

The scope of the PLO's tactical activity demonstrated a high degree of skill and efficiency. The methods used in message dissemination were characterized by threadbare resources that forced the Palestinians to devise unconventional means and the Israelis to fight a losing rear-guard battle. Besides the press and radio, the Palestinians possessed four other means for conveying information to the local population.[5]

Leaflets were the most important vehicle for message dissemination. They were cheap and easily produced in bulk, but they also had two drawbacks. The first drawback was the amount of information that could be printed on a typically one-page leaflet, and the second was that their circulation demanded a complex logistical layout. During the Intifada they were ubiquitous; they were found in public places, on walls, mosques, doors of homes, in mailboxes, they were also sent by fax or announced on PLO Radio and Radio Jibril.[6]

Graffiti was a widely used means for spreading messages and emboldening the populace. It was cheap, efficient, conspicuous, easy to produce, and its sources were hard to trace. It consisted of a few words or a line or two that had to convey an incisive idea, slogan, or graphic symbol that expressed a noble, inspiring idea. A good example was the word "Vietnam," which called to mind a small nation whose dedication and sacrifice defeated a superpower. Nothing more had to be added. Sometimes the graffiti carried Palestinian symbols; Hamas, for example, portrayed the al-Aqsa Mosque in Jerusalem with the Koran crowning its dome. All of the factions placed an icon of a rifle, a fist, or the Koran in the center of the map of Palestine. Other common images were swords, axes, and tanks. Graffiti was designed to drive home the messages of the Unified National Leadership, rouse the population to resistance, warn against collaboration, order the community to adhere to the leadership's commands, and announce the presence of various factions. Each organization had its own color: the PLO—black; communists—red; and Islamic organizations—green. All of the factions adopted Islamic motifs, such as verses from the Koran or the cry "Allahu Akbar" ("God is the greatest"). Some of the headings were written in English for the benefit of the foreign media, others in Hebrew for Israeli soldiers. The IDF waged a futile struggle against the street writing, and forced the owners of graffiti-painted walls to erase the slogans.

Facsimile. Intifada activists used fax machines on a wide scale because of their availability, accessibility, mobility, and operability. Information was communicated via fax machines and telephones for drafting leaflets, a process that demanded considerable coordination between Gaza and the West Bank, among the PLO factions, between the PLO and Islamic groups, and between the territories and Arafat, who was then in Tunisia.[7]

Loudspeakers have long been used in wartime at the tactical level to broadcast messages to the enemy: Palestinians employed mounted loudspeakers on vehicles to convey messages to the home audience. Loudspeakers were also used to relay sermons to crowds outside the mosques and were an integral part of the minaret where the muezzin calls the faithful to prayer five times a day. Palestinian activists in Hebron linked up most of the city's mosques to a single loudspeaker and promulgated the sermons and speeches to an extremely large audience. At the start of the Intifada most of the mosques were off-limits to the IDF. This made them a relatively safe place to hide in, hold meetings, make plans, and prepare weapons and leaflets. Megaphones were used to announce the time and place for demonstrations and report the number of casualties.

The Unified National Leadership and PLO oversaw information dissemination and integrated the different threads in a joint effort to magnify the impression of solidarity and determination. First, the leaflets were conveyed to the media, then distributed on the street (wall graffiti), and sent by fax to Israeli newspapers and simultaneously broadcast on Israeli radio.

The Israelis

IDF helicopters dropped leaflets exhorting the Palestinians to uphold law and order in the villages that had declared themselves "liberated areas." Sometimes the leaflets were scattered in public places or handed out personally. Settlers and soldiers (as individuals, not as part of an organized effort) spray-painted messages about the arrival of an army unit to a particular area or drew symbols like the Star of David and the map of Israel with a clenched fist (the logo of the radical rightwing *Kach* Movement). The IDF mounted amplifiers on jeeps to announce its presence in an area, curfews, or breaks in the curfew to stock up on supplies. Village leaders and notables also conveyed messages to the locals.

Persuasion Techniques

The Palestinians

Nonviolent Action

Nonviolent political activity is intended to catalyze political change without incurring loss of life. The most famous case in history is Mahatma Gandhi, who waged a successful struggle against British rule in India by taking the nonviolent path. Literature on the subject mentions over two hundred methods of nonviolent action for attaining an objective.[8]

The PLO adopted a policy of nonviolent resistance (in sharp contrast to its use of terror in the past) to dissuade the Israelis from forcibly breaking up mass demonstrations, and especially to countervail their justification in using force. Nonviolent resistance was introduced into the territories through the tireless work of Dr. Mubarak Awad, a Palestinian psychologist who lived in the United States and made an academic study of violent political activity. He returned to the territories in the mid-1980s and tried, without success, to promote his strategy. A few weeks after the Intifada broke out and the IDF and Shabak gained control over most of the events, the Palestinian activists sought another outlet for the people's pent-up revolutionary energy. First among the traditional leaders to believe that Awad's suggestions were worth reconsideration was Hanna Siniora (the editor of the influential newspaper *al-Fajar* that was identified with Arafat). Awad was followed by young activists who had grown up in the refugee camps and gone on to receive a university education. The Unified National Leadership's leaflets advocated disengagement from the Civil Administration and Israeli economy and later called for the founding of an alternative Palestinian leadership. Awad was a sought-after media personality because of his academic degrees, moral stance, and fluency in English. The Israeli government lost much sleep over him, and decided to deport him despite opposition from the US State Department and American public opinion (Awad held American citizenship). The Israelis claimed that his rejection of violence was only a public veneer. To prove this they quoted passages from his books stating that nonviolent resistance is merely a preparatory stage to violent activity for ousting Israel from the territories.

Awad's deportation did not stem the spread of his ideas. They were a major aspect of the Intifada since nonviolent resistance was perfectly suited to the situation in the territories. The IDF avoided indiscriminate fire on Palestinian crowds out of ethical considerations, strict rules of engagement, a legal system where appeals to the Supreme Court is common practice, and close monitoring of events by foreign and local journalists. The Palestinians' nonviolent resistance kept the Intifada on the world agenda for several months and strengthened the PLO's position in the territories after years of waiting in the wings.

The Palestinians' nonviolent techniques had three basic goals: to erode Israel's bureaucratic and political control of the Palestinians; to frustrate and exhaust the soldiers in the face of Palestinian determination by purposely inculcating a sense of angst and absurdity over Israel's continued rule in the territories; and to contrast the Palestinians' peaceful civil rights demonstrations with the IDF's cruel and thuggish conduct. The nonviolent resistance techniques were political, legal, economic, and religious.

Political Techniques

Demonstrations. The Palestinians' short-range goal was to mobilize the masses and ensure that the statehood issue retained its lead position on the international stage. The activists strove to maintain the highest degree of nonviolent confrontation with Israeli security forces by holding daily demonstrations in the territories. Their aims were to expand the circle of violence, escalate the conflict, and recruit a much greater number of activists by incurring losses among the Palestinians (a cynical but highly effective revolutionary technique for increasing support). As soon as the demonstrations reached a critical mass the troops would move in, often causing many injuries. When Palestinians were killed, wounded, or taken into custody, even if they had only been bystanders, their families immediately entered the fray and joined the ranks of the activists. For this reason women and children were instructed to take part in the protests: their presence served as a deterrent to the use of live ammunition or other heavy-handed means of crowd dispersal. There were two types of demonstrations: planned initiatives and local initiatives.

A few weeks after the spontaneous stage passed and the PLO gained control of the Intifada, the activists experienced in crowd control began plying their know-how. They organized demonstrations according to political exigencies, which quickly evolved into a game with mutually recognized rules. The foreign media working in close cooperation with the local population had the impression that the demonstrations were spontaneous outbursts. In reality they were usually timed to coincide with historical dates on the Palestinian calendar in an attempt to inculcate a national consciousness. (For example, March 30, "Land Day," was first celebrated in 1976 when the Arabs in Israel protested the expropriation of lands in the Galilee; November 29 commemorates the UN Decision of 1947 to partition British Mandate Palestine into two separate states.) Both sides prepared for clashes on these days. Demonstrations were generally held on Fridays, when the agitated congregations flooded the streets at the end of sermons in the mosques.

The time and place of the demonstrations appeared on leaflets. At first, organizing the event required choosing the right messages, preparing flags, composing slogans, and planning where to plant the banners. Next, the routes were decided on, cheering teams recruited to embolden the leaders, and strategic positions determined for the leaders and their bodyguards. The activists received placards, leaflets, and loudspeakers, escape routes were arranged, and spotters stationed to warn of the IDF's arrival. Details of the demonstration and the places where confrontation was most likely were conveyed to the media. The organizations videotaped the demonstrations in order to improve their tactics. Several weeks passed before Israeli security forces realized that it was more effective for counter-insurgency units to arrest the leaders than for IDF troops to quell large crowds. These units used cameras to record the leaders who were directing the demonstrations from the sidelines. The activists tried to hide their identity by covering their faces with a kaffiyeh or ninja mask.

Some of the spontaneous demonstrations were the result of local initiatives; others were initiated on order from above. In the first stage a small group of activists marched through the streets, banging on improvised drums and shouting slogans. They burned tires that sent thick black gusts of smoke spiraling in the air. A favorite tactic was to hold a demonstration as bait in order to ambush a military patrol. When the vehicle stopped because its tires were punctured by nails, the Palestinians pelted it with rocks. Sometimes when the soldiers left their vehicles to light off in pursuit of the rock-throwers, the Palestinians set the vehicles on fire and photographed the scene. These actions naturally had a very negative effect on the IDF's deterrent capability.

International Fact-finding Teams. The Palestinians had been using this technique widely since the 1970s, and the Civil Administration appointed a senior officer to deal with these teams. The number of investigating teams in the territories multiplied during the Intifada—some came on their own initiative, but most were sponsored by the PLO (generally arriving from the United States and EU countries). The delegation members visited villages and refugee camps and met with Palestinian leaders, academics, and professional colleagues in the field that the delegation represented (education, labor, community work, social welfare, etc.). Israelis who supported the PLO and who were highly critical of Israeli policy also joined the fact-finding teams. Many UN groups visited the territories. Since Arafat's first appearance in the UN in 1974, the PLO spared no effort to be accepted into the organization and prove itself responsible and respectable.

Marches. The "shock committees" (also termed the "popular army") had many young activists in its ranks and began to hold marches in the second year of the Intifada—first in remote villages and then in the cities. At first the marches were clandestine, with bystanders positioned to whistle if the army approached. Details of a march were announced only a short time before it was scheduled to begin so that the Israelis would be left in the dark. The procession set out from a central point in a village or neighborhood, with marchers donned in uniform and head coverings. They brandished axes, swords, or rifles, and carried the Palestinian flag. At a given point, journalists who had been invited became eye-witnesses of the event. In this way the world learned of the clandestine marches. Additional goals were also attained: deterring the population from collaboration with Israel; strengthening the morale of the Palestinian audience and creating the impression that an organization with armed members is in complete control of events whereas Israeli control is ineffectual; and proving that a strong Palestinian leadership exists and the Intifada has a good chance of succeeding. The IDF felt that the marches posed a threat to its standing, and tried to halt them with curfews and closures.

Sabotage. This is a simple, commonly used, low-risk technique for disabling the economy of an occupying state. Years before the Intifada broke out Palestinian workers in Israel perpetrated willful damage as a means of protest, such as pouring cement into water pipes in buildings under construction. Since the leaflets explicitly called for sabotage, the number of acts rose significantly. The Palestinians set fire to Jewish National Fund forests and natural woodlands. These acts made the headlines and the scars in the landscape were visible for a long time afterwards. The Palestinians quickly realized that setting ablaze trees and vehicles enraged the Israelis, incurred heavy costs, and had a profound psychological effect.

Sit-in strikes were a routine activity that came in the wake of IDF operations in the territories. The strikes were mainly held in the offices of international organizations, such as the Red Cross, or the US Consulate in East Jerusalem.

Lobbying. The Intifada also instilled national awareness in the Arab citizens in Israel, who began organizing demonstrations and solidarity marches with their Palestinian brethren in the territories and donating material to areas under curfew. The political representatives of Israel's Arabs took an active part in the struggle by initiating protest rallies and giving vent to their feelings in Knesset speeches. The Palestinians labored tirelessly to convince neutral audiences, such as the US Congress and Senate, of the justice of their cause. The American Jewish lobby obstructed Palestinian efforts to open a PLO office in the United States and gain an entry visa for Arafat, but the Palestinians overcame these obstacles through its network of front organizations such as the Arab Student Union and the Coalition for the Middle East. Palestinian political activity in the territories was modeled after the methods of the Jewish and Arab lobbies in the United States. The first Arab lobby was organized in 1968 and was followed by more groups. All of them endeavored to promote the Palestinian cause and increase American awareness of Arabic culture as a springboard for advancing political interests.

Legal Techniques

Overloading the Legal System. The smooth functioning of the legal system in the territories was of major importance for Israel, and the Palestinians' goal was to destroy this image. Palestinian lawyers had to struggle with their conscience whether or not to represent their clients in the Israeli courts. The argument against it claimed that legal representation was nothing short of de facto recognition of occupation rule and helping Israel maintain the image that it was administering the territories according to proper legal procedure. Other lawyers, however, argued that deals could be cut with the prosecutor that would lessen their clients' punishment and reduce their families' suffering. As the months passed and arrests increased, the number of Palestinians facing trial skyrocketed, and the chief military prosecutor had to reinforce his staff in order to cope with the growing pressure. Judges had to sit on scores of cases everyday and Palestinian defense attorneys felt it incumbent upon them to reach some sort of agreement with the military prosecutor for their clients' sake.

Ordinarily the military courts employed the criminal code in Palestinian cases, which indicated that the state regarded the crimes as matters of criminal conduct. However, Palestinian attorneys argued that their clients should be treated as political prisoners and that justice could not be meted out in a court that tried dozens of cases every day.[9] By the third month of the Intifada the Israeli prisons were filled to capacity and it was decided to set up a detention facility tent camp in Ktziot (western Negev). The camp's physical conditions were tolerable, and incarceration became a status symbol for young Palestinians, especially when the camp became an arena in the struggle against Israel. Despite the efforts to overtax the legal system in the territories, Israel has managed to preserve the image of a law abiding state. The Swedish government helped the Palestinians during the Intifada with generous monetary grants to finance the detainees' legal defense.[10]

The Supreme Court. The Palestinians made extensive use of the Israeli Supreme Court in its role as the high court of justice. In most cases of deportation and the demolition of homes the court accepted the position of the IDF and Shabak. However, in many instances of administrative arrest and prisoner rights, the Palestinian lawyers, in tandem with Israeli citizen's rights organizations, won the cases. As a result, the IDF had to examine the legal implication of every action to be sure it would be confirmed by the Supreme Court, which greatly impaired its ability to counter the Palestinians.

Economic Techniques

The Destruction of the Civil Administration. With the outbreak of the Intifada the Palestinians made a signal effort, via persuasion and force, to liberate themselves from Israel's bureaucracy and replace it with Palestinian institutions. In the decade before the "official outbreak" in 1987, various PLO factions set up hundreds of organizations to deal with charity collection and distribution, education, and employment. Palestinians who worked in the Israeli Civil Administration were ordered—via leaflets, phone calls, letters, and graffiti—to quit their jobs. The same order was issued to workers in local councils, beginning in February 1988. Many who refused to quit learned the hard way: beatings, death threats, and execution in a few cases. Most of them got the message.

The Civil Administration met this challenge in a number of ways. It secured its offices with metal doors, supplied Palestinian workers with emergency beepers, and replaced the tax collectors with private individuals who received monetary remuneration. These actions were effective, but the economic privation in the territories forced many workers to return to their jobs. The PLO realized that it had to offer some degree of economic assistance to the unemployed if their resignation was to be permanent. The policy of job resignation was flexible. While it is true that the PLO wanted to destroy the systems it believed were working against it, it did not pressure white-collar workers to give up their jobs. Medical staffs, for example, continued working since the alternative system could not supply a comparable level of medical services.

Strikes were one of the most common means of protest in the territories. The Palestinians began to apply this tactic shortly after the Six-Day War and kept it up on a wide scale. The first practical step in calling a strike appeared in a Unified National Leadership leaflet. There were different types of strikes. One was a general strike that forbade work in Israel and ordered shops and schools closed. Carrying out a strike demanded considerable preparation and exacted a heavy price on the population, especially when the economic situation was precariously sustainable. The second type was the commercial strike—closing shops for different lengths of time (hours or days). Other strikes pertained to certain sectors, such as drivers and teachers. Israel realized that the strikes were designed to achieve a number of goals: first, to show that Israel was no longer in control of the territories and thus reduce the psychological aspect of the population's deference to the occupation; second, to sow anarchy in the economy and thus jumpstart the population into an uprising; the third goal was to transfer the events from the political arena to the economic sphere and prove that Israel oppressed the population in this area too; and fourth, to hurt Israel economically, especially by keeping workers away from their jobs in Israel.

The activists maintained the uprising's image of popular consensus, especially by calling strikes when the enthusiasm waned and the enervating economic reality took its toll. Strikebreakers were threatened or assaulted; on occasion their stores and vehicles were torched. The activists endeavored to balance a contradictory reality—the population had to purchase staples, but the Intifada leadership wanted to demonstrate that the masses supported its decrees and was willing to close the stores. The storeowners quickly adapted themselves to this debilitating situation by opening stalls near their shuttered shops. Wealthy merchants opened warehouses at a discreet remove from residential areas. The Palestinian leadership generally turned a blind eye.

The Palestinians initiated a successful campaign with these commercial closures in order to create aversion in the Israeli public toward military service in the territories and prove to the local population that they had won a tactical victory. The method was not new but was carried out on a broader scale than expected. The idea was to demonstrate who controlled daily life in the territories. The leaflets announced the closing hours and warned that "enemies of the revolution" would be seriously punished if they disobeyed the instructions. The IDF understood the ulterior motive of the plan, therefore it compelled the storeowners to leave their shops open. The struggle raged on for ten weeks, and the IDF had welders lift the shutters or cut the locks on the doors so that the stores would remain open. But it was hard pressed to explain these steps to the troops, let alone to the general public, and the army's portrayal on television appeared farcical. The IDF finally gave up on the idea of forcing the stores to stay open. The Palestinians had inveigled the IDF into a no-win situation and emerged with a great moral victory.

Economic Separation from Israel. A few weeks after the outbreak of the rioting the Palestinian public was informed of the goal of economic autonomy. The veteran leadership, under Hanna Siniora, made the announcement in a press conference in East Jerusalem, and the message soon spread to the Intifada activists and appeared in leaflets. Basically the idea held that political independence would be achieved through the struggle for economic independence. But there was another aspect to it: one of Israel's basic arguments against an independent Palestinian state was that because of its unsustainability the Palestinians would request assistance from another Arab state that would soon dominate it and was liable to be hostile toward Israel. Therefore, the Palestinians believed that gaining economic independence would be the first step in pacifying Israel's fears of a Palestinian state and the first step in weakening the Israeli economy.

The leaflets also called for boycotting Israeli produce, though this decree later referred only to products that the Palestinians had an alternative for. The popular committees encouraged the purchase of local produce, such as home-made goods, and supported self-sufficiency through the cultivation of vegetables as ways of alleviating the economic stress. Media hype aside, these efforts proved effective only temporarily.

The Palestinians' main effort was directed toward crippling Israel's economy by preventing Palestinian workers from arriving at work in Israel. The campaign began very successfully while enthusiasm was running high, but as daily hardships increased, the off-limits policy could only be enforced by torching buses that transported workers, beating up laborers, and confiscating their identity cards. A few weeks later the Unified National Leadership ordered the public to burn Israeli IDs. If the anti-Israel campaign succeeded, it would be a severe blow to Israel's economy and its administrative control in the territories. But the leadership plan went awry. The IDs were a lifeline—especially in the Gaza Strip—for employment in Israel and the Gazans continued to work in Israel even at the height of the demonstrations.

Despite the prodigious time and energy invested in economic separation (including radical steps such as burning stores that sold Israeli goods), the effort failed, mainly because both economies were inextricably linked. The Palestinians' dependency on Israel increased because of the economic crisis in the Gulf States that forced many Palestinian workers to return home to the territories. Regardless of the result, the attempt at economic autonomy provided the media with a good story for several weeks.

Refusal to Pay Taxes. In November 1988, in the predominantly Christian town of Beit Sahour, east of Bethlehem, the local popular committee refused to pay taxes. Its battle-cry "no taxation without representation" was echoed in the media, press, and promulgated to Church organizations throughout the world. For all practical purposes it implied the establishment of a Palestinian state. The slogan was taken from American history and the colonists' struggle for independence from Great Britain. The Civil Administration realized that this campaign was a test case and could determine Israel's future in the territories. Therefore, in a carefully planned operation, tax collectors, accompanied by police and soldiers, went from house to house and appropriated household valuables according to the amount owed in taxes. The revolt eventually ran aground despite the volume of the protest and media coverage.

Religious Techniques

Religious issues played an important role in the Arab-Israeli conflict and were also incorporated into the Palestinians' nonviolent activity. The Palestinians made a great effort to highlight the Christian side of the Intifada. The death of a young Christian in a violent demonstration in early 1988 was a valuable tool in the activists' hands for mobilizing all sectors of society. When a Christian was wounded or killed, religious differences were set aside and the family received full support. The churches, too, played an important role in the struggle. The theory of nonviolent activity specifically mentions the church's potential for attracting outside support. Over the years the Palestinians developed a vast network of contacts with Christian groups in Europe and the United States. It will be recalled that the activists tried, with partial success, to organize demonstrations at famous Christian holy sites, such as the Church of the Holy Sepulcher in East Jerusalem and the Church of the Nativity in Bethlehem. They would eventually succeed in the Second Intifada.

Respect for the Dead. This is a common technique in nonviolent activity. A funeral is an emotionally volatile event that the authorities generally avoid interfering with. It allows the demonstrators to exploit the cracks in the government's authority. In Islam, the concept of the *shahid*—a martyr killed in a *jihad* (holy war against nonMuslims)—rewards the victim with an exalted place in Paradise and pleasures beyond imagination.[11] Those who were killed on the first day of the demonstrations were immediately declared martyrs and their funerals became rallying points (sometimes against the family's wishes) for additional martyrs to join their ranks. Thus, the flames of the Intifada were continuously refueled. The dead were granted *shahid* status: honors on special days and their pictures displayed in meetings and posted on walls, which bestowed a religious patina on the Intifada.

Other Techniques

The Use of Symbols. The Palestinians made effective use of three elements—music, clothes, and the colors of the flag.

Music. The Palestinians chose the song "Biladi, Biladi" (My Homeland, My Homeland) as their national anthem and as part of the PLO's wider cultural effort to inculcate a Palestinian national consciousness. For decades there were songs with nationalistic themes and musical productions that were performed at political and cultural rallies. Israel prohibited the playing of "Biladi, Biladi" and confiscated music tapes with nationalistic lyrics that were considered provocations. The Palestinians charged that the Israeli authorities were oppressing them not only politically but also culturally.

The Kaffiyeh. The traditional, usually white Arab headdress became a political symbol when its color was changed to checkered black and white. Arafat habitually draped his checkered kaffiyeh over his suit, with the kaffiyeh folded in the shape of the map of Palestine.

The Colors of the Flag. Like most Arab flags, the PLO made its national colors green, white, black, and red. Israel declared the Palestinian flag illegal, thus launching an ill-conceived tug-of-war against its public display. During the Intifada the Palestinians became adept at advertising the colors: for example, storekeepers advertised their wares in the window with the national colors and families hung the laundry in the color pattern. This kind of "game" frustrated and morally eroded the soldiers, especially when they appeared as buffoons trying to stop groups of children from flying flags.

Reiterating the Message. This is a tried and true persuasion technique, and the Palestinians were exceptionally adept at it. For example, they played the same song again and again at demonstrations. Activists repeated their messages, but not interminably lest they dull the audience. PLO leaflets reiterated the themes: "the PLO is the sole representative of the Palestinian people" and "no peace without the PLO—negotiations within the framework of an international conference." Messages directed to the neutrals included: "Israel violates civil rights" and "the Palestinians will struggle until they gain an independent state on the West Bank and Gaza." Palestinian power was strengthened by focusing on a few basic themes directed toward a single political goal.

Strengthening Feelings. The Palestinians awakened deep-seated feelings in two target audiences—the local population and IDF troops. A martyr's funeral required very little to turn it into a violent, uncontrollable demonstration, and inevitable clash. These events usually ended with further loss of life and a growing ring of violence. Sermons in the mosques were also an effective tool for stirring up passion. Cursing the troops was designed to infuriate them and provoke them to open fire. Such events were generally perpetrated in the presence of and for the benefit of the foreign media.

Rumor Spreading. Most Palestinians live in crowded villages, cities, or refugee camps. Their social structure is traditional—based on clans and extended families—therefore the population relies mainly on personal communication for obtaining information. The fast pace of events left the door open for rumors to spread like wildfire. The Intifada broke out, as noted, because of a road accident in Gaza which, according to the rumor that sped through the strip, had been intentionally caused in revenge over the death of an Israeli shopper the day before. In a matter of hours the rumor ignited a firestorm. Rumor spreading was a basic weapon employed by Palestinian activists to enflame the population in its political war against Israel.

Half Truths. This is a very effective technique that does not use absolute lies, which runs the risk of being revealed and detracting from credibility. It is much harder to uncover a partial truth and far easier to defend it by emphasizing the true part of the story or claiming that due to pressure the event was not thoroughly verified. Palestinian information sources frequently employed this technique to their advantage. A good example is their habit of counting the number of people killed in the Intifada along with people who died natural deaths or lost their lives in road accidents. These figures were practically impossible to confirm since it required exhuming the bodies and performing an autopsy—an act the Palestinians would have violently opposed. Thus Israel gave up trying to validate the figures the Palestinians presented.

Another example was the Palestinians' claim that Israel used nerve gas. In a sense it was true, Israel did employ tear gas—as most Western countries do—which affects the nervous system, inducing nausea and tears. Its effects last a few hours. But under no circumstances did it use illegal chemicals as the Palestinians insinuated.[12] Yet it was enough to create an impression of the illegal and immoral use of forbidden materials.

False Accusations were a major element in the Palestinians' psychological offensive. The goal was to occupy Israel with marginal matters by forcing it to channel its resources to a "wild goose chase," thus diverting them from an attack. The strategic assumption held that it made no difference whether the allegation was true or not as long as it kept the enemy on the defensive. Moreover, the actual issue will usually be quickly forgotten given the nature of the media that discards yesterday's stories and rarely owns up to its mistakes. This technique required a constant flow of trumped-up charges to have issues remain on the public agenda. The technique was suited to the intermediate stages of the campaign, after credibility had been achieved. There is no formal, general strategy for using false accusations in psywar. The technique is simple, demands little effort, is accessible to any group with a creative imagination, is risk-free, and can be shifted from one area to another. If the slur campaign takes a negative or mistaken direction, it can easily be corrected by instructing the activists to suppress it or by blaming a lower echelon and claiming it was a local initiative.

For example, PLO Radio reported that the IDF had transferred a wounded Palestinian to hospital by helicopter and sent the bill to the family, and that the IDF helicopters sprayed nerve gas. Other fabrications claimed that three Palestinians were tossed out of an IDF helicopter, and that Israel has a policy of neutralizing the Palestinian "demographic bomb" by manhandling pregnant women and spreading a special gas that induces abortions. The idea behind these accusations was to insinuate that Israel violates universal ethical standards.[13]

Armed Activity. The Palestinians carried out a number of terrorist acts against Israeli targets during the Intifada as part of their ongoing guerilla war. The most famous incidents were the attack on a civilian bus in the Negev (March 1988) and at Nitzanim Beach (May 1990). It is not clear whether they were carried out by an oppositionist group or planned by Arafat to deflect criticism of the PLO's nonviolent strategy. Several attempts were made at penetration from the Lebanese border that Arafat avowed were perpetrated by a group of Palestinian dissidents over whom he had no control. Israel portrayed these attacks as proof that the PLO was still bent on murdering Jews.

The Israeli Side

Demonstrating Strength. After the initial shock of mass rioting had passed, the IDF adopted an aggressive strategy of demonstrating strength. Dozens of regular army units were transferred to the territories to replace the older reservist units that had proved ineffective in chasing the rock-throwing youth. Paratroopers were ordered to wear their red berets even though this was no longer an effective deterrent symbol in the Intifada, especially since the paratroopers received no better training or equipment for police action than other infantry units.

The Ministry of Foreign Affairs. Documents in the MFA's archives reveal that it failed to take aggressive measures to counter Palestinian propaganda. Its response to Palestinian allegations concerning Israel's operations in the territories was rational and apologetic. The Ministry's most far-reaching move was to publicize Arafat's contradictory statements, and in one case publish Arafat's 1989 support of the Chinese government's suppression of the students who demonstrated in Tiananmen Square. One of the reasons for *hasbara*'s weak performance may have been its inability to overcome the gentlemanly, diplomatic tradition. The training provided to the Ministry staff and the attitude cultivated in the Ministry were unsuited for the challenges the Palestinians forced on them.

Messages to the Palestinian Population. Israel tried to dissuade the Palestinian public from marching in the demonstrations. It published a statement that the cessation of violence was a condition for negotiations. But this announcement went nowhere since the Intifada activists had driven home the message that rioting would continue until the political goals were attained.

Rumors. Israel dealt with hostile rumors by quickly disproving them. Whenever the IDF or Shabak heard of a possible new outbreak of violence, they would contact local Palestinian leaders, identify themselves by name, and provide facts that could be corroborated or denied regarding the rumored event. Another method was to supply information via Israel's Arabic-language radio and television programs that the Palestinians and even the Arab states considered extremely credible. This method staved off a number of anti-Israel demonstrations.

Military Actions. Israel employed this method in two ways. The first was large-scale operations aimed at maintaining freedom of movement on the roads, renewing the Civil Administration (including tax collecting), arresting Intifada activists, and regaining control of Palestinian villages that had declared themselves liberated. The second was a series of small-scale counter-insurgency strikes to capture members of the "shock committees" accused of murdering Israelis and Palestinians. These surgical strikes were intended to undermine the target audience's sense of security and faith in the political leadership's ability to lead it to victory. Two main factors hindered this activity: one was the late date of the operations (mid-1988); since the Intifada had already progressed beyond the spontaneous stage to the organized stage, that is, by the time the counter-terrorist teams finally made their presence felt in the territories, the Intifada had already peaked. The second factor was the nature of the military operations which obligated the soldiers to use weapons. This sparked protests and demonstrations and made it easy for the Palestinians to accuse the IDF of murder in cases that they themselves had perpetrated in the internecine struggle between warring factions. The Palestinians called these teams "liquidation squads" which reversed much of the political gain of having reduced the level of violence. The Palestinians' exposé of Israeli "hit teams" was one of the reasons that Israel publicly acknowledged their existence.

Black Psyop (message conveyed under a false identity).[14] In one of the weekly meetings of the "Territories Forum" headed by the defense minister and Chief of Staff, diverse nonviolent approaches for ending the riots were broached. One of them was the use of psychological warfare. Military Intelligence was responsible for this activity, but had been applying it only minimally due to certain constraints: unwillingness on the part of senior officers to engage in it, lack of equipment (loudspeakers, printing machines for leaflets, and so forth), and the absence of psywar training programs. Psychological warfare had been used in the First Lebanon War in 1982 but was discontinued in the five successive years. The IDF probably churned out a small number of bogus leaflets during the Intifada.[15] The Unified National Leadership's leaflets repeatedly warned the public of counterfeit messages. This proves that phony leaflets did appear and were successful to some degree. The Palestinians claimed that they checked the leaflets and found them to be very amateurish, filled with grammatical mistakes and stylistic flaws; furthermore, all of the leaflets had come off the same typewriter. The imitation leaflets may have had two goals. The first was to neutralize the general effectiveness of the Palestinian leadership's leaflets (for example, by misleading the local population about the dates of the demonstrations and strike schedules), thus spreading confusion and detracting from the people's willingness to take part in mass protests. The second goal was to sow division and enmity in the Palestinian camps and between the public and the Unified National Leadership (especially when financial corruption was alleged).

According to published Palestinian material, the Israelis devised various methods to make their leaflets seem credible, such as interspersing a large amount of truthful information with a small amount of falsification, or circulating a special leaflet that urged the Palestinians to keep an eye out for Israeli forgeries, thus deepening the Palestinians' suspicion of all leaflets.

Symbols. Israel lacked a powerful visual symbol to compete with the Palestinians' kaffiyeh. In the early years of the state there had been a visual national symbol—the simple, cotton *tembel* cap that farmers and laborers wore. The *tembel* cap became a popular symbol in the Jewish world (and to a lesser degree in the West) and conjured up the image of Israeli heroes and Zionist pioneers. But following the economic development in the last decades of the twentieth century and ethos shifts toward industry and technology, the naïve symbol was abandoned. The army was left only with uniforms, while the blue and white flag of Israel was increasingly identified with the settler movement and not the general population.

In conclusion, the Palestinians' effective use of psywar in the Intifada was the result of a unique combination of a handful of creative, energetic activists who correctly identified the enormous potential in psywar for achieving national goals, and a population that was eager to contribute to this effort. The similarities between the Palestinians' use of psychological warfare and the Yishuv's use of it in the struggle for independence against British rule is striking, especially regarding the Jews' willingness to take an active part in demonstrations, settlement activity, and clandestine immigrant operations. The main difference between the two peoples is that in the Jewish case, independence was achieved with minimal resort to internecine bloodshed.

From the material published to date it cannot be determined whether the Palestinians made a conscious effort to emulate Jewish psywar activity, but they made an impressive cultural effort in the last forty years to translate the works of Zionist thinkers and biographies of leading Zionist figures (such as Menachem Begin) into Arabic in order to "know thy enemy." However, Israel's activity in publishing was limited to Palestinian ideological works such as Abou Iyad's *My Home, My Land: A Narrative of the Palestinian Struggle*, a small number of books by left-wing intellectuals (published more out of empathy with the Palestinians' suffering than a desire to gain a profound understanding of their culture), and classified intelligence material.

The Palestinians manipulated the foreign media intuitively and shrewdly. They effectively exploited the Palestinian and Arab diaspora, and above all they initiated a large number of events that kept the Intifada on the international agenda for three years. By any standard this was an impressive achievement.

CHAPTER 11

The Second Intifada (2000–2005)

Ariel Sharon's visit to the Temple Mount on September 28, 2000, when he was the opposition leader, is generally believed to have been the trigger that sparked the bloody riots and deaths of seven Palestinians. These clashes launched the violent confrontation known as the "Second Intifada" or "Al-Aqsa Intifada" (the IDF officially used the term "Ebb and Flow Events"). Both the international and domestic media almost immediately picked up the first two names. The important innovation was the religious connotation that Al-Aqsa gave to the national struggle, and the appellation Al-Aqsa Intifada served as a battle-cry for recruiting the Muslim world to the Palestinians' political cause by conjuring up a war of religious freedom on the Temple Mount. At first Israel overlooked the significance and transcending power of the new term and made no attempt to pose an alternative Hebrew name. Both Al-Aqsa Intifada and the more prosaic Second Intifada remain the epithets for this chaotic period. It is hard to say whether the chairman of the Palestinian Authority (PA), Yasser Arafat, initiated the fighting following the stalemate in political negotiations with Israel, or whether the Second Intifada was a spontaneous outburst of anger and frustration. In either case, by late 1999 both sides sensed that a new eruption of violence was only a matter of time, and both sides, especially Israel, went all-out in preparing for the expected clash.

In 2000 two major events exacerbated tensions and spurred the Palestinians to shift from political negotiations to violent action: the IDF's hasty withdrawal from Southern Lebanon in May and the failure of the Camp David Talks in July in reaching a final solution, notwithstanding the combined efforts of Prime Minister Barak, Chairman Arafat, and President Clinton. The Palestinians perceived the first as indicative of Israel's susceptibility to public opinion on security matters, Israelis' inability to slug it out in a protracted, violent confrontation, and especially their hyper-sensitivity to the loss of life. The second event proved that negotiations would not bring Israel to adopt flexible positions; only violence would.

A decade after the First Intifada and five years after the Oslo Accords a sea change took place in the Palestinian struggle: During the First Intifada the Palestinians had stayed clear of violence and armed attacks, now in the Second Intifada they began using small-arms fire, Qassam rockets, improvised explosive devices (IEDs) against tanks and strongholds in the Gaza Strip, and suicide bombings. They exhibited boldness, determination, and originality in carrying out dangerous missions, and succeeded in surmounting the IDF's sophisticated defense equipment. Their strategy, of course, was to narrow the power imbalance that was heavily biased in Israel's favor. Their acts of terror were often spectacular, so that more than serving purely military objectives, they demonstrated the classic psychological dictum: propaganda by deed.[1]

One of the reasons for the shift to violence may have been Arafat's assessment that Israeli society was divided over the question of an independent Palestinian state, and that a terror campaign could increase support for Palestinian national sovereignty—the ultimate goal. Also, Arafat may have received assurances from certain world leaders that they would pressure Israel into accepting Palestinian independence and would protect the PA from military steps that Israel might take.

Other factors that convinced Arafat to embark upon a campaign of violence were the PA's significant military build-up after the Oslo Accords, numbering in the tens of thousands of trained troops. In addition, it acquired large stockpiles of weapons (light arms and antitank missiles). Also, the fact that Israel refrained from serious operations following terrorist outrages, after incurring heavy casualties (in the period between Oslo and the Second Intifada), boosted Palestinian self-confidence and convinced the PA that violent activity worked to its advantage. Whatever the case, Arafat's decision to begin an armed struggle was probably based on rational considerations, especially after Sharon's visit to the Temple Mount and the ensuing firestorm.

At the start of this period, two events grabbed the media's attention and gained wide coverage: the death of the young boy Muhammad al-Dura in the Gaza Strip on September 30, 2000 during an exchange of fire between the IDF and armed Palestinians; and the lynching of two Israeli reservists by Palestinians on October 12, 2000. A few months after the rioting commenced, violence took a sharp upswing. The Palestinians went from mass demonstrations (à la First Intifada) to live-fire ambushes against settlers and troops. Next they shifted into higher gear—suicide operations—first in the territories, then inside Israel. The Islamic organizations (Hamas and Islamic Jihad) joined the Fatah activists. The IDF responded with air strikes and targeted assassinations.

In early 2001 Israel dramatically expanded its military steps: raids on PA facilities in Area A (Palestinian autonomy), arrests, the demolition of homes, and targeted killings. In the beginning of 2002 Israel escalated its counter-insurgency operations after the US government agreed to remove restrictions on Israel's responses. This turnabout came in the wake of September 11 and President Bush's declaration of war on global terror; and Israel's seizure of the Palestinian weapons ship *Karine A* on January 2, 2002 with the huge quantity of arms that Iran had sent to Gaza and evidence of Arafat's personal involvement in terrorist activity. Under these circumstances, Washington gave Israel the green light to accelerate its assassination policy and even reoccupy Palestinian cities. The latter took place in Operation "Defensive Shield" (March 29–May 10, 2002), an Israeli military operation that came in response to the sharp escalation in suicide bombings inside Israel and especially to the attack in the Park Hotel in Netanya on Passover Eve. Although the operation did not completely quell terrorist attacks, it was a turning point: The number of terrorist strikes declined and the Palestinians began seeking channels for negotiations.

In late June 2002, the PA and Islamic organizations agreed to a *hudna* (ceasefire in Arabic) for half a year. There were several reasons for this: Abu Mazen's appointment as prime minister (March 2003); American pressure on the PA to halt its terrorist activity; the Palestinians' fear of large-scale Israeli military operations in the West Bank (along the lines of "Defensive Shield"); and the targeted killings of Hamas leaders in the Gaza Strip. The ceasefire kept for a few weeks until the next suicide attack, followed by Israeli retaliation and the next cycle of violence.

The Second Intifada tapered off in 2005 as the disengagement from Gaza approached. This resulted from Israel's development of a war-fighting doctrine that integrated the Shabak (high-quality intelligence on the activists), air force interdiction, and special forces teams for capturing or killing a great number of terrorists. The roster of leaders who were assassinated included the Hamas activist Salah Shahada (July 2002), and the heads of the Hamas organization Sheikh Ahmad Yassin (March 2004) and Abd al-Aziz Rantissi (April 17, 2004). Also, progress was made in the construction of the separation fence (early summer 2002) between Judea and Samaria, and Israel that significantly curtailed terrorist operations. In addition, Israel took various steps in preparing for the disengagement from the Gaza Strip and Northern Samaria (implementation was scheduled for August–September 2005). On the Palestinian side there was Arafat's demise in November 2004, and the Palestinians' exhaustion from the prolonged violence that had failed to produce the hoped-for results in either the neutral or Israeli audience. The Palestinians realized that their original assessment had been illusory: the Israeli public was capable of mustering a high degree of stamina, resolve, and solidarity in the face of terrorist attacks and was willing to put its full weight behind the government's iron-fist policy.

Palestinian Leadership and the Islamic Organizations

The Oslo Accords essentially legitimized the PA and accorded it all the mechanisms of de facto political independence: a flag, national hymn, enlarged police force (its army, in effect), a passport, an Internet suffix (ps), tax collection, and centralized control of the mass media (radio, television, and press). It was through the media that the PA conveyed messages and promoted its political goals, especially to the home audience. In the realm of security, the authority had no less than eight organizations whose leaders were loyal to Arafat. But the chairman of the PA cunningly played them off against each other so as to weaken their relative strength. The organizations, some of them engaging in terrorist activity,[2] competed for the support of Arafat and public backing.

In addition to the PA and its security mechanisms, two Islamic organizations—Hamas and Islamic Jihad—began terrorist operations against Israel that enhanced their status both militarily and politically after a long period of decline. Iran, Syria, and Iraq (until the destruction of Sadaam Hussein's regime) provided them with financial assistance, as did the vast network of charity funds and front organizations in the United States and Europe. But above all, the Islamic groups won the growing support of the Palestinian public, especially in Gaza. In contrast to the First Intifada, when the two organizations generally refrained from violent acts against Israel, this time the activists heeded the instructions of their spiritual leader, Sheikh Ahmed Yassin, and his *da'wa* (preaching) on long-range goals. They launched a massive wave of terrorist strikes. It is hard to determine the exact degree of coordination between the Islamic organizations and the PA, but they were a convenient scapegoat for the PA to blame for excessively violent attacks that incurred sharp criticism and heightened the tension with Israel.

In psywar the Islamic organizations had a different agenda from the PA's. Instead of setting forth goals to be attained within a certain time frame, they presented the vision of an uncompromising struggle of unlimited duration. National objectives combined with a religious envelope to create an electrifying message for recruiting the oppressed and disheartened, especially since it downplayed the importance of temporary failure.

Hamas and Islamic Jihad dictated a formidable religious agenda, exclusive of the political struggle, when they enlisted volunteers for suicide missions. The terrorist strikes and their messages were fodder for the media because of their dramatic nature (death and suicide). They magnified the Islamic organizations' image as martyrs and fearless warriors and conveyed the basic political message ("propaganda by deed"). Their leaders embellished the messages with aggressive themes, such as "every activist is thirsting to kill ten Israeli civilians which will end the occupation and establish an Islamic state." Their strategy was predicated on continuous armed struggle until Israel was destroyed, though under certain circumstances a ceasefire was permitted. The Israeli public suddenly became versed in Islamic political terms, such as *hudna* (ceasefire) and *tahadiya* (temporary quiet).

Palestinian Psywar Techniques

The Palestinians' successfully applied two main principles in psychological warfare during the Second Intifada:

"From Asset to Liability"—This message emphasized the exorbitant price that Israel had to pay for maintaining control of the territories. The violence in the Second Intifada and soaring number of Israeli casualties (over one thousand dead)—unlike the First Intifada when Israel suffered chiefly political and image damage—put the message "from asset to liability" in a completely new light.

Inculcating Guilt Feeling—The Palestinians used this principle on a wide scale as they had in the First Intifada, given the surge in the number of casualties from IDF fire, especially civilians (over three thousand). It was intended to undermine the IDF's sophisticated operational mechanism. For example, the Palestinians published details on cases of civilian deaths, children in particular, from IDF fire. They cleverly termed construction of the separation fence the "apartheid wall" and presented the untold misery that it caused Palestinian families whose lands were expropriated or that fell on the "wrong side" of the fence, or who were now cut off from family members and municipal services, such as schools, health clinics, and workplaces. The Palestinians highlighted these cases, especially in the Israeli media, while taking special care not to mention that the reason for the fence was the porous border that facilitated murderous attacks on Jewish civilians.

Israel's Responsibility—The Palestinians used this theme to great effect during the Second Intifada to repeatedly attack Israel and downplay the need to present the facts accurately. The goal was to instill in Israelis (officers and non-commissioned officers [NCOs] were particularly singled out) hesitation before taking measures against them. In practical terms, after every terrorist attack the Palestinians broadcast messages to the Israeli audience emphasizing the despair that the occupation was causing them and the realization that their frustration and desperation could only be released through violence.

"Not Our Fault"—A very common theme that complemented the previous one, guilt acquittal was designed to avert criticism from the PA after each suicide attack. After each strike, the Palestinian leaders officially immediately condemned the atrocity but quickly added that they sympathized with the motivation since it sprang from the anguish and hopelessness in the face of Israel's continued occupation of their land. In this way they neutralized much of the shock effect of the pictures of the carnage.

Neutralizing Israel's Weapons—Preventing the enemy from employing their weapons is a cardinal principle in psychological warfare based on the simple logic that if the weak lack comparable weapons then they have to convince the strong not to use theirs. During the First Intifada the Palestinians employed this principle to only a limited extent because Israel did not apply its force on a large scale. They concentrated their effort on pressuring the Israeli public to limit or cease entirely the use of nonlethal weapons such as billy clubs, rubber bullets, and tear gas. However, in the Second Intifada the Palestinians increasingly adopted this message when the IDF began sending rocket-armed helicopters and fighter aircraft armed with smart bombs to take out terrorist leaders. Since the Palestinians had no answer to such sophisticated devices, they made a maximum effort to foment a moral discourse in Israel on the legitimacy of their use, stressing the death and maiming of innocent bystanders.

This is how the Palestinians waged a successful campaign after Israel's assassination of Salah Shehadeh, head of Hamas military wing in Gaza, with a one-ton bomb that also caused collateral damage to adjacent structures (sixteen bystanders killed, including ten children). The event ignited a vociferous public debate in Israel over the justification of assassinating the heads of terror organizations when civilians were liable to be in the line of fire. The Palestinians intensified the debate by supplying details on the victims. In one case they exerted pressure on commercial companies that sold equipment that could be used for combat to Israel. The outstanding example was the American Caterpillar Company that produced the large bulldozers that were the IDF's mainstays for breaking into Palestinian villages, razing homes, and clearing away ("exposure procedures") crops and orchards along the sides of patrol roads.[3] The Palestinians also employed this psywar message against IDF roadblocks and the Separation Wall (see below).

The Linkage—The Palestinians applied this classic psywar technique in much the same way as they did in the First Intifada. The idea is to create a dependency between one's actions and the enemy's; to show that it is a case of cause and effect: "we responded to your actions." The aim is to plant the seeds of doubt and self-criticism in the enemy and force them to understand that if they refrain from action they won't receive a punitive counter-punch. The more the technique is employed the more the enemy begin to question the justification of their policy; and their maneuverability becomes limited. Thus, the Palestinians linked the shooting incidents at the beginning of the Second Intifada (October 2000) to the visit of the "infidel" Ariel Sharon—"the butcher of Sabra and Shatila"—to the Temple Mount. Later they justified their murderous acts against Israeli civilians to the targeted killing of one of their leading terrorists.

Expanding the Ring of Victims—The aim of revolutionaries is to recruit as many people as possible to their cause and turn them into activists. In guerilla warfare this is accomplished by provoking the enemy to retaliate by opening fire in a civilian surrounding and unintentionally killing and wounding innocent bystanders. The victims' friends, families, and the general population will be primed to join the guerillas. In psywar this is done by fanning the flames of passion. For example, a beneficial, albeit unplanned, side effect of the suicide bombings was the increase in the number of Israeli roadblocks in Judea and Samaria and the imposition of stricter measures for security checks that seriously impeded the Palestinians' daily life. Sometimes IDF soldiers acted callously and depreciatingly toward the Palestinians. The number of victims rose exponentially and the Palestinians' desire for revenge reached breaking point.

Exploiting Opportunities—The Palestinians exploited unplanned events to convey their messages to target audiences. Two outstanding examples were the staged killing of a young boy—Muhammad al-Dura—in the Gaza Strip and the alleged massacre in the Jenin Refugee Camp during Operation "Defensive Shield" (April 2002).

Recruiting Activists from Abroad—The Palestinians recruited young activists from neutral target audiences, such as the ISM (the International Solidarity Movement) through a lengthy vetting and training process. After receiving detailed instructions on the Palestinian perspective, the activists came to the territories, obtained assistance from the local population, and sometimes even tried to physically stop IDF bulldozers with their bodies. The American Rachel Corrie and British Thomas Hurndall were the prominent examples of international sympathy that was won by this method. In March 2003 Corrie was accidentally crushed by an IDF bulldozer when she threw herself in front of it in an attempt to stop the destruction of a Palestinian home in Rafah; Hurndall was caught in crossfire in Rafah and succumbed to his wounds nine months later. These events received wide media coverage in Britain and the United States and, with Palestinian help, galvanized harsh responses that blackened Israel's activities in the territories.

The Use of Themes in Psywar

Israel's Themes

The innovations in Israel's themes during the Second Intifada came in reaction to the radicalization of the Palestinians' struggle. The messages aimed at the home audience strengthened solidarity and boosted morale in the aftermath of Palestinian terror, and graphically illustrated to the home and neutral audience the Palestinians' cruelty and inhumanity by transmitting pictures from Israeli hospitals and sites where civilians had been slain. However, the attempt to halt the suicide bombings by addressing the enemy audience proved futile.

Themes to the Home Audience

Given the change in the nature of the events and their influence on the civilian population, Israel began conveying to its home audience, for the first time, the scope of the casualties, the loss of personal security, and the decline in the public mood. The themes focused on Palestinian terror and psywar activity.

Strengthening National Morale. In the first half of the Second Intifada Israel used this theme to buttress faith in the country's direction and the willingness to suffer for a better future. This came in the wake of gruesome terrorist strikes, mostly suicide bombings in urban centers, that culminated in March 2002 (131 Israelis killed), and the IDF and Shabak were unable to prevent them. Until Operation "Defensive Shield" the government vacillated over ordering the IDF to recapture West Bank cities and refugee camps in particular, for which there were military (Palestinian resistance would be fierce, the cost in human life exorbitant) and political reasons (not to weaken the PA). Therefore, the IDF embarked upon a limited static war and nervously awaited the next attack. It refrained from applying its full might against the terror organizations. The messages that the Israeli audience received spoke of "cutting off the hand of terror"—"we shall overcome"—"our arm will reach the murderers." Also, in response to the wave of suicide bombings the government reverted to the methods it had adopted in the First Intifada: state funerals with media coverage of speeches by ministers and Knesset members; the "Benefits for Victims of Hostilities Law" that compensated victims of terrorist attacks and symbolized official recognition of the fallen (that is, civilians were granted the same status as soldiers); interviews with somber-faced politicians and high-ranking reserve officers.

In early 2002 the government gradually changed its policy and began deploying infantry brigades in Jenin and Nablus, the main terrorist bases. Following the success of the first operation in the Balata Refugee Camp adjacent to Nablus, journalists quoted the paratrooper brigade commander: "The tiger of Balata turned out to be a pussy cat." The statement was made for public consumption, dismissing the terrorists' much-touted ability to oppose the might of the IDF. During preparations for Operation "Defensive Shield" the government increased public support for IDF activity. The operation was designed to recapture the West Bank town of Jenin, strike at the heart of the terror cells, and indirectly restore the IDF's deterrent capability. An exceptionally high number of reservists reported to their units.

Strengthening National Unity. The Palestinians' struggle against the Jewish settlers also took its toll on the troops. The mounting casualty rate triggered a heated public debate over the justification of remote, isolated settlements. The government campaign stressed that the settlers' fate is the same as that of the population "behind" the Green Line. The *hasbara* campaign also noted that the Palestinians were waging a ruthless war of terror to drive the Jews out of the country (not just the territories). This is a "battle for our homes," the government spokesmen warned, therefore "the fate of Nitazarim and Kfar Darom [Jewish settlements in the Gaza Strip] is the same as that of Tel Aviv."

Themes to the Home and Neutral Audiences

Israel used the same themes as in the First Intifada: reviling the enemy, blaming the media, and demonstrating how the PA depicted itself as a peace-seeking entity while in reality it abetted terror (especially in the second half of the Second Intifada). In addition, two new themes came into vogue: atrocity propaganda (demonization) and Israel as the victim. Both were the byproduct of the upturn in violence.

Vilifying the enemy was intended to condition the hearts and minds of the home audience to absorb the second theme—demonization of the enemy.[4] A similar effort was made with the neutral audience, where the objective was to disparage the enemy, undercut their support, and co-opt the audience to Israel's side.

Delegitimizing the enemy (aimed at the neutral audience) **and driving a wedge in the enemy's ranks** (aimed at the enemy audience). This theme was designed to make the enemy so hated in the eyes of the home audience that it was willing to kill them. Another way of instilling hatred of the enemy was to blame them for the evils of the occupation and for forcing Israel to employ brutal policies.

Demonization assumes that people will support any accusation, no matter how contrived or preposterous, if they hear it enough times. The party behind the message wants the target audience to internalize the theme, first to the lunatic fringe that will believe anything and then the political center. At the same time, in order to facilitate absorption of the message the target audience has to receive information that substantiates the accusations so that an overall impression of credibility is achieved.

Demonization. Israel frequently used this theme in response to the Palestinians' wave of suicide bombings against civilians. Its message was that Palestinians attribute little value to human life, but glorify and sanctify death instead. The key event in the first month of the Second Intifada was the savage lynching of two Israeli reservists in Ramallah. The soldiers took a wrong turn, ended up at a Palestinian roadblock, and were taken to a detention house. Rumor of their capture spread and a mob stormed the jail, murdered the two, and desecrated their bodies for several hours. The Palestinian leadership immediately recognized the potential fallout from such an event and appropriated all the video tapes taken by camera crews, but missed those of an Italian team. The IDF purchased the Italians' tape and then exploited it for all it was worth. The newspapers published two photos from the tape—one that captured the Palestinians throwing the body of one of the soldiers into a courtyard, and the other of a Palestinian flaunting his blood-stained hands to a cheering crowd. The Israel information mechanism scored a major victory with this video that portrayed the Palestinians as blood-thirsty beasts.[5]

Other cases where Israel highlighted the barbarity of the Palestinians were the murder of the infant Shalhevet Fass by a Palestinian sniper in Hebron on March 26, 2001, and the murder of Revital Ohayon and her two children, Matan and Noam, in Kibbutz Metzer on January 9, 2002. The point that Israel made in demonizing the Palestinian terrorists in these cases was that they knew exactly who their victims were: Jewish children. In another unbearably gruesome case, the Israeli media publicized the photo of masked Palestinians flaunting the body parts of IDF soldiers when their vehicle detonated an IED in the Gaza Strip on May 11, 2004.

Vilifying the Enemy. This theme dealt with the following subjects:

Palestinians Firing on IDF Troops from Behind a Human Shield (women and children). This tactic was deliberately designed to cause civilian deaths from the return fire, yet the topic received minimal media coverage compared to what the Western media accorded importance, events in which Palestinian women and children were killed. For three decades the storyline was about Israelis killing Palestinians.

Cynical Exploitation of Children As Martyrs or As Carriers of Explosives. Israel publicized the fact that the Palestinians took advantage of the IDF soldiers at the roadblocks who abstained from thorough body searches on children and their personal belongings. Israel scored a publicity coup when it published the picture of a Palestinian child with an explosive belt strapped to its body.

Corruption in the Palestinian Authority. By headlining this reality Israel tried to delegitimize the PA in the eyes of the neutral audience and pressure Arafat to deal with terror more determinedly (following threats that unless he took serious steps to counter Palestinian terror, the Europeans would cut off their funds to the PA). The Israeli campaign against the corruption of senior PA officials peaked with the publication of documents that IDF troops confiscated in the Mukata'a, Arafat's headquarters, in Ramallah. At first top-level IDF officers tried to enlist Military Intelligence's research section to *hasbara* and come out with a "White Book" containing incriminating information on Arafat's involvement in corruption and terrorism, but Prime Minister Ehud Barak vetoed the plan. Eventually the incriminating documents were incorporated into a book published by the journalist Ronen Bergman.[6] The question of whether or not to exploit this theme became a watershed in Israel's Intifada policy: the information was in Israel's hands,[7] but it withheld its publication for political motives.

The climax in Israel's coordinated campaign against Palestinian terror came after the debate in the International Court of Justice in The Hague (February 23–25, 2004) on **the legality of erecting the Separation Wall** as a border between Israel and the Palestinian territories on the West Bank (the wall was built mainly to the east of the Green Line, that is, inside Judea and Samaria). Israel claimed that the wall was absolutely necessary to protect its citizens from the unrelenting killing of civilians. It presented photographs of the victims and the charred remains of a bus to garner support in the international arena. But the judges remained unconvinced, and in July 2004 determined that the fence was illegal and had to be dismantled.

Exposing the Palestinian Method of Indoctrination. The government publicized the flagrant anti-Israel campaign in school textbooks and summer camps, and hatred of Israel as a common theme on children's television programs. The subject of the Palestinian Authority's schoolbooks has become a never ending controversy ever since.

The Victim Theme. An Israeli (and by association, a Jew) is now the victim of a ruthless, cynical enemy. This was a contest for the sympathy of Western public opinion and an attempt to wrest from the Palestinians the fruits of their all-out effort in portraying themselves as the victims of Israeli brutality. In effect, it was Israel's new psywar tactic, and included the wide-scale circulation of images of suicide bombings and grisly photos of the wounded in the hospitals. The use of this theme came from a decision related to Israeli identity. The Israeli stereotype had always been presented as the antithesis of the Diaspora Jew, a pillar of strength as opposed to the weak, exploited, and downtrodden Jew. In the beginning of the Second Intifada Israel avoided displaying the pictures of the victims lest they shock the viewer by dint of their gory content, and out of consideration of individual privacy, the families' feelings, and respect for the dead. Therefore photographers and editors were discouraged from capturing the bombing sites and hospitals on film. But after a few months, the Ministry did a *volte face* and changed its no-show policy, once it realized the potential profit to Israel's image that could be gained in the international arena. Thus, all the obstacles barring photographs were removed, and the world bore witness to Israel's suffering.

At the same time the Ministry, which until now had been the paragon of moderation and restraint, began producing short documentaries, in video format made up of synthesized images, to bring to the international audience the results of Palestinian terror. Albeit a sense of discretion was maintained, that is, the clips did not depict the shredded remains of children, but rather pictures of their blood-stained school bags on the floor of a gutted bus, or the opposite, images of a burned out bus and blood-spattered belongings of the passengers shown alongside images of children romping in a playground next to smiling moms. This technique went straight to the viewers' viscera and created a sense of outrage, illustrating in vivid imagery the savagery of the terrorists, but without inducing nightmares in the audience.

Blaming the Media. On several occasions in the first stage of the Second Intifada Israel challenged the foreign outlets' reportage and demanded balanced coverage. To accomplish this it recruited supporters in the United States. This was the case in 2000 of Rula Amin, a Palestinian journalist working at CNN. Israel charged that she inserted political views into her reports. Pressure from pro-Israel groups forced the network to cancel her program for several months. After a lull she was reinstated and resumed broadcasting. Her articles remained, however, blatantly anti-Israel. During Operation "Defensive Shield" Israel stated that she was practically a mouthpiece for the PA.

Another prominent case was CNN's in-depth program in June 2002 on suicide attacks. Chen Keinan, who lost her mother and daughter in a suicide bombing in Petach Tikva about a month earlier, was interviewed for the show. The producers promised that her tragedy would be aired, but when she tuned in to the "International Hour" she was shocked to discover that the interview with her was marginal and the bulk of the program was devoted to an interview with the mother of the suicide bomber. The Israeli cable company announced it was removing CNN and its programs from the network. CNN's vice president immediately flew to Israel and guaranteed greater even-handedness in reporting. The following day CNN broadcast the entire interview with Chen Keinan on cable TV.

The use of this theme tapered off because of the exasperation and futility in fighting the networks. The dominant opinion in the Ministry was that no matter how much Israel growled and threatened the foreign media would continue to be anti-Israel.

Revealing the PLO's Hypocrisy. Israel employed this theme in the First Intifada and increased its use when the Palestinian organizations, including Fatah, turned to acts of violence. The PA took over the PLO's place and

Arafat continued to play a central role in the organization. Israel declared him an "enemy" and "the main obstacle to peace," and "sought to get rid of him," threatening him with expulsion, and even seriously considered eliminating him. Although Arafat was isolated from the external world since the summer of 2002, Israel continued to blame him for all its problems. It published a document showing that senior PA officials, including Arafat, supported and financed terrorism, and it accused them of playing a two-faced game that allowed them to reap the benefits of both worlds. On the one hand, PA officials publicly condemned the murder of innocent victims; on the other hand they maintained the "rotating door" policy, which basically released terrorists immediately after their arrest and instructed clandestine groups to continue the suicide attacks.

Explaining the Logic and Justification of Israel's Struggle. In the First Intifada Israel aimed its messages primarily at the neutral audience, presenting its version of the struggle and the roots of the conflict, and showing that Israel acted in accordance with international law; for instance, the West Bank had a different legal status than the Golan Heights, as it had been occupied by Jordan from 1948–1967 and didn't exist as a sovereign entity.[8] During the Second Intifada these themes were cast aside. The psywar that the two parties waged left little room for rational information; it became a gut-wrenching, smash-mouth struggle. Once the Palestinians gained ready access to the international stage, Israel realized it was useless to discuss these issues. Introducing themes such as "Israel is the only democracy in the Middle East" into the public discourse merely elicited a rise of the eyebrows and resounding chuckle of "so this is how a democracy acts." The basic question that remained was how Israel could end the violence. This was the result of the Palestinians' success in creating the impression that the Oslo Accords expressed Israel's willingness to make concessions to the Palestinian people. The generous cooperation that the Palestinians found in the West enabled them to embark upon full-scale psywar activity in Europe and the United States. In the foreign parliaments and campuses they organized demonstrations and rallies that enhanced the sense of injustice and suffering that Israel was perpetrating daily.[9]

Themes Aimed at the Enemy

The most conspicuous theme was the neutralization of suicide bombers as human weapons. Simultaneously Israel continued to convey information on the main issues of the conflict.

The Suicide Bombers. Israel tried, albeit to no avail, to limit the Palestinians' use of suicide bombers by emphasizing the amorality of murdering innocent civilians. Despite its efforts it immediately encountered basic obstacles, such as the enormous discrepancy between Israel's positive message of "the world we live in" (the benefits of peace, prosperity, and quiet, in the spirit of liberal Western democracy) and the Islamic organizations' messages of the "other world" (spiritual joy and sexual gratification according to the Muslim ideal). The mental barrier between these worlds made it impossible for Israel to get its messages across to Palestinian society, and technically there was a lack of channels for conveying information, excluding leaflets that contained only a minimal amount of information. (See below: Israel's distribution methods.) Most important, the suicide bombers' desire to carry out their mission (whether willingly or under pressure) precluded addressing them, since psywar's message to the enemy had always been based on the sanctity of life as the highest principle. Throughout the twentieth century, psywar operators had tried to convince the enemy (in their cultural terms, of course) to prefer the principle of life and living to other values, such as blind loyalty to the homeland or belief in an infallible leader.[10] However, the "sanctity of life" principle is neutralized when the target audience willingly chooses its own death.

The accumulated experience from a century of psychological warfare cannot answer the challenge of radical Islam. All attempts of Israel's intelligence bodies to thwart the suicide bombers by destroying the recruiting infrastructure failed. The Shabak tried to compose a profile of a suicide bomber in order to identify the potential shahid as early as possible. Prime candidates included desperate bachelors, followed by childless, unemployed husbands, then husbands with a job, husbands with families and jobs, and finally women and children. In other words, a profile of the suicide bomber defied characterization since the organizers recruited their quarry either willingly or by manipulating their weaknesses. In this light, the efforts to counter the suicide bombers probably should have focused on the religious level and practical psychology.

An analysis of Israel's messages to the Palestinian audience reveals many lost opportunities. None of the themes are new. Some were used during the First Intifada and others even earlier. The reason they were not exploited can be attributed to psywar's low status in Israel. The following points illustrate this:

The Schism in Palestinian Society. The factions waged a bitter internecine struggle with messages as well as physical violence. Israel could have exploited the vulnerability of Palestinian society in order to widen the internal conflicts and thus weaken it morally and structurally.

Corruption in the Palestinian Authority. The Palestinians themselves spread many leaflets on this theme as part of their internal power struggles. This subject could have easily been exploited with black psyop to drive a wedge in the Palestinian leadership.

The Conspiracy Theory (Arabic: *muamara*). This is a common theme in the Arab world, and especially among the Palestinians. According to *muamara*, politics is always a cunning device wielded from above (the ruling classes and national leaders) to exploit the downtrodden. Israel could have taken advantage of this theory to spread confusion and division among the Palestinians.

The Murder of Collaborators. Israel could have exploited the large number of Palestinians who had collaborated with it and were then summarily executed by individuals or groups. Sometimes, however, the killings had nothing to do with collaboration but were motivated by family disputes or criminal payback. The murders could have been presented in a way that showed that the PA's style of governing was similar to that of a Sicilian mafia gang, since this was assassination pure and simple, without any gloss of legal process and totally unrelated to collaboration with the enemy.

The Conflict between the Recruiters and the Suicide Bombers (a technique of subverting credibility). Israel could have pointed to the unethical methods used to recruit suicide bombers. For example, women who were handicapped or came from poor families, or who were stigmatized for having dishonored their families were the easiest prey. In other words, the recruiters exploited the misery of women who were deemed illegible for marriage and convinced them to become human dynamite sticks, and in exchange their families would be rewarded with money from Islamic funds. Men were recruited by similar methods (revenge on Israel for the death of a family member or performing a "sacred" religious precept to kill infidels). On one occasion Israel scored a relatively minor "win" that indicated the great potential in this approach. The Shabak publicized a tape in which the wife of Abdel-Aziz al-Rantissi (one of Hamas' founders) bitterly complained about attempts to enlist her son, a student, as a suicide bomber.

Palestinian Indoctrination. This subject was presented sporadically to foreign audiences and garnered minimal success. Israel failed to produce graphic images, like Palestinian murderers' hands dripping blood. Israeli decision-makers deliberated over the tapes sent to them by a private body (see below). When the Ministry finally integrated the tapes into films, they were of low quality and unsuited for TV, even though the images of little children parroting anti-Israel hate messages would have had a very powerful impact on TV.

The Muslims' Persecution of Christian Arabs in Bethlehem. This was the first opportunity to spread this theme, against the background of armed Palestinians shooting point blank into a Jewish residential area in the Gilo neighborhood (southwest of Jerusalem). The gunfire emanated from homes in the adjacent Christian town of Beit Jala. The second opportunity came during Operation "Defensive Shield" when Israeli troops laid siege to a group of wanted Palestinians that sought refuge in the Church of the Nativity in Bethlehem. Israel paid a heavy price for this incident in terms of world public opinion.

Palestinian Themes

The Palestinians' strategic aims in psychological warfare in the Second Intifada were similar to those in the First Intifada. To the home audience: solidarity with the organizations' military operations, demonization of Israel, willingness to sacrifice one's life; to the neutral audience: gaining its support for the establishment of an independent state; to Israel: presenting an image of unity, resolve, broad public backing for the national struggle, convincing Israel of the futility in persisting in its rule over the territories, driving a wedge between the settlers and general population, and encouraging soldiers to refuse service in the territories on moral grounds.

Themes for the Home Audience

Like in the First Intifada, the Palestinians' main theme to the home audience was to increase national unity and solidarity in the protracted struggle, that is, to strengthen the people's willingness to suffer casualties and hardship (because of the violent nature of the struggle), and to prevent the homefront from criticizing the PA and its militant wing. Three goals were derived from these themes: hatred of the enemy, absolute loyalty to the cause, and the cult of the hero. True, they had been present in the First Intifada, but then their scope was narrower and their intensity more subdued.

Hatred of the Enemy. This was the main theme for the home audience and was based on accumulated experience in the world of psychological warfare. It aims to unite the population, encourage self-sacrifice, and facilitate the destruction (read: murder) of the enemy. The "hate thy enemy" theme was commonly used in the First Intifada when Israeli troops were depicted as cowardly, venal, bumbling, and moronic but also capable of wielding tremendous firepower. Furthermore, in the Second Intifada Israelis were portrayed as drinking Palestinian blood. Every time Israel carried out a targeted killing, the bullet-ridden or shrapnel-mutilated bodies were photographed and next to them posed armed Palestinians whose hands were soaked in blood. These pictures intensified the hatred of a cruel and murderous enemy and presented Israel as a country that employs savage means to liquidate freedom fighters and the peace-loving civilian population. The Palestinian media described in detail the funerals of children killed by IDF fire. The most famous case, and one that symbolized the Second Intifada, was the death of the little boy Muhammad al-Dura who, the Palestinians claim, was cut down in a crossfire between the IDF and Palestinian terrorists at the Netzarim Junction in the Gaza Strip. The international media accepted the Palestinian version that he was killed by IDF rifle fire and almost completely ignored evidence that the Palestinians regularly staged events in order to score a propaganda windfall.[11]

The inconveniences and annoyances of daily life also exacerbated the population's hatred of Israel, especially because of the strict security checks at the roadblocks and the damage caused by the separation fence that forced people to spend hours traveling to reach schools, health clinics, and fields and orchards where they worked. Additionally, the Palestinians shelved the themes of religious oppression and school closure, which became irrelevant after the PA was established and assumed responsibility for the education system and religious institutions.

Absolute Loyalty. The subtext of this theme was that anyone who collaborates with the enemy is as good as dead. The Palestinians employed this theme in the First Intifada to break Israel's physical and psychological hold on the population. They increased the deterrent factor, leaving no room for the imagination, by putting the bodies of executed collaborators on public display. During the Second Intifada there was a sharp rise in the use of this theme. The PA turned the punishment process into a media event: trial, announcement of the verdict, and public execution. It also carried out a psyop campaign in schools, universities, and media that instructed how to avoid being entrapped by Shabak coordinators.

Cult of the Hero. This was the most frequently conveyed theme to the home audience during the Second Intifada since it expressed a key principle of Islam—waging jihad against the infidels. The leaders emphasized that any Muslims killed in a jihad are martyrs whose reward in the next world is guaranteed. The struggle with Israel was a religious war therefore anyone killed in an anti-Israel demonstration was considered a shahid. The definition was expanded on the theological-practical level to refer to anyone who sacrificed their life for Palestinian independence. The use of suicide bombers for achieving political goals is known from other parts of the world—Sri Lanka, Kashmir, and various al-Qaeda incidents. The Palestinians employed self-sacrifice on an unprecedented scale and elevated it to the noblest value in their struggle.

The organizers of the suicide bombings adapted the theme to the objective circumstances—the debilitating inconveniences of occupation and the hopelessness stemming from dire economic conditions. The theme was further strengthened by the highly developed indoctrination program, the layout for spotting potential martyrs, and the official media's unparalleled praise of self-sacrifice. For example, PA television aired children's programs that glorified martyrdom, mosque loudspeakers blared sermons on self-sacrifice as a holy commandment, pictures of martyrs appeared everywhere, and memorial sites were erected in honor of the dead heroes. Religious figures blessed this activity—as they did during the First Intifada to those who were killed during riots—despite Islam's injunction against suicide.[12]

The same recruiting themes were employed as in the First Intifada—unity, Islam, inevitable victory, "*sumud*" (determined resistance), and Jerusalem. Popular support for Arafat was also strengthened in 2002, in answer to Israel's sporadic siege of the Mukata'a that was designed to weaken the chairman's power. For example, in September 2002 when a senior PA official discovered Israeli sappers in the Mukata'a kitchen examining where dynamite charges could be planted, he reported this to an Al Jazeera correspondent and warned that if the gas tanks exploded the entire Mukata'a could blow up. The publication of this information made a powerful impact on the local population. Late that evening tens of thousands of Palestinians poured into the streets to demonstrate support of Arafat in defiance of the IDF curfew. Israel's efforts to introduce reforms in the PA were designed to limit Arafat's authority, but only sparked more demonstrations and visits of delegations to the Mukata'a in support of Arafat. Opinion polls showed that Arafat's popularity peaked in October 2002 following a series of Israeli sieges on the Mukata'a.

The Palestinians continued to laud women's contribution to the cause but they adapted the theme to the new nature of the struggle. During the First Intifada women had been urged to join the popular struggle (leave their place in the kitchen and take part in mass demonstrations, hurl rocks at the enemy, and assault IDF troops who were arresting their loved ones). But in the Second Intifada they were encouraged to strengthen their support of families whose sons and daughters disintegrated themselves on suicide missions.

Themes Aimed at the Neutral Audience

The Palestinians attributed great political importance to the neutral audience and invested enormous resources in gaining its support. They generally succeeded in conveying an image of solidarity to the outside world by using simple messages, such as "the occupation is the core of the problem." Thus, when Abu Mazen was appointed prime minister of the PA in March 2003, he devised a strategy that focused on American public opinion rather than on domestic backing. He had to convince the US administration that the PA honestly intended to introduce fundamental changes in its policy. This is why he chose the Aqaba Summit in June 2003 (in the presence of President Bush, Prime Minister Sharon, and King Abdullah of Jordan) to recognize the suffering of the Jewish people and avoid mention of the Palestinians' suffering, even though he knew he would have to weather bitter rebuke from the home audience because of this. His strategy succeeded—President Bush invited him to visit Washington after having kept Arafat at bay for three years.

Further evidence of Palestinian investment in international opinion is its huge diplomatic layout—101 diplomatic consulates, most of them at the ambassadorial level. The financial investment involved in this representative feat far exceeds that of a middle-sized country. For example, Israel maintains only seventy diplomatic consulates. Established in the mid-1970s, the Palestinian diplomatic machinery has played a major role in transforming the PLO from a terror organization into an independent authority that enjoys worldwide support in its effort to achieve national statehood.

During the Second Intifada, the Palestinians, like the Israelis, made extensive use of the new theme: demonization of the enemy. At the same time they continued to convey the themes of Palestinian justice and themes that castigated the enemy.

Demonization. This theme was rarely used during in the First Intifada because of the relatively small number of people killed in clashes with the IDF. The low casualty rate is attributed to the Palestinians' intentionally nonviolent activity that eschewed terror and guerilla warfare. However, in the

Second Intifada both sides incurred heavy losses because of the dimension of the violence that the Palestinians initiated (shooting incidents and suicide bombings) and because of the IDF's use of live ammunition (in encounters with armed Palestinians). It was only natural that demonization of the enemy became a commonly used theme on both sides. Palestinian spokespersons employed the media to accuse Israel for a wide range of imaginary atrocities: from kidnapping Palestinian children and harvesting their organs to handing out poisoned candy, using female soldiers to infect Palestinians with AIDS, and poisoning wells. Chairman Arafat's wife, Suha, brought up the last allegation in a conversation with Hillary Clinton (when the latter was First Lady) during her visit to the territories in February 2002. Foreign journalists scoffed at these accusations and regarded them as the fruit of a fertile Oriental imagination. Nevertheless, they should not be taken lightly. This was a familiar psywar technique to vilify the enemy. Demonization has two goals: to delegitimize Israel abroad (messages aimed at the neutral audience) and to render the enemy an object of hatred and prevent dialogue (messages aimed at the Palestinians).

The first major use of this theme came after an IDF raid on the village of Beit Rima north of Jerusalem in October 2001 in which five Palestinian policemen were killed, five wounded, and one civilian hurt.[13] The PA accused Israel of killing the wounded police officers and covering up the results. It also exploited the fact that the IDF prohibited media crews and ambulances from entering the village during the operation. This was the start of the Palestinians' atrocity propaganda that culminated in the claim of a 'massacre' in Jenin half a year later. Unfortunately, the IDF failed to learn the lesson from this event in its relations with the media.

The Palestinians applied the same theme in the Jenin Refugee Camp during Operation "Defensive Shield." The IDF put the number of Palestinians killed at fifty-three, including five civilians. (The IDF lost twenty-three troops in the operation.) The IDF's lack of coordination with the media (as a result of its decision to prohibit journalists from accompanying combat troops) created an information vacuum and led to a spike of rumors in Israel that the Palestinians were quick to fill in via interviews, photographs, and news reports.

The battle in the refugee camp involved great destruction. Because of the high number of wounded troops, the IDF ordered bulldozers to raze scores of buildings. This enabled the Palestinians to exaggerate the claim that a massacre had been carried out. Senior PA officials put the figure at three thousand dead. Later they whittled it down to five hundred. And finally, when world interest moved on to the next big event the number settled at fifty-six Palestinians killed. To substantiate the initial claim of an Israeli slaughter they recruited supporters like Terje Larson, the UN envoy to the Middle East, who quickly flew to the scene clad in a light blue UN helmet and flack jacket and was photographed from every possible angle while examining "first-hand" the Palestinians' charges of Israeli war crimes. The impression was created that atrocities had been committed a few days after the battle, especially when the Palestinians dragged the carcasses of horses and donkeys into the camp center to visualize the sense of carnage. The success of Palestinian atrocity propaganda of the alleged massacre was realized when the UN Secretary-General announced on April 19 that an investigating committee under his auspices would examine the events in Jenin. Israel's unwillingness to cooperate with the committee, combined with pressure by the pro-Israel lobby on the Secretary-General and US government, forced the Secretary-General to announce the dismantling of the committee on May 2.

A few weeks later, Muhammad Bachri, an Israeli-Arab actor, produced the documentary *Jenin, Jenin*[14] that underscored the theme of IDF demonization. It opened with the title announcing that the photographer was killed by Israel. It did not mention, however, that he was killed with an AK47 rifle in his hand while shooting at IDF forces. Naturally Bachri is not a psywar operator, but his work reflects the technique of exploiting an opportunity to stain Israel's image. Israel's statements to the effect that its soldiers knowingly sacrificed their lives in house-to-house fighting in order to reduce the risk to Palestinian civilians and that the IDF refrained from calling in the air force for the same reason made little impression on the international media.

Another prominent example of demonizing Israel is what occurred at the Church of the Nativity in Bethlehem in April 2002: the IDF laid siege to the edifice where scores of terrorists had found safe haven. The Palestinians launched a massive Israel-bashing campaign addressed to the Christian world, implying that Israel had desecrated a Christian holy site. The smear campaign began losing steam when reports were published that the armed terrorists had damaged the church and had stolen precious artifacts.

Disparaging the Enemy. The Palestinians used the media to convey a great amount of visual information on casualties and property damage resulting from Israeli-initiated activity. In the case of a targeted assassination, they made sure to downplay the target's history and to stress the details surrounding civilians who were killed by being in the wrong place at the wrong time. This was especially true when the bystanders were women or children. In this way they presented Israel's targeted assassination policy as the cold-blooded murder of civilians, and emphasized Israeli brutality when noncombatants were killed in the proximity of the target due to identification error or the destructive power of the missiles fired from helicopter gunships.

In one case, five children from the same family in Khan Yunis (Gaza Strip, November 2001) were killed by an explosive device that Israel planted to counter activists preparing missile launchings. The Palestinian media assailed Israel, accusing it of willfully murdering young innocents and using lethal weapons, such as assault rifles, tanks shells, and even tactical nuclear weapons (no less)[15] for crowd dispersal.

The First Intifada themes were repeated: the Jewish lobby's control of the US administration, Israel is a nuclear power, Israel commits atrocities in the territories, and Israel is a Middle East version of South Africa. At first glance, the last theme seems inapplicable given the fact that South Africa returned to the family of nations after its apartheid regime was ousted in 1994 (that is, half a decade before the Second Intifada) but the Palestinians remodeled the image, which still packed a wallop in the international consciousness, in order to halt construction on the separation fence that they termed the "apartheid wall" because of the severe disruption of daily lives that it caused.[16]

The Palestinians continued to spread the theme of human rights violations—a secondary theme in the calumniation of the enemy. The idea was to create another front against Israel while exploiting the wholesale presence of human rights organizations in the territories, such as Amnesty International. The Ministry was unprepared for the flood of petitions that it received as the Palestinians continued to churn out devastating reports. Israel grew tired of calling attention to the egregious disproportion between the passing mention of slaughter in Sudan and Congo where hundreds of thousands of Africans were butchered and the lengthy reports of human rights infringement in the territories.

A secondary demonization theme was to portray Israel as a Nazi state. Here too (as in the First Intifada) the Palestinians continued to make freewheeling use of the terms genocide, ethnic cleansing, and liquidation. They added a historical-psychological twist to Israel's conduct: the Zionists were merely doing to the Palestinians what the Nazis did to their fathers.

As the casualty rate rose, the Palestinians adopted themes related to conscience and the Holocaust. At the same time they made wide use of the international law theme, especially after the erection of the separation fence, its debate in the International Court of Justice in The Hague, and the adoption of international law by many European states for punishing war criminals. Given these developments, Israel began blurring the faces of officers in photos taken during operations. In addition, high-ranking officers who served in the Second Intifada avoided travel to European countries.[17]

The Palestinians relentlessly attacked the head of the enemy camp: Prime Minister Ariel Sharon, Yitzhak Shamir's successor. Sharon was described as drinking the blood of Palestinian babies and graphically depicted as a lip-smacking ogre who had brutalized the Palestinians throughout his military and political career—from retaliatory raids by the elite 101 Unit in the 1950s to the liquidation of terror in the Gaza Strip in the early 1970s, the massacre committed by Christian Phalangists in the 1982 War in Lebanon ("the butcher of Sabra and Shatila"), the massive expansion of Jewish settlements in the territories in the 1980s and 1990s, and finally the targeted assassinations of senior Palestinian military activists and political leaders in his role as prime minister.

The political messages aimed at the neutral audience reflected the changes in the region and world. The following themes were jettisoned: Palestinian self-determination and convening an international conference (no longer necessary because of the establishment of the PA); Soviet Jewry (the period of mass immigration ended); and American aid to Israel (the Palestinians also became recipients of American assistance, including police sniper training by CIA instructors). The theme of the Palestinians' right of return remained, though it was downplayed in messages to the Israeli public.[18] Long-standing themes were still applied—justice, oppression, and morality; but gone were brotherhood, nonviolence (given the changes in the nature of the fighting), and democracy (following the establishment of the PA).

Use of Force

These themes remained essentially the same as in the First Intifada. The Palestinians' sought to undermine Israel's solidarity by driving a wedge between Israelis living within the Green Line and the settlers. They continued to view the settlers as the most hostile target audience since they presented an ideological, religiously motivated alternative to the fate of the territories. Therefore the Palestinians tried to terminate the settlement enterprise in every way possible. Militarily, they attacked the settlers, and in particular the soldiers protecting them and manning the roadblocks. These ambushes eroded national solidarity since they strengthened the claim that there was no need to have IDF troops pay with their lives for the defense of small and isolated settlements such as Netzarim in the Gaza Strip. A Hamas leader, interviewed by the Israeli journalist Avi Issacharoff (Channel 1, September 11, 2004), said that the Israeli Left's "Refusal to Serve Movement" inspired his organization to pursue its military activity. One of the Palestinians' biggest mistakes in the Second Intifada (beginning in March 2001) was to transfer their violent struggle from the territories to Israeli cities within the Green Line, a move that bonded Israeli society much tighter than in the past.

The Palestinian Information Layout; its Relations with the Foreign Media

The most significant change in the Palestinian information layout in the Second Intifada was that the PA controlled the state media. This enabled the Palestinians to get their messages across much more effectively than before, especially to the home audience. (Previously Israel had been able to clamp down on the Palestinian press—censoring material and prohibiting circulation). With the newly gained autonomy, the Palestinian Ministry of Education published schoolbooks with scores of hate references toward Israel. As in all the Arab states, the Palestinians coordinated the distribution of information through an information ministry that worked in conjunction with a PR director. The centralization of information distribution added substantially to its effect.

Aware that the networks were the main vehicles for transferring messages to the neutral audience, the Palestinians maintained their cordial and cooperative relations with the foreign media. They continued to ply foreign journalists with human interest items. The Jerusalem Media and Communications Center (JCMM), established in 1988 by Ghassan Khatib, is an excellent example of the institutionalization of the Palestinians' relationship with the foreign media.[19] The center contacted foreign reporters in their home countries and invited them on study tours in the territories where they received red-carpet service: translators, access to many areas, and interviews with Palestinians and Israelis (the latter, naturally, were of politically correct persuasions). The journalists were not told what to write, but their Palestinian chaperones brought them to the right place at the right time, and together with the special interviews and background material the foreign correspondents generally advanced the Palestinian cause in the international media.

Interestingly, the foreign media's coverage of the territories led to a drastic reduction in the number of foreign journalists and photographers at the scene of events, and their replacement by Palestinian stringers. This was because the armed guerillas and Israeli countermeasures often put the foreign reporters in the line of fire, thus increasing their insurance premium. Therefore the foreign network heads increasingly relied on Palestinian stringers.

The surge in the number of Palestinian teams can be traced to the economic situation (lack of employment for young Palestinians); the establishment of PA-controlled media channels (that created a need for spreading messages to the home audience); the Palestinians' ideological commitment to promoting national interests; and the low cost needed to produce news (cameras, camcorders, digital stills, scanners, computers, and cellular phones).

The large networks, especially Reuters and the French news agency Agence France-Presse (AFP), enthusiastically adopted this arrangement. They obtained the photographed material, its quality improved over the years, without endangering the lives of their reporters and at very low cost (in most cases credit was given to the news agency without mention of the Palestinian photographer). The Palestinian stringers gradually became proficient at stills and video photography (the rough and jumpy footage from the scene of an event, taken close to real time, enhanced the drama and often overcame the substandard quality of the filming[20]). The foreign news agencies were not part of the Palestinian information distribution mechanism, but the Palestinian photo stringers exploited the events, chose the story, the angle of the filming, and the timing for relaying the story to the agencies. Thus they served as a direct link to the world media.

The PA was careful about its image on the international stage, therefore it made sure to remove incriminating evidence that Israel could use against it. For example, it got rid of the photographs of the lynching in Ramallah and ordered a halt to the celebrations in the Palestinian towns over the 9/11 attacks. It issued regulations to local reporters forbidding pictures of Palestinian children carrying weapons. This order was designed to counter Israel's messages that the Palestinians were educating their youth to engage in a violent struggle rather than pursue a path of dialogue and co-existence.

Israel's Information Layout

During the Second Intifada there were three main official bodies for distributing information and maintaining contact with the media: the Government Press Office (GPO), the Ministry, and the IDF. The severity of the events highlighted the immense difficulties these bodies faced (shifting priorities, cutbacks in funding, stagnation in developing a modus operandi, and reduction in manpower training). Private bodies were also a conspicuous feature of this period.

The Government Press Office. The steady decline in the importance of the GPO after Operation Peace for Galilee can be attributed to a number of reasons. One, technological advances in information gathering diminished the network's dependency on government sources and simultaneously enhanced the importance of private information channels that operated through the Internet, mobile phones, and independent satellite services. Two, structural change in the world of news gathering, such as additional news-only TV stations (CNN, Fox) that demanded quality, real-time information on a 24/7 basis; and an increase of unofficial information sources (government and company officials and military officers) who often replaced state-supplied sources. Three, Israel's growing diversity of political opinion and greater willingness to publicize it over the media, and the decline in importance of public consensus, resulted in Israeli political elements often wooing the journalists and newscasters. Four, the Palestinians applied the policy of establishing alternative information layouts. The JMCC, for example, worked in conjunction with the foreign media and furnished it with extremely valuable material, thus diminishing the need for obtaining official information from Israeli spokespersons. Five, the heads of state and senior officials wanted to retain control of information distribution. Prime Minister Ehud Barak, for example, transferred many job quotas from the GPO to the new media unit that he installed in the Prime Minister's Office in order to systematically track publications in the Israeli media (the quotas were not returned to the GPO at the end of Barak's tenure). Finally, the trend to relegate *hasbara* to the bottom rung of the national agenda with regard to the allocation of resources (budgets and personnel).

All these factors combined to create a gradual decline in the GPO's raison d'être. Its operations shrunk to merely issuing government licenses that allowed journalists easier access to interviews with senior officials and granting them a slight reduction in entry restrictions to areas of confrontation. The head of the office came under harsh criticism from the foreign journalists because of his refusal to issue press cards to the Palestinian stringers and his claim that they exploited them for PA political goals.

The Ministry of Foreign Affairs—Despite the blow to Israel's image in the First Intifada, the Second Intifada saw no fundamental policy change in the Ministry's priorities for improving Israel's image overseas or in the Hasbara Unit (that was upgraded to a department) regarding information distribution.

The gap between the need for effective *hasbara* and the reality on the ground was so glaring that the State Comptroller issued a scathing report in October 2002. The document criticized the failure to define objectives and goals, the absence of basic guidelines, the inefficient use of manpower, the shallow ties between overseas *hasbara* volunteers and the Ministry, and an absurdly small budget (most of which went to salaries in Israel and abroad). In addition, it stated that the Ministry had failed to address the problem of Palestinian control of the campuses in Europe and the United States—the breeding ground of the next generation of leadership—and the lack of coordination between government organizations (the Prime Minister's Office and the Ministry of Foreign Affairs) and security bodies (the IDF) in ordinary times, and especially during major operations such as "Defensive Shield."

There were several reasons for this sorry state of affairs. First—ideological dissent resulted in an ambiguous attitude toward relations between Israel and the world (in stark contrast to the Palestinians' sharply defined messages). For example, should Israel convey an image of power and resolve (by stressing the liquidation of terrorists) or weakness (by publishing pictures of the victims of terror strikes)? Is anti-Semitism so universal and deep-rooted that no effort on Israel's part can change inherently hostile attitudes? Should Israel withdraw from the Gaza Strip and Judea, and Samaria in order to appease international pressure (as opposed to maintaining an ongoing *hasbara* campaign)? Second—the people chosen to fill senior roles in Israel's overseas consulates were often political appointees unsuited to the task. They lacked ability and training in public relations, and were often ignorant of the target country's culture and language. Third—the high-handed attitude of Israel's representatives toward the local Jewish communities, undermined and was thus counterproductive to *hasbara* efforts. Fourth—there was a basic misunderstanding of the role of Israel's official overseas public relations representatives and the frivolous dismissal of the need for thorough training and serious study. But in reality *hasbara* is a complex task that demands lengthy training, innate talent, and considerable experience.[21]

The Ministry's inadequacy in *hasbara* came to light when it tried to challenge the Palestinians' control of overseas campuses. Palestinian success in this area was the result of a long-range policy that began in the early 1970s and the investment of tremendous resources in coordination with Arab and Islamic groups. The American and European students eventually graduated and some became politicians and media executives in the 1980s, and gradually worked their way up the hierarchy. Parliamentarians, journalists, writers, and intellectuals gained powerful impressions from their visits to the territories and participation in seminars and lectures organized by the Palestinians. Palestinian public relations received huge financial and organizational backing. In the same period the Israeli MFA employed one part-time worker in charge of *hasbara* on campuses overseas.

Private Bodies. Alongside the official bodies that engaged in information dissemination, private Jewish bodies and non-Jewish sympathizers also rose to prominence in the Second Intifada by exploiting the cyber revolution to spread vast amounts of low-cost visual information to decision-makers and neutral audiences. These independent initiatives, whether privately backed or community financed, provided an answer to the extensive, far-reaching operations of the Palestinians and their Arab and Muslim supporters whose websites were dedicated to maligning Israel and reinforcing their political messages. Over the years the pro-Israel private bodies expanded their activities and gained the image of credible databases on the Israeli-Palestinian conflict. The leading groups were The Middle East Media Research Institute (MEMRI) headed by Yigal Carmon, a former advisor to the prime minister on the war against terror; Palestinian Media Watch under the directorship of Itamar Marcus; and the pioneering work of a private individual, Sonia Bayefsky, who operated out of her small Jerusalem flat. Bayefsky was the first to document the Arab networks around the clock, taping their news broadcasts and documentaries on Israel. Private groups translated material from Palestinian television into English and conveyed the PA's negative side. For example, they published an exposé on Palestinian summer camps where "arts-and-crafts" and "outdoor sports" included weapons assembly, military exercises, anti-Israel incitement, and oaths to enlist as suicide bombers. Other reports described how women were recruited to undertake suicide bombing missions; how the PA extolled the female suicide bomber Wafa Idris, who carried out a suicide attack in Jerusalem on January 27, 2002; substantial monetary grants to the families of suicide bombers and terrorists;[22] and the PA's support of Sadaam Hussein (prior to his demise). The independent reportage also detailed the

Palestinians' emphasis on violent anti-Western themes, such as a jihad against the United States and the West,[23] the demonization of President Bush after the occupation of Iraq, and the depiction of the United States as the enemy of Islam.

The IDF. Two IDF units are officially tasked with directing and supplying information—the IDF Spokesperson's Unit and the Psyop Unit.

The IDF Spokesperson. During the Second Intifada two people from different backgrounds filled this role. The first was Brigadier General Ron Kitri, a former intelligence officer who was called back to military service from civilian life by the Chief of Staff—Ehud Barak. Kitri lacked training and experience in the media. He replaced Brigadier General Oded Ben-Ami, a journalist, who succeeded a long list of intelligence officers. The appointment of Ben-Ami's predecessors had been problematic because of their lack of media training and their attitude toward information, which, given their background in Military Intelligence, was the opposite of what their new role demanded. Instead of publishing information, they tended to block it as much as possible. One of the reasons for Ben-Ami's appointment may have been the outstanding work of another journalist, Nachman Shai, during the First Gulf War (1991).

Ben-Ami's appointment was designed to improve IDF-media relations especially with the foreign media, but it also raised another problem. Since he was outside the military system, he lacked the trust of officers in the field, and this interfered with the transfer of information to the media in real time.

In 2002 Brigadier General Ruth Yaron became the spokesperson. Yaron was borrowed from the MFA where she had gained invaluable experience working with foreign outlets. She succeeded in slightly improving the unit's organizational structure and its relations with the media. However, no basic change took place in the IDF and defense ministry's middle and senior levels regarding military-media relations.

In short, the IDF Spokesperson's Unit did not provide an effective answer to the challenges of the media revolution and its focus on Israeli actions in the territories. Despite the best intentions and dedicated labor of its personnel, the unit failed to supply the media with convincing information during the two Intifadas. Worse, the IDF made no systematic attempt to increase its officers' awareness of the growing importance of the media and psywar in the twenty-first century. Staff officers' course routinely included just one day devoted to relations with the media. Field officers generally harbored deep reservations over the media—especially foreign journalists—and tried to conceal as much information as possible from them. This was only natural given the prevalent view in the IDF that any information leak to foreign elements compromised state security. As expected, this attitude did little to enhance Israel's or the IDF's image.

One of the army's major innovations in the Second Intifada was the integration of photographers in combat units. Since this type of filming is essentially for civilian consumption, the IDF mulled over the idea of training combat troops in photography or integrating professional photographers into combat units. In 2004 the IDF weekly, *Bamahane*, reported the establishment of a new unit ("Amit") comprised of troops who completed a photography course (video and stills) and accompanied combat missions armed with their cameras. In April 2003 one soldier of the members of the unit was killed while filming the search for tunnels and weapons in Rafah. Today, troops from elite units are sent to operational photography courses. But the IDF still seems to have a long way to go to internalize the full import of filming events during battles.

The IDF's Relations with the Media. The IDF's relations with journalists can best be characterized as ambivalent. Although the army was quick to exploit the media for conveying messages, as in the case of the *Karine A* arms vessel, still, it feared the media as a double-edged sword that could harm Israel, for example, by quoting soldiers who criticized military and political policy. Therefore, it refused to allow reporters to accompany the fighting forces in Operation "Defensive Shield" in the northern West Bank. This move, however, backfired when a wave of rumors inundated Israel about a "catastrophe" that had occurred (which was exacerbated by censoring reports on events in Jenin). The upshot of this ill-contrived policy was to hand the Palestinians a golden opportunity to exaggerate their claims of an Israeli massacre in the Jenin Refugee Camp. Only after the IDF permitted journalists entry into the camp did the truth come out: the accusations were unadulterated fabrications. The Chief of Staff Lieutenant General Moshe Ya'alon admitted that the decision to slap restrictions on the media had been a mistake.

The IDF and Israel police made judicious use of media exposure—local and foreign—during the evacuation of Israeli settlers from Gaza and northern Samaria in August 2005. This is not to say that the media has to be "in" on every operation, but the IDF should examine the benefits of the media's presence, especially the foreign press and networks, in each action it undertakes.

The Psyop Unit. A few months before the Second Intifada, this unit suffered heavy cutbacks. An Israeli journalist reported that the IDF psyop unit was using the London-based Arab press to influence Iran and the Arab world. The chief of military intel panicked and almost dismantled the unit. The drastic reduction in manpower and allocations was the final step in the long erosion of psywar's importance in the IDF. As a result the unit's ability to introduce strategic moves was severely hampered.

Nevertheless, the army's attitude toward the media and psychological warfare altered somewhat in 2005. Chief of Staff Moshe Ya'alon introduced the term "consciousness" and spinoffs such as "consciousness burning" into the IDF's lexicon. Under Ya'alon's command a series of operational moves were introduced that testify to the growing importance accorded the media in combat operations and the army's improved ability in conveying messages to the Palestinians.

These rectifications included improved coordination between the IDF spokesperson and military units; photography courses for combat troops to enable the immediate supply of visual material beneficial to Israel's image in the world media (not only for debriefing, as before); and courses for junior officers (company commanders) that explained the media's importance and role in combat. (Although this is still a far cry from other armies—the US Army, for example—where officers who receive intensive training in military-media relations and public affairs have a respectable military career track.)

CHAPTER 12

The Psyop War

The Israeli Side

Psywar Planning: Definition and Aims

Following the breakdown in the political process with the Palestinians in late 1999 Israel planned a military response, but nothing is known of special preparations for psychological warfare or if its goals were defined. This is another example of the basic shortcomings—limited resources of the information warfare unit, and psywar's lowly status in the IDF—even though the decision-makers were aware that psychological warfare could be extremely advantageous (as the Palestinians had proven). The traditional mindset remained: the struggle with the Palestinians would be decided by military force alone; psychological warfare was of negligible importance.

From the shreds of available information it turns out that close to the outbreak of the Second Intifada Israel could have defined two main objectives in its psywar: deepening the schism in Palestinian society and lowering the morale in order to sap popular support for the military struggle. Ironically, prior to the Second Intifada, Israel had defined one of its goals as strengthening the PA and its chairman. Only in 2002 did the government change its policy and work to undermine the Palestinian leadership and even get rid of Arafat.

Main Actions

Under Prime Minister Ariel Sharon and Chief of Staff Shaul Mofaz's leadership, Israel responded swiftly to every terrorist attack—striking Palestinian targets and liquidating key terror activists. This activity reflects the minimal importance that Israeli decision-makers attributed to psychological tactics—especially regarding neutral audiences—such as the "Israel is the victim" theme and the savagery of Palestinian terror that makes no distinction between soldier and civilian. However, Israel's retaliations only diverted the media's attention to the Palestinian casualties and strengthened the Palestinians' parallel themes of victimhood and enemy brutality. Nevertheless, the decision-makers may have wanted to influence other audiences of greater importance than the neutral audience—the domestic and enemy audiences—by demonstrating Israel's power and determination: the message that the enemy could expect no respite from Israel's vengeance raised the domestic audience's morale and bolstered its sense of security.

The most outstanding case of prioritizing a targeted killing for political and *hasbara* reasons was the liquidation of the Tanzim activist Raed Karmi in Tulkarem in January 2002. Yet this incident caused Israel strategic damage and was vilified in the world press for jumpstarting the cycle of violence and rehabilitating the PA's status after its nadir (following Israel's exposé of Arafat's personal involvement in the *Karine A* arms smuggling ship).

The IDF did not formulate a psywar doctrine in the Second Intifada. The few initiatives that were made came from the information warfare unit in the months preceding the unit's decommissioning, the establishment of a new body,[1] and from commanders who realized the value of this type of activity in a low-intensity conflict (LIC). The following steps had direct and indirect implications on the psywar:

Karine A. Using state-of-the-art intelligence, the Israeli navy seized a vessel transporting a huge quantity of weapons from Iran to the Gaza Strip in mid-sea in January 2002. The cargo included long-range rockets and highly lethal explosive devices. Unlike the navy's capture of the *Santorini* six months earlier, this time Israel decided to exploit the operational success for a public relations windfall. Unfortunately, the publicity of the operation was poorly staged and missed the mark. The enormous array of weapons (fifty tons) was spread out for view on a wharf in the Port of Eilat, according to weapon types, and offered visual proof of the Palestinians' intentions to continue the violent struggle, cause an untold number of Israeli casualties, and fire missiles into the Gaza Envelope. The "show," however, came off as rather dull. A ship in dock at an Israeli port did not spark particular interest even if a vast quantity of weapons was on display. Had the authorities conveyed videos of commandos rappelling from helicopters and seizing control of the vessel or advancing in assault boats, the foreign media would have shown much keener interest.

Some logistical difficulties—such as the lack of spokespersons with knowledge of foreign languages—were also apparent as the cache appeared in the international media. This probably stemmed from the fact that the official information bodies—the IDF and others—became privy to the operation only at its conclusion because of security exigencies. Coordination between the IDF and government *hasbara* agencies—the Ministry and GPO—was defective.

A few weeks later another *hasbara* attempt was made, this time to a specific target audience—an Israeli intelligence delegation brought proof to the US administration of Arafat's direct involvement in arms smuggling. This stood in flagrant contradiction to Arafat's letter to the President denying any knowledge of the ship prior to its seizure. This information in effect scandalized the PA and its leader and confirmed the link between the PA and world terror that had struck the United States only a few months earlier (September 11, 2001). The fruits of this revelation soon ripened when the Bush Administration removed its restrictions on Israel's response to terrorist activity.

Aerial Activity. Surgical attacks by helicopter gunships induced severe psychological distress among the Palestinians since it gave the impression that the enemy was ubiquitous and omniscient but unseen and invulnerable. To counter the threat the Palestinians covered broad stretches of the urban terrain in the Gaza Strip with carpets and camouflage canvas sheets to blur visual ground data.

UAV Photographs in Psychological Warfare. Two highly regarded, yet almost fortuitous successes were attributed to *unmanned aerial vehicle* (UAV) photos. The first was the video recording of a Palestinian staged funeral in Jenin immediately after Operation "Defensive Shield." One of the pallbearers tripped and the deceased got off the litter to stretch his limbs. The IDF conveyed the film to the television networks and Internet sites with the express purpose of shattering the Palestinians' credibility and refuting their charge that Israel had perpetrated a massacre in the city. In the second case a UAV photographed armed fighters being transported in Red Crescent ambulances and exploiting the protection guaranteed the vehicles at Israeli roadblocks. Israel proved the Palestinians to be liars who made a mockery of the Geneva Convention.

Driving a Wedge between Groups. On August 18, 2004, security prisoners went on a hunger strike (a common practice in political struggles and one that the Palestinians had been employing since the 1970s). Israel published a picture of Marwan Barghouti, the head of the Tanzim in the West Bank, eating heartily in his cell. By disseminating the photo Israel sought to discredit one of the leading symbols of the Second Intifada.

Terminology. Aware of the effect that terminology has on persuasion, Israel devised some of its own and borrowed others: "targeted assassination" for liquidation, "clearance" for uprooting trees and crops on roadsides, "collateral damage" for noncombatants unintentionally killed in the course of military action (a term borrowed from the US Army in the Vietnam War).

Exploiting Captured Documents. During Operation "Defensive Shield" reams of documents were confiscated in the recaptured Palestinian Mukata'a. The IDF was fully aware of their *hasbara* potential and a special Military Intelligence team was set up to sift through the batches, translate them, and convey the material to the media and later to Raviv Drucker, an Israeli journalist who published it in a book.

Means of Dissemination

Radio and Television. Israel's Arabic-language broadcasts continued to decline during the Second Intifada, thus squandering an effective means of getting messages across to the Palestinian public. The Voice of Israel in Arabic, once extremely popular in the Arab world, was steadily downsized since the 1980s and not even available in all parts of Gaza. Israel's Arabic language programs went downhill in the 1990s as the old generation of Jewish journalists who grew up in Arab countries gradually retired. In addition, Arab Israelis had a far larger selection of channels to choose from with the revolution in satellite TV, such as Qatar's Al Jazeera, Saudi Arabia's Al Arabiya, Hezbollah's Al-Manar. Israel's state channel, in a longtime state of decline, reduced budgets and manpower instead of increasing its efforts to confront the competition.

Leaflets. In the absence of alternatives, Israel dropped leaflets from the air on the Palestinians in the territories. The procedure was a logistical nightmare: writing the messages, getting them approved, printing the leaflets, packing them, and coordinating the operation with the air force, and finally dropping them on the target audience. This was only one technique for conveying messages and a very limited one at that—a single page—containing minimal information (often a warning. Naturally the PA scrambled to collect and burn the leaflets, though a small number may have reached their targets. On the messages' effectiveness—no data is available.)

A famous leaflet that appeared in the Israeli press dealt with the launching of Qassam rockets into the western Negev. It had an illustration of Palestinian activists firing a Qassam: The missile veers off course, boomerangs back in their direction, and slams into a Palestinian home blowing it to smithereens. This was a tried-and-true technique that different armies applied in the past: using visual means to cut through rational mechanisms and convey a visceral message even to the illiterate. Although the target audience was ordered to "search and destroy" the "venom being spread by the enemy," in the fraction of a second before throwing the leaflet into the dustbin the people were exposed to the message. Israel also used the leaflets to warn Palestinian noncombatants not to shelter terrorists.[2]

Worried that Israel would drop bogus leaflets (black propaganda), the Palestinians circulated their own leaflets warning the population to take heed and giving tips on how to identify "Zionist" material. The Hebrew daily *Ha'aretz* reported one case in which the Palestinians discovered such a ruse.[3] This was a leaflet supposedly sent by Christian Arabs in Beit Jala (a Palestinian town south of Jerusalem) but the wording showed that it was definitely not written by a Christian. Perhaps the unprofessionalism is indicative of the sorry state of affairs in the IDF information warfare unit at this time due to sweeping cutbacks. Inexperienced personnel may have tried their hand at a "little" psychological initiative only to have their activity immediately exposed.

Persuasion Techniques

Demonstrating Strength. Israel's main persuasive technique—the application of force—reached its climax in Operation "Defensive Shield." Only in early 2002 did Israel begin to demonstrate its strength, after Palestinian terror rose to intolerable levels following murderous attacks against military targets that included antitank explosives in Gaza, ambushes at roadblocks in the Ramallah district, and suicide bombings in Israeli cities. In February the IDF launched its first assaults on the refugee camps adjacent to Jenin and Nablus, eliminating scores of armed activists.

On one occasion the IDF exploited a military operation to boost its deterrent strength. The Golani Infantry Brigade raided the Tulkarem Refugee Camp in March 2002, surrounding hundreds of armed activists who, after negotiating, surrendered en masse. Television crews were on hand to document hundreds of male terrorists stripped bare to the waist marching out of the camp in a conga line with their hands on their heads.

The brigade commander admitted that the inspiration came from Hezbollah activity in Lebanon. The timing of the action was just as important as the operation's success—conveying to the home audience, as well as to the Palestinians, the message and image of a powerful army that knows how to quash terror. The Tulkarem raid came at the height of suicide attacks in Israel and after a streak of IDF setbacks.

Operation "Defensive Shield" furnished the Palestinians, for the first time since the Six-Day War, with tangible proof of the IDF's might. The scores of tanks and APCs rolling through Jenin's streets physically demonstrated Israel's determination, reinforced by unprecedented public support, to crush Palestinian terror, whatever the cost.

During Operation "Defensive Shield" the IDF and Shabak maintained that superlative cooperation that had been institutionalized since the mid-1990s. As IDF forces encircled Jenin and closed in, the Shabak made contact with armed terrorists in the city and advised them to surrender. These conversations undoubtedly had a powerful psychological impact since they proved that Israel's intelligence was omnipresent (knowing the activists' exact whereabouts and even their phone numbers).

After "Defensive Shield" the IDF carried out massive arrests and sent in snipers, special forces, and attack helicopters to eliminate terrorist leaders. The government adopted various defensive measures to quell Palestinian terror, such as the construction of the separation fence (beginning in the summer of 2002), and other actions of limited success for securing roads in the territories and protecting public institutions and entertainment centers in Israel.

The air force's increased involvement in ground operations also supplied valuable material in the "battle for the minds." The surgical assassinations by helicopters instilled an overriding fear in the population that Israeli intelligence had inside knowledge and could find whoever it targeted. The buzz of a camera-equipped UAV cruising in the skies generated deep anxiety in the Palestinians and left them with many a sleepless night.

Message Conveying to the Palestinian Population. One example of establishing ties with the Gaza population was the press announcement in November 2003 by the general of the Southern Command congratulating the locals on the approaching Id al-Fitr holiday and calling for peace.

Another Example: The Shabak published a picture of one of the terrorists who had taken part in the lynching of the two IDF reservists in Ramallah at the start of the Second Intifada. The photo of the murderer handcuffed and behind bars illustrated Israel's ability to capture anyone who perpetrated an attack.[4] The Israeli press assisted in the transmission of this message by publishing it juxtaposed with the famous picture taken immediately after the lynching by the terrorist brandishing his blood-stained hands.

Symbols. Israel circulated two symbols that summed up Palestinian terror in all its barbarity and ferocity: the charred and twisted remains of buses destroyed in suicide bombings (the remnants of one were sent to the Hague where the International Court of Justice was debating the legality of the separation fence) and the Palestinian flourishing his hands dripping with the blood of the victims of the Ramallah lynch. The Ministry distributed a videotape of the lynching to the participants in the international conference in Sharm al-Sheikh held under the auspices of the United States in October 2000.

The Palestinian Side

Planning Psychological Warfare: Definitions and Goals

After the Oslo Accords the Palestinians continued to spread information to advance their political goals and convince the target audiences of the justification of their cause. The establishment of the PA enhanced their information-disseminating capability. Thus, when the uprising shifted to the violent stage in November 2000 they only had to modify their propaganda tools rather than build new ones. According to Palestinian press reports, in preparation for the renewal of violence they opened a number of courses that instructed cadres how to neutralize Israel's psywar efforts.

Their goals were the same as in the First Intifada except for the nature of the struggle: the use of violence.

Means of Dissemination

The PA's main development in this field was the establishment of independent media networks that diminished the need for the earlier simpler means—graffiti, loudspeakers, leaflets, and so forth.

It quickly set up an independent television station (the "Palestinian Broadcasting Corporation"), a radio station (Voice of Palestine), two official newspapers—*al-Hayat al-Jadida* (The New Life) and *al-Ayam* (The Days), and seems to have control over dozens of independent papers.

Hamas and Islamic Jihad's independent radio stations are extremely popular. To counter this, the PA established a new radio station in September 2005—Al-Karama (The Voice of Honor) that broadcasted twelve hours daily. Another important Islamic radio station, Voice of Jerusalem, transmits from Syria and is identified with Islamic Jihad. Its programs are mainly geared to the Palestinian audience.

Internet Sites. The Palestinians' main vehicle for conveying messages is the Internet. Contrary to conventional wisdom about the Palestinians' technological backwardness, it turned out that the opposite was the case, and at an early stage they went cyber to reach the largest possible target audience. Until the PA was officially installed, the Internet served as an effective tool for circumventing Israeli press censorship and conveying messages relatively safely. IDF troops who entered ramshackle abodes in the refugee camps were amazed to find sophisticated electronic equipment. The abundance of computers probably stemmed from the interminable curfews and closures. One of the Palestinian sites with the most "hits" is still the "Palestinian Ministry of Information"—www.minfo.gov.ps—that appears in Hebrew and is addressed to Israelis. The site offers dozens of major links to NGOs, human rights organizations, and anti-censorship organizations, as well as to what the Palestinians term Israeli provocation organizations: Rotternet, the Makor Rishon (Primary Source) newspaper, and MEMRI.[5]

Palestinian universities are actively involved in information dissemination. Bir Zeit University specializes in the neutral audience[6] and its site was the first to include hundreds of links related to the Israeli-Palestinian conflict directly or indirectly, and personal sites of media and academic figures who visited the University and uploaded photos of their visits.

The use of simpler means of message dissemination may have diminished in the Second Intifada but were still used. For example: Leaflets remained the basic means employed by the independent terror organizations—Hamas and Islamic Jihad—and their messages were often covered by the media; graffiti was employed by the Islamic organizations and splinter groups; and loudspeakers in the mosques and megaphones in demonstrations are still prevalent.

Persuasive Techniques

Nonviolent action, the hallmark of the First Intifada, became anachronistic in the Second Intifada and was replaced with alternative techniques: symbols and military operations.

The Use of Symbols. The Palestinians adopted the golden dome shrine on the Temple Mount as their main symbol. This expressed the centrality of Jerusalem in the political struggle over a permanent settlement as well as opposition to Israeli rule over Islamic holy places (and was a leading factor in the breakdown in the Camp David Talks between the Prime Minister Barak and Yasser Arafat in the months preceding the Second Intifada). The symbol also gave a religious patina to the national struggle and was designed to mobilize support in Arab and Muslim countries. To Western eyes the golden dome is incomparably more impressive than the bleak stones of the Wailing Wall (actually, the "Wall" as a religious symbol was rather downplayed in official Israeli publications).

Another key symbol of the period were the suicide bombers—the heroes of the Palestinian public and a source of national pride, inspiration, and emulation to Palestinian children and teens. The pictures of the suicide bombers were draped everywhere—on billboards, schoolyards, and the walls of houses. Palestinian children tied discs of the martyrs' pictures around their necks. The PA took several steps in transforming the suicide bombers into the symbol of national liberation: official visits of condolence to the bereaved families; extolling the martyrs in the official press; transferring money to the families; and holding official memorial ceremonies. Children killed in the Second Intifada also became major symbols, such as Mohammad al-Dura, who, the Palestinians claim was cut down at the Netzarim Junction.

The Mukata'a—Arafat's Ramallah residence for most of the Second Intifada—served as a symbol of Palestinian sovereignty. Israel's fitful siege of the facility (that housed the PA's offices and administrative centers) in 2000 was translated into the symbol of the heroic struggle of those trapped inside. After the siege Arafat was still forbidden to leave the premises, almost until his death. (He was buried in the Mukata'a in November 2004.)

The roadblocks were the paramount symbol of the Israeli occupation and the focus of perpetual friction between the local population and the troops manning the points. During the Second Intifada, the number of roadblocks rose dramatically and the monitoring procedures became stricter. Personal belongings were checked thoroughly and people were frisked to make sure they were not smuggling explosives or that they themselves were not suicide bombers. Palestinians had to suffer long hours in lines for the security checks, undergo a painstaking body search, have their personal belongings scrutinized, and were sometimes called in for impromptu interrogations. The soldiers and border police did not always follow instructions to the letter (due to exhaustion or hostility toward the Palestinians especially after a suicide attack). Thus, the searches were occasionally accompanied by humiliation. The Palestinians used the Internet and media to great effect in railing against the checks and conveying the daily suffering they had to endure. All of this had a powerful negative impact on Israel's image.

On November 25, 2004, one of the most image-tarnishing incidents occurred. An IDF soldier manning a roadblock asked a Palestinian to open his violin case for a security check and the individual took it out and began playing—as stated in the IDF investigative report—to demonstrate that it was only a musical instrument. In the photo, the soldier is seen examining other Palestinians and not even looking at the musician. The point was that many Israelis associated the picture (and the Palestinians were quick to remind those who had forgotten) with that of Jewish musicians in the extermination camps during the Holocaust. In other words, the Palestinians had purposely and cleverly created a powerful image: the Jews are doing to us what the Nazis did to them.

Military Actions

Firing on Jerusalem's Gilo Neighborhood. The Palestinians employed a highly effective and sophisticated psychological technique: firing on the Gilo neighborhood from homes of Christian Arabs in the town of Beit Jala. They picked a target that served the double purpose of hurting the enemy and advancing their political agenda. The main effect of the shooting was psychological: They hoped it would break the spirit of the neighborhood's residents and shock the Israeli public with a relentless threat to their capital city. The Palestinians' grand strategy was to reopen the question of Israel sovereignty over Jerusalem—the most complex element in the core issues of the Israeli-Palestinian conflict (the military significance of the shooting was slight as the distance from the border houses in Beit Jala to Gilo was beyond effective range of standard issued rifles). By claiming that the Jewish neighborhood was built on occupied land, the Palestinians hoped to blunt the accusation of injuring civilians. The Jewish population witnessed its government instruct the residents of Gilo to defend their homes with sandbags and stay clear of danger areas, while it postponed ordering the security forces to gain control of Beit Jala (that was under the PA's full responsibility according to the Oslo Accords). The government's limp response mirrored the political dilemma that Israel faced in the first stages of the Second Intifada regarding the PA. A few weeks were to pass until the government ordered the IDF to suppress the fire—which it promptly did.

Suicide Bombers. The suicide bombings were the most lethal and effective means that the Palestinians applied in the Second Intifada, causing almost half of all Israeli deaths and leaving an indelible impression on the nation. The Palestinians regarded the suicide bombers as strategic weapons, a supremely effective answer to Israel's F-16s and Merkava tanks. Thus, the human bomb served as a game evener and deterrence equalizer. The Palestinian plan was to sow fear among Israelis, strengthen the fear to serve in the military, and widen the divisions in the Israeli public over the future of the territories. In the Palestinian perspective, Israel's disengagement from the Gaza Strip in August-September 2005 was the direct result of the suicide attacks.

What undoubtedly encouraged the Palestinians to escalate the use of this weapon was the Western media's affinity for acts of self-sacrifice and its keen interest in human drama. There were numerous other contributing factors: the ease with which suicide bombers could slip into Israeli territory, especially where the separation fence had not been erected; no escape route need to be planned for a suicide bomber; the freedom to choose the place and time for an operation to produce maximum casualties; a large reservoir of volunteers.

The murderous strikes were designed to demoralize Israeli society and make it despair of continuing its control over the territories. Paradoxically, they did just the opposite, even if only temporarily. They buttressed world opinion in support of Israel and united Israeli society. The Palestinians countered with a sophisticated deception tactic: they upgraded the lethal effect of the explosives while at the same time hastened to condemn the attacks in order to stave off sympathy toward Israel because of the premeditated murder of civilians. They issued noncommittal statements in which they deplored any attack against civilians. No matter what Israel did to diminish the Palestinians' support of the terrorist attacks and prove that terror was futile, popular support for the suicide bombings reached unprecedented heights in the Second Intifada, and martyrdom in jihad remains a cardinal virtue in Palestinian society.

Firing Qassam Rockets into the Western Negev. Like the concentrated fire on the Gilo neighborhood, the launching of Qassam rockets at the Western Negev was not designed to achieve military goals but psychological ones, that is, to motivate the Israeli public to pressure the government to withdraw from the Gaza Strip. In response to the rocket fire, the IDF frequently entered areas where the fire emanated from, eliminated the armed terrorists though often inadvertently injuring civilians. The Palestinians exploited this to the hilt to intensify hatred and atrocity propaganda. When the IDF sent tanks to provide maximum cover to the infantry, the Palestinians circulated pictures of the heavy-armored vehicles against a background of houses teetering on collapse, thus creating a powerful image that was widely publicized in the world media.

Firing on the Roadblocks. The Palestinians ambushed Israeli roadblocks in Judea and Samaria (three such events took place in the Ramallah district in February-March 2002 where the security checks were the most manifest symbol of Palestinian suffering throughout the occupation). The most successful operation, from the Palestinian point of view, occurred in Wadi Kharamiya on March 3, 2003 when a sniper killed ten Israeli soldiers and escaped uninjured. He left behind an old M1 carbine with a wobbly butt attached with nails. Rumors spread in Israel that the sniper was an IRA mercenary, but these were proven false when the terrorist was caught—in effect, a Palestinian from a nearby village.

Firing on Settlers' Vehicles. At the start of the Second Intifada the Palestinians focused their struggle on the settlers. They hoped to render the settlers' lives intolerable thus forcing them to leave their homes, and to drive a wedge between the settlers and Israeli society west of the Green Line, and create the psychological effect that rather than a pioneering vanguard the settlers were a burden on Israeli society. But the preferred targets were soldiers traveling on the roads of Judea and Samaria or guarding civilians there since this would strengthen the claim—especially by left-wing Israelis—that the troops' deaths were in vain. Be this as it may, the attacks within the Green Line achieved the opposite goal since they obliterated the difference between the settlers and Israelis living within the borders of 1967.

CHAPTER 13

Psychological Warfare in Operation "Cast Lead"

Although the IDF has never invested heavily in psychological warfare, Operation "Cast Lead" demonstrated a long-needed change. For the first time Israel embarked on a military venture with a psywar plan devised by a designated unit in coordination with the tactical forces. The unit—the Center for Consciousness Operations (MALAT)—was established at the end of the Second Intifada and became operational in the Second Lebanon War.

The goals of the operation as was instructed in the order of battle for the MALAT (a refreshingly new phenomenon in recent IDF operations) were to cripple Hamas' psychological warfare capability, channels of conveyance, and credibility of content; to undermine Hamas' control over the Gaza Strip and to highlight Israel's achievements and Hamas' failures, and demoralize Hamas and its support circles. The MALAT focused on three target audiences: Hamas militants, civilian supporters, and the general Palestinian society in Gaza.

The Messages to Hamas Fighters Were: "You haven't a chance against IDF special forces units and their weapons. Your leaders fled the field, they deserted you." During the operation the press reported that the IDF gained control of Hamas' communications networks and was conveying messages directly to Hamas militants. Addressing them in the heat of battle on their own networks induced the feeling that the enemy "knows everything."

To the Civilians: The messages assailed the leadership—"your leaders have abandoned the people" . . . "They misread Israel's response and are, therefore, unfit to lead" . . . "Hamas has turned the civilian population into a human shield" . . . "The leadership steals from the international aid intended for the people" . . . "The IDF will embark upon a retaliatory incursion into the Gaza Strip."

These were the themes of the airdropped messages. Other leaflets exhorted Gaza's civilians to save their lives and property by reporting on arms caches and ambushes. Each leaflet contained a phone number. Thousands of responses came in, most of which were obscene calls. But Hamas' concerted reaction in the media to vilify the "informer" leaflets seems to indicate that the organization feared its Palestinian rivals might exploit the opportunity and disclose the whereabouts of military positions and weapons stockpiles. The scope and intensity of Hamas' responses show that Israel's psychological warfare was successful in this case. In effect it was the classic example of driving a wedge between Hamas and the general population and factionalizing the enemy—one of hundreds of techniques in psywar to undermine the ruling power's legitimacy.

Messages regarding the IDF's undeterred resolve to invade Gaza were designed to subvert the local population's confidence that it had nothing to fear from an IDF ground operation. They also aimed at shattering Hamas' assurance of its lethal network of traps and ambushes set for Israeli troops and armored vehicles.

Information Channels to the Palestinians

Traditional psywar doctrine distinguishes between two means of conveying information: the conventional media (television, radio, and the press); and the alternative media used by the side with limited means (leaflets, fax machines, graffiti, and loudspeakers). Today digital technology has co-opted the rules of the game. The Internet is the main theater of operations, integrating TV, radio, the press, email, blogs, and social networks such as Facebook and Twitter. Added to this is the mobile phone, which enables any user to become a radio broadcaster and consumer of accessible messages. These devices were employed in Operation "Cast Lead."

Although a century has passed since the first massive dropping of printed leaflets onto the battlefield, this is still the easiest method for conveying messages in conventional warfare. Millions of leaflets were scattered across Gaza during the operation. This demanded a major effort on the part of the IDF, especially since the fighting took place in winter when rain and wind impeded the work. The leaflets instructed the population how to conduct themselves and contained information on humanitarian matters such as how and when food would be distributed. The number of droppings was limited so as not to overplay the dramatic effect.

In electronic warfare, Israel's main method of conveying messages was to seize control of Hamas radio and TV stations. This was preferable to broadcasts from Israel-based stations since it forced the enemy to listen to or watch the messages. Also, Israel's Arabic-language channels are not picked up in the Gaza Strip since the transmission antennas were removed in the 1990s. And even had the programs been broadcast their rating would not have gone up prior to the operation. The radio and TV channels seized by the IDF transmitted alternative news programs and clips with messages produced by the MALAT.

Preparing the Messages

The nature and length of the message determines the medium for conveying it: a leaflet can contain a few short lines; a radio broadcast can elaborate.

Every message has to overcome the enemy's suspicion and instinctive rejection. These are powerful psychological blocks that can be neutralized only if the audience feels that the messages are vital or stimulating. The experience of twentieth-century wars has taught that the most effective format for message delivery is a news broadcast, since the demand for credible news and information in wartime is insatiable. Information on humanitarian matters is also an effective means of attracting viewers or listeners.

Thus, the IDF tried to win the hearts and minds of the Palestinians by initiating actions rather than just circulating the messages. The leaflets, in effect, conquered the physical space. But when a foreign element gains control of a radio frequency, let alone a television channel which is a much more intimate medium like a guest in the living-room, then the impact of the invasion of privacy is at its height. TV messages were conveyed in the form of news programs, replete with the synthesized opening audio-visual themes. In order to enhance the programs' attraction, the shows led off with important details on humanitarian assistance, and only afterwards presented reports on the fighting. The leaflets were written in spoken Arabic, but the radio and television transmissions were in standard literary Arabic.

Operation "Cast Lead"—Hamas' Psywar Campaign

Hamas engaged in psychological warfare to a greater extent before and after the fighting than during the actual combat. Prior to the war it tried to deter Israel with messages about turning the Gaza Strip into a death trap of tunnels and IEDs.[1] After the war it chalked up some impressive achievements, such as the Goldstone Report, which caused Israel severe political injury. During the fighting Hamas' attempts at psychological warfare were negligible because of limited human and technological resources, but it did address the home audience—the Palestinian population.

Having come to power in a violent takeover, it nurtured the Palestinian society's support since it could not rely on the loyalty of the entire population—especially under Israel's military pressure. The campaign waged by the MALAT was designed, therefore, to widen the divide in Palestinian society and increase opposition to Hamas.

Western society—especially the United States and Europe—was the neutral target audience whose influence could provide an added advantage to one of the sides. Hamas' goal was to get the West to pressure Israel to cease combat operations and withdraw from Gaza. Another goal was to render Israel's defensive steps illegitimate so that its hands would be tied in the event of a future war.

The Israeli audience was Hamas' last priority. Messages stressed the destruction of Palestinian property and the suffering of the Palestinian people as a result of the IDF incursion. With the conclusion of the fighting, Hamas intensified the psywar campaign in order to rend Israeli society. This happened just as the level of patriotic mobilization was declining and the nation was beginning to review the impact of the war on itself, the IDF, and the international community. This campaign—like the one directed at Western society—was intended primarily to thwart the defense establishment's moves in the next confrontation.

Hamas' Messages

The operation Hamas conveyed two main messages: first, the Gaza Strip is a giant firetrap waiting for the IDF and, by association, for Israeli society; second, the main victims of Israel's embargo are innocent civilians. Once Israel launched the operation, Hamas set its sights on maintaining its hold on Palestinian society. The internally directed messages dealt with Israeli aggression and the need to preserve unity.

At the end of the operation, Hamas leaders emerged from the bunkers and took up the cudgels to establish the identity of the victor. In Israeli eyes this was patently absurd, but the lesson to be learned here is that victory or defeat in such wars is not based on objective facts but on subjective feelings that can be molded or manipulated regardless of their connection to the reality on the ground.

Hamas' Channels for Conveying Its Messages

War is prime time for the media since the populations on both sides of the conflict are hungry for information. Because the private media is generally considered reliable, each side strives to win its favor for message conveying. In Hamas' effort to address Israel's citizenry, it took advantage of the openness of Israeli society and fed the Israeli (and international) media information via telephone and the Internet (entry to the Gaza Strip was forbidden to reporters). Israel's injustices against Palestinian noncombatants were highlighted in order to imbue guilt feelings in the general public and in the hope that soldiers would also be affected. This technique was used with great success in the First Intifada.

At the start of the operation Hamas media consisted of newspapers, radio stations, a satellite TV station (Al-Aqsa) and ground station (Al-Quds), and Internet sites.[2] Several of its official sites were threatened by hackers (through organized or individual efforts). Most, however, are Islamic sites that are not directly identified with Hamas but that thrive on Hamas' ideology and convey its messages. Hamas also ran an information center that collected the messages. The head of the center was Fathi Hamad, a member of parliament in Gaza. Photographers who remained in the Gaza Strip furnished the news agencies (for example, the Ramatan Agency) with pictures of IDF attacks.

Even when the IDF gained control of the radio and television stations, Hamas was still left with websites, mobile phones, and radio and television programs that continued broadcasting. (After a station is overtaken, transmission is always left on, thus allowing the enemy to continue broadcasting, albeit intermittently, so that the populace will stay tuned to the channel.) Hamas supplied the news sites with information via mobile phones that Israel failed to block due to their great number. The IDF quickly dealt with the problem and established a designated branch within the IDF Spokespersons Unit to track the social networks and feed them information.

Despite Hamas' military inferiority and the heavy pressure from the IDF, it tried to adopt Israel's modus operandi. It succeeded in jamming the

IDF's public radio station in the south, and journalists reported that it launched a balloon into Israel that scattered leaflets in broken Hebrew. In addition, text messages were sent to mobile phones in the south, with mistakes in the wording that only elicited ridicule.

Hamas spread rumors about the number of IDF casualties. But the reports caused little damage. In one case, however, Hamas did succeed in frightening the Israeli public when it transmitted the message that Gilad Shalit, the captured Israeli soldier, had been wounded in an IDF bombing. This illustrates how even unsophisticated equipment can have serious psychological repercussions on the enemy.[3]

The Influence of the Psychological Warfare Campaign

In conventional warfare it is relatively easy to examine the effect of steps taken against the enemy and then make the necessary corrections. In psychological warfare it is much more difficult. Few people will admit (even to themselves) that they were influenced by the enemy's messages or psywar campaign (soldiers and officers are no exception). For obvious reasons it is impossible to hand out feedbacks and questionnaires like in a marketing survey on the effectiveness of the enemy's psychological effort. Therefore the side implementing psywar has to find alternative ways of measuring the influence of its campaign.

The first criterion is whether the population has followed instructions, that is, if it has altered its behavior. The impression is that in "Cast Lead" the Palestinian population did obey the IDF's directives. It is difficult to estimate how many of the millions of leaflets were actually read, how many Palestinians listened to the radio or watched the video clips that Israel broadcast. From the Palestinians' complaints in blogs and websites, the number of listeners and viewers seems to have been rather high.

Hamas' messages reiterated the theme that the Palestinian people stand behind the organization. Another message conveyed day and night was that Israel's psychological warfare was ineffectual. The fact that Hamas had to continuously drum home these messages indicates, albeit indirectly, that Israel's psywar campaign did have a powerful impact. Further evidence that Hamas constantly listened to the messages Israel broadcast: every time the MALAT accused Hamas of war crimes, the organization immediately presented counterclaims.

In an after-war victory speech, Prime Minister Ismail Haniyeh praised the people for their heroic stand in the face of IDF brigades and hundreds of psywar troops. The personnel in the center could only smile wistfully: pleased with the compliment, but regretting the implacable gap between the unit's needs and the meager resources allotted to it.

Judging by Hamas' response, the MALAT did a magnificent job: its messages penetrated all levels of the population, including Hamas militants, which naturally caused the leadership dismay. The center nearly succeeded in implanting the sense that Hamas' hold over Gaza was disintegrating. This forced the leaders to work overtime in proving that it was still in control. The IDF unit stressed Israel's humanitarian activity (actually this should have been the job of the IDF Spokesperson's Unit but it lacked the means to broadcast to the Arab population).[4]

In accordance with the basic tenets of guerilla warfare, Hamas avoided direct confrontation with the enemy. Its psywar effort was also kept on a low flame. Parallel to battlefield operations, it tried to lure IDF troops into abduction ambushes. Its psyops were limited mainly to damage control of Israel's messages. After the war it concentrated on political persuasion, which, as Clausewitz wrote almost two centuries ago, is the main battlefield.

Once hostilities ended, the organization began ingraining a victory consciousness that it defined as "the triumph of the spirit." It demonized the Israeli enemy (satanic children-killers) and trumpeted the irrefutable fact that the Hamas government was still in power. The prewritten victory speech was broadcast as soon as danger passed. No connection existed between the awareness or sense of victory that was marketed to the Palestinian public and the reality on the ground, but Israel failed to grasp the meaning of the dissonance. For Israelis, the images of rubble in Gaza symbolized the IDF's incontestable victory, while Hamas paradoxically exalted and mythicized the ruins into the triumph of the spirit over the material.

Israel's relatively low-scaled "battle for the mind" was directed at the Palestinians in Gaza, Judea and Samaria, and especially at the neutral parties. This was based on the axiom that Israel is dependent on the good will of the West, and that whatever inhibits the West from extending its moral and political support of Israel also inhibits its military and economic aid, and without these assets Israel will be swept away in the tsunami of Islamic fanaticism. The Goldstone Report is just one link in the long chain of Hamas' psychological warfare efforts. Israel's leaders and the IDF general staff must remember this.

CHAPTER 14

The Mavi Marmara Affair

The *Mavi Marmara* affair of May 2010, offers a fascinating case study of how psyop works. The *Mavi Marmara* Affair encapsulates the deployment of all components of the current theory of Information Warfare.[1] These include computer network operation, psyop, deception, electronic warfare, and operation security. This chapter will relate to these elements, with the emphasis placed on psyop.

The event began with six ships comprising a flotilla originating from Ireland, Turkey, and Greece, assembling thirty km south of Cyprus, with the aim of anchoring in Gaza in the face of the blockade established by the Israeli government searching every vessel approaching Gaza for weapons being carried for Hamas. One of the ships was the *Mavi Marmara*, an anonymous vessel; another was the *Rachel Corrie*, a name which raised much more alarm in Israel (see Chapter 11). The flotilla operation had been transpiring for over a year, completely overt, conscripting peace activists from all over Europe. It appeared on Israeli radar but was placed on the lowest priority because there was no immediate foreseeable danger. In retrospect, this was a costly mistake for Israel. The explicit goal of the flotilla was to break the "Gaza siege" and to bring supplies to "the hungry children of Gaza." In reality, the actual humanitarian needs of the Gaza population are equivocal. (Gaza at that time, and currently, enjoyed modern shopping malls and a variety of gourmet restaurants.)[2] Convoys from Israel with essential provisions enter Gaza regularly, but the main channels of supply originated in Egypt through the tunnels of Rafah.[3] The flotilla carried some food and expired medications.

One ship of the flotilla was organized by the *IHH,* a Turkish Jihadi organization with strong contacts to the Turkish government. They had essentially politically hijacked the entire operation.

The idea of a ship breaking a siege within the context of the Arab-Israeli conflict was not a Palestinian invention.

A precedent can be traced to the *Exodus*, which sailed from France with 4,500 Jewish Holocaust survivors in July 1947 in order to smuggle them through the blockade in British-mandated Palestine. In case they were apprehended the goal was to turn it into a political confrontation. Following wide media coverage, the British Royal Navy seized the ship and deported all its passengers back to Europe.

The Palestinians organized a similar siege break attempt during the First Intifada in February 1988. They chartered the *Sol Pheryn,* formerly an Israeli ferry, and renamed it *Al Awda*—The Return. They planned to board the ship with two hundred Palestinian deportees from the West Bank and many journalists and reconstructed the plight of the *Exodus* with the underlying theme: "you are doing to us what was done to you." For an entire week, international journalists were invited to Athens for the occasion. It proceeded as a brilliant media event, but when it came to boarding the ship in Limassol, Cyprus, a mysterious explosion caused the ship to sink in the harbor.

Afterwards, there were a number of minor events in 2008 and in 2009: yachts with peace activists managed to break into Gaza but these efforts did not attract much media attention.

It is not clear whether these sails were coordinated, but the overall effect was that the Israeli security forces had been caught completely off guard. The flotilla was not ranked very high on the Israeli priority list. As this priority list is so extensive, there will always be attempts to avoid overburdening the Israeli defense system. In fact, the process of determining prioritizing criteria may hold a key for the Israeli defense establishment in deriving possible conclusions from this affair.

The flotilla rendezvoused south of Cyprus, with the ships maintaining minimal distance from each other—less than a hundred meters—and sailed in the direction of Gaza. They were accompanied by a Turkish warship. This sudden addition to the flotilla revised the whole perspective for the Israeli navy and constrained the available actions.

The lead ship, as it turned out, was to be the *Mavi Marmara*; all the others were essentially decoys. In addition to the peace activists, the ship was manned by *IHH* members, trained for violent engagement, possessing firearms and cold weapons. Weapons had been concealed on deck and preparations were made to produce weapons instantly when needed, for example: iron rods taken from the ship's railing. A number of the *IHH* participants had recorded a Jihadi suicide testimonial video before boarding ship.

The ship was fully equipped with a broadcast-quality television studio. It held broadcast cameras and editing suites. It served Al Jazeera and two other stations. In addition, there were dozens of available laptops with editing software for delivery of material to Internet recipients. All in all, by the end of the operation, hundreds of cameras were confiscated by the Israelis and their contents copied. One impediment to confiscating the extensive anti-Israel footage was that many had the memory cards and sticks secreted on their bodies.

Anticipating the central role to be played by mass communication, the IDF used media-jamming equipment, but it was hardly effective as the jamming had breaches and material went out during these breaks. The main difficulty faced by the Israelis was that the passengers were using civilian satellite phones and this equipment apparently makes total jamming difficult.

The Military Aspect

The military takeover lasted forty-three minutes. Based on past nonviolent experience the Israeli navy began implementing a takeover with crowd-dispersal means. The challenge was that while naval commando techniques were needed in order to board the ship, policemen were needed for dispersing a demonstration. Israel did not have that mix of manpower, so the navy commando Unit 13 was assigned the entire mission. They were equipped with paintball guns, stun grenades, micro-submachine guns, and handguns. Four helicopters accompanied the mission, with only one intended for landing. They departed on the mission at 4:30 in the afternoon with the intention of taking the ship by surprise at night. The commandos were met by the *IHH* who instructed all the other passengers to go downstairs below deck. The Israeli commandos were met with crowbars, some were fired at, some were stabbed, and all were beaten with metal rods and crowbars. Some commandos were dragged below deck. At that stage the Israeli commanding officer realized they had suffered casualties, and then ultimately instructed his soldiers to use their firearms.

The *Mavi Marmara* affair was orchestrated to be a political trap for Israel, into which Israel fell. It was meant to portray Israel as aggressive, intolerant, insensitive to human rights, even as Hamas continued to shell

Israeli towns in the South with mortars and rockets and continued to hold the kidnapped Israeli soldier Gilad Shalit, which in itself was another brilliant Hamas-staged psyop operation.

This was a win-win situation for the Palestinians and it was designed to invoke internal social and political dissent which eventually, at the end of a long trajectory, would lead to the disintegration of Israel's political will.

The media, old as well as new, covered the event for days, since coverage of the Arab-Israeli conflict poses no imminent dangers to outside parties. A self-proclaimed peace activist or a journalist can travel a short distance of four to five hours to Israel, get a story in the afternoon, and then return in the evening to a luxurious hotel.

Media Management

The flotilla affair was executed according to a textbook campaign. There was a *before*, a *during*, and an *after*. The overall goal is naturally to capture as much attention for as extended a time as possible. During the weeks before the event, information was leaked as to the whereabouts of the flotilla, the intended participants, and various other details. Then, there was the event of the takeover itself, and then the aftermath. The on-board studio broadcasted throughout the journey, with the most crucial segment being that of the IDF soldiers trying to board the ship and the "heroic" nonviolent resistance of the peace activists. Here was a hard decision for the Israelis to make. The Israeli navy realized from the training drills that images are important and it should board with as little violence as possible. One participating helicopter was assigned to get the visual material to shore. But the commanding officer after seeing one of his soldiers lying on the deck of the *Mavi Marmara* severely wounded ordered the helicopter to revise its mission and to evacuate the wounded. That caused a substantial delay in Israel's providing the incriminating, violent, visual images of the *IHH*. In addition, internal conflict between the parallel IDF spokesman unit and navy spokesman unit resulted in a further delay. Furthermore, there were two additional crucial links in the chain of command: the Field Security Branch (OPSEC) had to clear the material for release, and the analysts had to identify the instruments with which the *IHH* were striking. This took considerable time. In the meantime Al Jazeera controlled the hub, and that put the new media into operation. The ship's media headquarters broadcast on the web from the cameras positioned on board, while editing out the *IHH*-initiated violent segments. The violent segments accessible to the

Israelis were limited to those recorded from the helicopters and only later from the ship's security cameras.

Afterwards, the event was prolonged successfully by the *IHH*, with the story transformed into the inhuman treatment accorded by the Israeli prison authorities, as hundreds of the flotilla participants were taken into custody. The next day, when the participants relieved themselves and pulled the memory sticks from where they were hidden inside their persons, came the next phase. Fortified with this new material, The Turkish media disseminated the images of the beaten soldiers, which damaged the deterrence of the Israeli forces and caused Israeli demoralization and frustration. In addition the media continued with breaking stories of the funerals of the 9 *IHH* casualties. Mass funerals were transformed into mass demonstrations, and so Turkey's Erdogan was able to use this as a final justification to sever contact with Israel.

The mission to handle new media was assigned to a small section of two junior officers and three soldiers from the film section of the IDF military spokesman unit. They were doing twenty-four-hour shifts, watching the materials and selecting those segments deemed suitable for the new media.

They also hadn't anticipated that this was going to be a very stressful month, as they had dealt with small flotilla events in the past—this perspective constituted an additional factor related to Israel's defense establishment having been caught off guard.

The Israeli chain of command was particularly long. The first to see the material were the commanding officers, then the spokesmen for the IDF and the navy, than the OPSEC unit needed to review it, and once the air force and navy intelligence people cleared the material then it was all made available to the new media. By that time, of course, it was plainly too late to have the desired effect.

The main platform receiving the material initially was the IDF's website.

The main strategy the IDF used was to work with bloggers, a contact that started prior to the sailing of the flotilla. The recently established new media section of the IDF had mapped out a group of bloggers and divided them into three categories: pro, neutral, and against. They were all briefed on the information from the time of the first visual contact. From the start, they faced a setback as they released a clip where the Israeli navy was calling the ships to halt over the radio and the ship responded with foul language, such as "f***ing Jews, go back to Auschwitz." This was deemed inappropriate language by the blogosphere. Once the foul language was edited out, the blogosphere response continued to be negative, including negative talk-backs that indicated they had proof that the IDF material was a forgery, and so on. Yet things began to fall into place as the hours passed on. The junior team traced the equivalent of what the news agencies were to the old media—the feeding blogs, those that supply material for bloggers. One such was *MEMEORANDUM*, which sums up the most influential posts at any given moment and they were naturally the first to get fed. They were in contact with about two hundred bloggers. The Israeli staff also realized that not all material would be useful to all bloggers.

The affair continued when the *Rachel Corrie* ship arrived, and a smaller event took place with the holding of the passengers by the Interior Ministry clerks, and so on, which prolonged the event a couple of days more. Libya's Gaddafi entered the fray with a ship he sent—the *Irene*—but by then the story was already dead.

Thus, by a handful of organizers, NGOs, modest funding, and the support of a hostile state, Israel, a regional superpower, was again placed with its back to the wall, attempting to explain its just cause, unable to use its physical force, and its citizens gaping at the TV sets and computer screens unable to understand how their costly defense organizations performed so badly. The *Mavi Marmara* is a case study of contemporary psychological warfare.

Conclusions

A number of conclusions can be drawn from the use of psychological warfare in the Middle East:

1. The power of psychological warfare. Psywar is a flexible tool that strategy planners can model to their needs. Even when messages change radically on short notice, it can still be used by every type of regime (though democratic regimes find it difficult because of the profusion of communications channels). In many cases, when backed by the requisite financial, human, and intellectual resources, psywar can alter the viewpoints of various audiences.
2. In democratic countries the psywar layout is also maintained in peacetime; otherwise it could become rusty and unserviceable. However, democratic states harbor reservations about employing psychological warfare in peacetime as it conjures up unethical practices that are unpalatable to free societies. But when war erupts, these states quickly recalibrate their priorities and lose little time in establishing a mechanism based on two major advantages. One, they recruit talented staff mostly from the universities and the media, who bring highly creative skills to the job (unlike citizens in totalitarian regimes where original, open-ended thinking is discouraged). Two, the absence of bureaucratic tradition and a top-heavy hierarchy makes it easier to apply innovative ideas. For psychological warfare to succeed the layout must be based on high managerial efficiency, resource allotment, open-mindedness, and above all prestige and priority in the eyes of the decision-makers. Despite psywar's proven success in wartime, once the guns fall silent democratic values take precedence over security considerations and the psywar layout is dismantled or relegated to the realm of clandestine operations far from the public eye.

3. Nothing new under the sun (except for technology). In World War I the British laid the foundations for modern psychological warfare, beaming messages to the battlefield and homefront. Today every side engaged in psychological warfare—from the superpowers to terrorist organizations—employs the principles that the British developed (demonizing the enemy and driving a wedge between enemy camps). The technology of message dissemination, however, has changed. In World War I the press was the main instrument for conveying messages; in World War II the radio; in the Korean War (early 1950s) television came into vogue; in the Vietnam War (1960s and early 1970s) television totally revolutionized news coverage. In Israel's wars too, technological innovation has played a key role in conveying messages: in the First Lebanon War the satellite was widely used; in the First Intifada the Palestinians employed fax machines to bring messages to the Israeli media; in the Gulf War of 1991 satellite phones were used for the first time; and the War in Iraq in 2003 witnessed the massive use of sophisticated technological innovations (video phones, digital cameras, email, and the Internet). Despite technological development, the main factor in psywar's success remains the creative thinking of its operators.
4. The weak side in the conflict uses psywar as a force multiplier, that is, it strives to offset the asymmetry by making wide-scale use of means that are inexpensive, accessible, and effective. The weaker side's smallness is actually an advantage since it often implies the absence of institutionalization, thus greater flexibility in adapting its messages to the changing needs and the easier implementation of innovative, unorthodox ideas. Officers in an institutionalized, compartmentalized army are accustomed to teamwork and pattern-based thinking where an unexpected obstacle is more likely to stymie one of the lower rungs in the chain of command.
5. Military-media relations—a vital element of information strategy. The twentieth century witnessed the clash between the public's right to know and the state's need to safeguard operational security. In the last thirty years many attempts have been made (especially by the US Army) to reach a modus operandi acceptable to newspaper editors and military officers. During the War in Iraq journalists accompanied combat units. The rationale behind the change in policy was that if journalists experience what the troops are going through, they will tend to write about the soldiers and military operations in a favorable

light. This was a revolutionary change in the concept of operational security. Classified information had always been an inseparable part of the state's security apparatus, and the reason why so much effort was invested in protecting secrets and trying to discover the enemy's plans. In the last quarter of the twentieth century this tradition underwent a *volte face*, and today's militaries tend to increase the output of information. The concept of "secrecy" is still important—no one divulges the "where, when, or how" of operations—but in the "new" war a massive amount of information is deliberately and calculatedly released without incurring operational damage. The fear that the enemy will exploit the information is balanced by the political gain to be had. On the other hand, secrecy remains a dominant element in Israel's security thinking, so that defense agencies (excluding the Shabak, even though initial signs of change are visible) expend vast resources in keeping correspondents as far away as possible from the center of events. This is what happened in Operation "Defensive Shield" (2002) when the Palestinians skillfully filled Israel's information vacuum with their version of the events.

6. Psychological warfare and the "truth." The bulk of information dissemination is to advance political goals. This approach flies in the face of traditional thinking of psychological warfare as a cunning means of spreading lies far from criticism and the public's prying. The information campaign's greatest asset is its credibility. If the information is unreliable or misleading, then no matter how much energy and imagination go into conveying the messages the target audience will not be duped. This is why today's psywar units must concentrate on the truth and discard the residuum of secrecy, the roots of which lie in the exciting tales of black propaganda from World War II. Operations from the past may excite the imagination but hardly justify the prodigious effort that went into them and the incalculable risk to loss of credibility. A British study found that German civilians who tuned in to BBC broadcasts during the war were willing to put their lives at great risk because the BBC's principle was to "tell the truth, only the truth, and as far as possible, the whole truth." It reported both Allied mishaps and defeats, but maintained a spirit of determination and hope for the future.
7. For psychological warfare to be effective it must convince the state's citizens of the need to support the war, accept economic hardship, suffer the loss of loved ones, and make the ultimate sacrifice. It has to

encourage patriotism at home and pacifism on the enemy homefront. The first task of every army is to define the war aims in the clearest terms possible and convince the troops of the war's justification. Regardless of the type of regime, unless the troops have internalized the grounds for going to war, their motivation will be low. Examples of failure in this area are the Vietnam War and First Lebanon War.

Whither to? Psywar in the Twenty-First Century

The current trend is to limit the size of conventional armies and increase the scope of mobile, highly technological special forces. Fire power, like digital power, is going miniature—more power on smaller platforms. In the past an army's strength was measured in rifles and cannons; today the key to victory is the "system," a generic concept that encompasses weapons integration, remote guided systems (for casualty reduction), precision tracking of the enemy (to increase fire effectiveness and lessen collateral damage), command and control of overall wartime activity, and the psychological dimension (collecting and conveying information to designated audiences as quickly as possible). The psychological factor is of paramount importance for neutralizing the enemy's attempts to exploit events for political advantage.

Massive amounts of information are often relayed in real time given today's technological advances in connectivity. But this readily available free-flow is a double-edged sword. On the one hand, countries now have the means to extend their messages to every citizen and foreign audience; on the other hand, connectivity offers unprecedented manipulative power to forces that threaten (with minimal investment) the world's social structure and political order. Connectivity brings war atrocities into the viewers' homes immediately after they occur. This is a technological and psychological feat that aids the side interested in galvanizing criticism of the war or encouraging military or political action even when the public gains nothing from it.

The armies and security agencies are preparing for the new interconnected reality, but they still have a long way to go. Unlike small, flexible terrorist organizations and guerilla bands, large, cumbersome, hierarchy-based armies struggle to adopt new strategies. High-ranking officers immersed in group thinking conform to the strict rules of the organizational game, having spent their entire careers in the "system." Waging effective psywar, however, demands skills of an entirely different nature—flexibility, playing in a field of inconsistency and dichotomy, asserting one thing and its opposite simultaneously, conveying the same message in a variety of packages to diverse audiences, exploiting breakthroughs with lightning speed and bombarding the enemy with so many messages that they can barely raise their heads. An organization or small state tends to present an image of weakness facing a large and powerful enemy, and then turns to the international media and slams the enemy's actions as illegal and inhumane.

Modern armies invest in developing fighting equipment geared to the mass media (mini-cameras mounted on soldiers' helmets and rifles, for example). Some of the pictures are immediately relayed to the networks. A greater challenge in psywar lies in devising a new warfighting doctrine, the goals of which include the transmission of live images from the battlefield. This requires troops trained in photography, news editing, and film directing, in addition to regular combat skills (fieldcraft, fighting in built-up areas, designated marksmanship, and so forth).

The US Army and other Western armies have increased the range of psychological warfare after its success in Afghanistan and the two Gulf Wars. Psywar operators and cyber warriors receive larger budgets and sharper attention from the decision-makers. Advances in the social sciences (anthropology, sociology, social psychology, and marketing) have been translated into precise analyses of foreign target audiences, with special "banks of messages" prepared for them. Experts in foreign cultures and social mosaics are now an integral part of the military's rapid deployment units.

The technological infrastructure has always been of utmost importance for military planners. This is especially true in psychological warfare—when the side that conveys pictures from the battlefield first gains control of the media, while the other side is left to fend for itself. Battlefield images are transmitted to control centers and from there the international outlets (CNN and Fox News, for example) relay them, then the enemy's television networks pick them up and broadcast them. The pictures are also shown on a laser screen near the battlefield so that the enemy can view their approaching defeat.

Alongside the technological marvels in message dissemination, the traditional means of conveyance—paper leaflets, radio broadcasts, and loudspeakers—will probably continue to be used. The principle remains the same: to influence the finger pulling the trigger. The side that has more insight into the enemy's culture will find the means (technological, traditional, or unconventional) to get the messages to him and eventually defeat him.

Epilogue

This book went to print after the Second Gaza War when the first buds in the new stage in Israel's psychological warfare began to sprout. The war overturned many a long-held view in the IDF and defense establishment. No one can predict how these repercussions will influence hearts and minds in the future. The IDF displayed a high level of technological capability: taking over Hezbollah's Al-Manar television stations, scattering a huge amount of leaflets from aircraft, reaching Lebanese citizens by phone (according to foreign reports), building websites that masqueraded as Lebanese sites (gray propaganda), creating the machinery to make contact with Lebanese civilians and recruit them as informers, and reopening the Arabic-language radio station Voice of the South. All this testifies to Israel's bold moves and unprecedented development in psychological warfare.

The security establishment's examination committees will undoubtedly assess the effect of "winning the hearts and minds." The questions in this area must focus on Israel's handling of strategic information in wartime, especially since Arabic-language activity on the Voice of Israel that once courted the Arab audience has been rendered inconsequential. I suggest that the committee address the following issues: is Israel capable of fathoming Hezbollah and Iranian "cultural intelligence"; are the messages conveyed really effective (Nasrallah in the guise of a snake, for example) or merely wishful thinking; does a modus operandi exist that checks the messages before conveying them; have attempts been made to determine psywar's impact on the enemy and discover which efforts are convincing and which a waste of time.

This book, naturally, claims psychological warfare is invaluable. As the confrontational arena (Syria and Iran) heats up, psywar's relevance increases. A few hours before the ceasefire went into effect at the end of the Second Lebanon War many homes in Southern Lebanon—only fifty meters from the border with Israel—raised high the Hezbollah flag. A few days later

Hezbollah launched a symbolic psychological broadside: a never-before seen photo of the captured Israeli navigator, Ron Arad. This was one of the heavier weapons in its psychological arsenal (along with its regular threat of massive rocket attacks ever since Israel's withdrawal from Lebanon in 2000). The publication of the photo deepened the average Israeli's frustration and, given the enemy's diabolical inhumanity, generated criticism of the government's impotence toward Hezbollah and catapulted the public into a vicious cycle of disgruntlement and vexation.

The abduction of IDF soldier Gilad Shalit tore the Israeli society apart. Hamas dragged the incident for five long years until it felt the chain could no longer be yanked. A small group of activists determined to win despite risk to its civilian population managed to subdue a regional superpower. Psychological warfare could not ask for greater achievement.

Notes

1 Psychological Warfare Theory

1. In the war against the Midianites, the Israelite prophet Gideon employed noise and deception to demoralize the enemy's superior forces (Judges 7: 17–22). See also the speech by the Assyrian commander, Ravshakeh, to the besieged inhabitants of Jerusalem in 701 BC, urging them to surrender (2 Kings 18: 17–37; Isaiah 36).
2. Philip M. Taylor, *World Encyclopedia of Propaganda*, New York: Sharpe, 1998, pp. xv–xix.
3. Charles Roetter, *Psychological Warfare*, London: B. T. Batsford, 1974, pp. 35–37.
4. See the US Army manual on psychological warfare, accessible on the Internet: *FM 3-1-1, Psychological Operations Techniques and Procedures*. http://www.enlisted.info/field-manuals/fm-33-1-1-psychological-operations-techniques-and-procedures.shtml
5. JP 3-13.2 Military Information Support Operation, http://info.publicintelligence.net/JCS-MISO.pdf, January 7, 2010. Incorporating Change 1, December 20, 2011.
6. Socialism played an important part in shaping the worldview of the state's founders. Israeli leaders were fully aware of propaganda's tremendous potential in the hands of those appointed to wield it.
7. *Hasbara* comes from the Hebrew word "to explain." The term originated with Nahum Sokolow, an early Zionist leader.
8. Moshe Yegar, *Toldot Hahasbara Hayisraelit* (*The History of Israel's Foreign Hasbara System*), Tel Aviv: Lahav Publishers, 1986, p. 38.
9. These publications can be found in the Truman Research Institute Library, Hebrew University of Jerusalem, Mt. Scopus Campus.
10. The USIA is now part of the State Department.
11. *FM 3-1-1, Psychological Operations Techniques and Procedures*.
12. Deliberate action is being taken to prevent a repeat of the unwanted developments of the Vietnam War (1961–1973) and the wars in Afghanistan (2001–) and in Iraq (2003–2011) after the American occupation.

2 Principles of Psychological Warfare Management

1. Nazi Germany's propaganda system, prior to the invasion of the Soviet Union (June 1941), depicted Bolshevism as a menace to humankind. In recent years the Palestine Authority and the Egyptians have broadcast anti-Semitic diatribes that included the demonization of Israel.
2. For example, the orders "Encounter!" or "Forward, charge!" force every soldier to respond immediately.
3. The First Gulf War (1991) is the classic case of the US army utilizing the media to convey messages that served the military's aims.
4. The source for tracking the bogus leaflets is Dr. Saleh Abd al-Jawad from Bir Zeit. See, Saleh Abd al-Jawad, "Les Faux tracts," *Revue d'études palestiniennes*, 48, été, 1993; see also the B'Tselem report—*Collaborators in the Occupied Territories during the Intifada: Violations and Infringements on Human Rights*, 1994 [Hebrew].
5. Israeli Foreign Ministry representatives distributed a tape of the lynching to the participants at the Sharm el-Sheikh Conference (the PLO and United States) that was held one week after the event (October 16–17).

4 Psychological Warfare in the Arab-Israeli Wars (1948–1982)

1. Be this as it may, many people in the Yishuv joined the British army in World War II, and actually experienced psychological warfare first-hand by both sides in the conflict, such as radio broadcasts and air-dropped leaflets.
2. The American psywar unit in World War II encountered the same problem when air commanders refused to risk their crewmen in dispersing "pieces of paper." To counter this, psywar officers launched a "marketing" campaign, the gist of which was semantic—replacing the term "pieces of paper" with "paper bullets."
3. Captain Katz's letter to Lieutenant Colonel Herzog, chief of intelligence services, December 1, 1948; Herzog's reply was that he was very interested in Katz's work and would help him find a room and transportation, but his hands were tied (March 2, 1949, IDF Archives 2169/50/72).
4. In the 1950s Nawi retired from politics and was elected mayor of Beer Sheva, an office he held for many years. He published books on Arab folklore, the most important of which for understanding psychological warfare is: *Stories from the Old Middle East: Wisdom, Lechery and Lessons to be Learned* [*sipurei hamizrach hatichon hayashan: chochma, zima vimusar heskel*] (Tel Aviv: Tamuz, 2000).
5. Rafi Buchnik, "Voice of Israel Broadcasts Fail to Reach Most of the Gaza Strip—A Mess-up in Arabic Broadcasts," *Ha'aretz*, September 18, 2003.
6. The main sources of information on Mossad activity: Yossi Melman (ed.), *CIA Report on Israel's Intelligence and Security Services* (Tel Aviv: Erez Press, 1982)—an anthology of documents, removed by the Khomeini regime removed from the

United States Embassy in Tehran and later published; Meir Amit, *Head to Head: A Personal Look at Great Events and World Affairs* (Or Yehuda: Hed Artzi Publishers, 1999)—memoirs of the former chief of the Mossad; Victor Ostrovsky, *By Way of Deception: The Making and Unmaking of a Mossad Officer* (New York: St. Martin's Press, 1990)—a sensational book.

7. Paul Linebarger & Myron Anthony, *Psychological Warfare* (Washington DC: Combat Forces Press, 1954).
8. Based on the report of Nichols Van Damme of the Dutch Foreign Ministry. Van Damme stated that he exposed the case because he felt that remaining silent would have caused long-term damage to Druze-Israeli relations.
9. The Egyptians, wittingly or unwittingly, employed the system that the Germans had used in World War I—letting out bits of information on French war prisoners in order to get the French people to read their propaganda sheet.
10. Palestinian sources reported 700–800 killed, while official Lebanese reports put the number at 460.
11. Foreign journalists arriving in Lebanon for brief stays found accommodations in Beirut's Commodore Hotel. The hotel bar was, in effect, the nerve center for information on Lebanon. The Syrians, PLO, and other Palestinian groups did their best to get the journalists to publish their positions by employing the "stick and carrot method." The carrot was providing information, granting dramatic interviews with the underground, and allowing exclusive pictures. The stick came in the form of threats, kidnappings, and, on occasion, murder. Journalists—especially those who remained in Lebanon for extended periods—had to walk a very thin line when reporting the events.

5 The War between Israel and Hezbollah in Southern Lebanon (1985–2000)

1. Twenty thousand people were killed in the Lebanese Civil War, over half of them Shiites.
2. These include the break-away "Islamic Amal," a Shiite organization that split from "Amal" and carried out innumerable strikes against the IDF.
3. The Hezbollah was not the only one to threaten and blackmail SLA troops. When manpower in the Christian militia declined following widespread demoralization caused by Hezbollah's threats and attacks, the SLA high command began pressuring the local population, Christians as well as Shiites, to join its ranks. Dissenters and their families were sent to the SLA-controlled el-Hiam prison to ensure the troops' loyalty.
4. Jewish history is rife with cases of Jews being kidnapped and held for ransom. This became a major topic of discussion in Talmudic literature and the Responsa (rabbinical questions and answers).

5. After protracted negotiations, the bodies of the three soldiers were returned to Israel in late 2004 along with the very much alive Elhanan Tenenbaum, a senior reservist officer who had been kidnapped by Hezbollah and held in custody for three years. In exchange Israel had to release four hundred Palestinian prisoners and dozens of others from Arab countries, including Mustafa Dirani and Abd al-Karim Obeid whom Israel had abducted as bartering chips for information on the missing airman Ron Arad.
6. The Hezbollah leader Sheikh Fadlallah gave many interviews to the foreign press, such as *Der Spiegel* and *Le Figaro,* but his real attitude toward Western countries can be gleaned from the organization's Arabic-language publications and interviews in the Arab press. See M. Kramer, "Hezbollah's Vision on the West," *Policy Papers*, No. 16, (1989), The Washington Institute for Near East Policy, Ch. IV.
7. The sources for this chapter are Israeli newspapers and "Hatzav"—the military intelligence's unit that tracked the public media in the Arab world.
8. The messages are sorted according to target audiences, based on the theory of Maurice Tugwell who studied the connection between terror and propaganda in underground organizations, such as the IRA, the FLN in Algeria, and Etzel (Menachem Begin's paramilitary organization during the British Mandate).
9. Demonization is a highly effective psychological tool since it circumvents rational considerations and convinces people to obey orders automatically for the sake of a national idea or higher goal. Conversations with IDF troops who served in Lebanon reveal that they felt no overriding hatred toward Hezbollah. On the other hand, the Shiite organization employed religious and psychological motifs to instill an ideological and psychological hatred of Israel in its members.
10. The Hezbollah leader Subhi Tufayli described the sacrifice made by the organization's fighters: "The Islamic Revolution will continue regardless of obstacles. Islam is a way of life that views the world as a platform for action and struggle. Its prize is the Afterlife, and it is of no importance whether we achieve victory and hegemony in this world, only that we act in accordance with the will of God. If God's will is realized by self-sacrifice or monetary payment, then Islam commands the Muslims to suffer and strive for victory." The document was translated by Hatzav (17.4.90/843/007), taken from an interview published in the Lebanese newspaper *Al Ahad* on February 16, 1990.
11. Esther Webman, "Anti-Semitism as a Corollary of Anti-Zionism: Basic Tenet of Hezbollah, Ideology," *Justice*, No.6 (August 1995): 17.
12. After Israel's pullout from Lebanon, Hezbollah continued its struggle for additional territory in an area bordering Israel—the Shaba Farms—by launching terror squads into Israeli territory and firing anti-aircraft shells into the Galilee.
13. This theme was conveyed mainly on Internet sites.
14. Prior to Hezbollah, the Palestinians published a newspaper with this name. The Palestinian paper, which also came out in English, was designed to break the monopoly of Israel's daily *Jerusalem Post* that was a mouthpiece of the Zionist

Left (see below). The Palestinians also published a Hebrew edition of *Al Fajar* for a few months.

15. Mustafa Tlass, *The Israeli Invasion of Lebanon* (Tel Aviv: Maarachot, 1988) [Hebrew].
16. Moshe Yegar, *The History of Israel's Foreign Hasbara Campaign* (Tel Aviv: Lahav Publishers, 1996).
17. Various intelligence agencies obtained valuable information applicable for psychological warfare but were loath to release it lest they compromise their sources.
18. Identification with the weak side in a struggle is a well-known psychological phenomenon. Revolutionary movements and insurgency groups have exploited this to sway public opinion to their side.
19. Israel has been broadcasting radio programs to Iran several hours a day for many years. According to various accounts, the station has gained a large following.

6 The Arab-Israeli Conflict and the First Intifada (1948–1989)

1. In his monumental work on propaganda, the French sociologist, Jacques Ellul, noted that the propagandist simplifies complex things and presents them in easily digestible form so that the message serves the goal. Intellectuals, he wrote, are particularly easy prey to propaganda messages because, in the modern world, they are expected to have opinions on every subject. Here the propagandists come to their aid by providing them with ready-made information. Jacques Ellul, *Propaganda: The Formation of Men's Attitudes* (New York: Vintage Books, 1973).
2. Both sides employ the Holocaust for political bashing: the Israelis bring up the Nazi collaboration of the Mufti of Jerusalem—Haj Amin al-Huseini—the Palestinian leader during the British Mandate period. The Palestinians remind their audience that before and during the war the Zionist leadership cooperated with the Nazis in efforts to save European Jewry and salvage Jewish property. L. Brenner, *Zionism in the Age of Dictators* (London: Croom Helm, 1983).
3. They do this by presenting as evidence Arab radio broadcasts from the period. See Shmuel Katz, *Battleground: Fact and Fantasy in the Holy Land* (Tel Aviv: Karni Publishers, 1973).
4. In 1968 Arafat was almost captured in one of his visits to the West Bank, escaping by the skin of his teeth in female disguise.
5. The highly respected Israeli journalists Ze'ev Schiff and Ehud Ya'ari describe in their book *Intifada*, (Jerusalem and Tel Aviv: Schocken, 1990 [Hebrew]) an event that occurred half a year earlier in which members of "Islamic Jihad" (a small, clandestine terror organization) succeeded in pulling off a bold prison escape from Israeli custody in Gaza. Their vaunted claim that this feat proved Israel's incompetence

significantly hurt Israel's deterrent capability and, in retrospect, paved the way for mass rioting against IDF troops.

6. The chapter describes focuses on the first two years (December 1987 to December 1989).
7. During a government discussion (November 30, 2003) on Israeli *hasbara* on the international stage, the deputy foreign ministry's director-general for *hasbara* asked the ministers to stop using Palestinian terms. His argument was that this was helping the Palestinian cause. Instead of referring to events by the Arabic term *intifada,* he suggested the word *war.*
8. The Islamic groups agreed to cooperate unofficially with the PLO following its success, but stipulated that the leaflets also have Islamic terms inscribed on them (for example, "in the name of Allah"). Other commentators claim that Fatah initiated the use of Islamic terms on the leaflets in order to offset the Islamic groups' growing influence in Palestinian society.

7 Applying Psywar Themes in the Intifada

1. One of the first was the Institute for Palestinian Studies that dealt mostly with Israeli affairs. The PLO set up other institutes, such as el-Galil, that have databases on Israeli literature, newspapers, propaganda publications, and leading Israeli figures.
2. The sources for this chapter are: the Information Center Archives at the Israel Ministry of Foreign Affairs (Hasbara Department), foreign ministry files in the Israel State Archives, and internal memos in Israeli embassies regarding neutral target audiences. Foreign ministry memos classified as "hasbara papers" offer insight into the perspectives on the Palestinian uprising and the ministry's information policy in this period.
3. A senior Israeli officer explained the difference between Israel and other countries: On the day the Intifada broke out riots erupted on the Egyptian side of Rafah (Southern Rafah is in Sinai, Northern Rafah in the Gaza Strip); the Egyptian army fired live ammunition at the demonstrators and they dispersed immediately.
4. This theme was no longer used by the end of the Intifada. At that time South Africa had made the transition to full democracy (1993–1994) and apartheid ceased to be a relevant issue. (South Africa was subsequently welcomed back into the family of nations.) But the term "apartheid" lost its halo only temporarily; its revival came after a decade-long hiatus when Israel commenced construction of the Separation Wall.
5. The foreign ministry, for example, published the differences between Arafat's statements to the Western media (calls for peace and cooperation with Israel) and the Arab media (calls for jihad and the destruction of the Zionist state). At the opening

session of the UN General Assembly in Geneva in December 1988, the foreign ministry issued a long list of terrorist acts carried out by the PLO and recently uncovered terror cells. The message was that the PLO is a terrorist organization and not to be believed. Two months later Arafat recognized Israel, whereupon the foreign ministry modified its theme and charged that this was merely a tactical step toward the liquidation of Israel.

6. The Ministry's view reflected the sharp divisions in Israeli society over the future of the territories, and the political pressure that unavoidably resulted from the national unity government's biannual rotation of the prime minister and defense minister.
7. The most candid expression of the Ministry's view of the media was the speech by President Chaim Herzog stating that the media reflected an inherently anti-Semitic approach in the West, one that employs the stock accusation that the Jews are responsible for everything and have no right to exist. The Hasbara Center published a brochure on this subject, the ministry of education translated it into English, and the foreign ministry disseminated it abroad.
8. The themes for the neutral audience were taken from the PLO's official English publication *Palestine* (that reflected the positions of senior PLO members rather than local initiatives) and from the organization's other foreign language publications (most of which were printed in the Washington Office). As for the home audience, the main sources were Unified National Leadership leaflets translated into Hebrew for the Israeli Civil Administration by advisors for Arab affairs and daily Hatzav reports. The Palestinians reached the Israeli target audience via the Israeli media, although it is not clear whether the initiative came from the Palestinians or Israeli journalists and television correspondents.
9. The city of Khaybar was the scene of a seventh-century battle in which Muhammad defeated the Jewish tribes of the Arabian Peninsula.
10. This was a common theme in Hezbollah publications.
11. Nevertheless, when the uprising started losing momentum, equality for Palestinian women was stricken from the agenda and women returned to their traditional roles.
12. The spiritual meaning was also accompanied by generous financial support.
13. This theme was characteristic of underground movements and, as noted, Hezbollah made wide use of it.
14. The initiative's main purpose was to convene an international conference that would include Israel, a Jordanian-Palestinian delegation, and the five permanent members of the UN Security Council.
15. Since this theme contained anti-Semitic overtones (such as incriminations similar to those in the *Protocols of the Elders of Zion*) the pro-Palestinian organizations in the United States (especially the Anti-Discrimination League) avoided

raising it in their contacts with the media and US government, and preferred to relegate it to Arab fringe groups or the Black Muslim organization.

16. The Israeli government has never acknowledged it possesses nuclear weapons. But since the Mordechai Vanunu Affair (1986) the American and European media treat the matter as a foregone conclusion.
17. Torture was an issue that generated a harsh debate in Israel and abroad. The Israeli Supreme Court defined certain instances when the Shabak was permitted to apply "moderate physical pressure," and later handed down the criterion for a "ticking bomb" that allowed the use of force in extreme cases where Israeli lives were in immediate danger. These rulings were the result of Palestinian suicide bombers who had caused a great many Israeli casualties, and the surging public support of the Shabak's counterterrorist operations.
18. International law requires an occupied state to uphold the same legal system that existed prior to the occupation (*mutatis mutandis*).
19. They reinforced this assertion by claiming that the Jews never established an independent state in the country except for the short period of rule under the Hasmonean Kingdom in the second-century BC.
20. MUSLIMS: JESUS WAS 1ST "PALESTINIAN MARTYR". Yasser Arafat seen as figure who followed in Christ's footsteps. Published: 12/24/2010 at 11:20 PM. AARON KLEIN. Read more at http://www.wnd.com/2010/12/243545/#K7Zw1ZkwsCVG3FBE.99 and http://www.wnd.com/2010/12/243545/
21. Three leading female journalists are Raymonda Tawil (Suha Arafat's mother); Dr. Hanan Ashrawi of Bir Zeit University, who began her international career as a spokeswoman; and Mary Haas, in charge of elementary education for UNWRA in Gaza.
22. The Palestinians cooperated with Maxim Ghilan, a former Israeli poet and journalist from France who was an enthusiastic supporter of a Palestinian state. Ghilan established an organization in the United States whose stated purpose was to convince the US government to open its gates to Soviet Jews. Ghilan claimed that for the Jews' own safety they must not be concentrated in one place (Israel).
23. The PLO canceled the theme that justified terror by comparing its use in the Intifada to Jewish underground activity during the British Mandate. They did this when they realized that such a comparison was likely to induce a defensive psychological reaction on the average Israeli that would render the theme ineffective.
24. The National Unity Government was in power between 1984 and 1990. During the Intifada Yitzhak Shamir was prime minister and Yitzhak Rabin defense minister.

8 The Palestinian Information Mechanism

1. Alan Hart, *Arafat: Terrorist or Peacemaker* (Sidgwick & Jackson Ltd., 1984), later revised as *Arafat: A Political Biography* (Indiana University Press, 1989), was most well-known. Arafat's need for world publicity led to an impressive number of biographies being written by authors who were accorded full cooperation, excluding T. Keirnan, *Yassir Arafat: The Man and the Myth* (London, Abacus Press, 1976). According to Keirnan, the reason that Arafat withdrew his cooperation was Keirnan's refusal to meet his demand to have complete say over the contents of the book. Most of the biographies described Arafat's place of birth. Arafat claimed he was born in Jerusalem, whereas Israel insists that he was born in Egypt. The propaganda implications of his place of birth are obvious. See E. Karsh, *Arafat's War: The Man and His Battle for Israeli Conquest* (NY, Grove Press 2004).
2. An analysis of the PLO's official English-language bulletin published in Beirut in the 1970s and 1980s shows the organization's contact with the world media (especially in the East Bloc and Third World) and its manpower training in various areas of communications, such as photography, journalism, and film production. The paper reported the graduation ceremonies of PLO members in journalism studies in East Germany and cinema-photography in Bulgaria.
3. Evidence for this was found in the Egyptian and Syrian armies' activities in the 1948 War of Independence.
4. For example, the PLO's official publication, *Filastin al-Thaura* and the cultural affairs journal *al-Carmel*.
5. Needless to say, it served as a key location for planning and implementing terrorist activities, arms deals, and espionage.
6. The book *Harb al-Nafsiya* (*Psychological Warfare*), published in Egypt in the 1960s, describes these methods. A copy can be found in the Truman Research Institute library in Jerusalem.
7. In the few cases in which censorship officials apprehended journalists who violated the law, their Government Press Office journalist licenses were revoked, but photographed material was rarely confiscated.
8. Part of the PLO's rehabilitation of prisoners from Israeli jails included integrating them into the media. This provided employment and proved that the organization did not abandon the victims of the revolution.
9. This advice presumably came from various sources, such as veteran PLO leaders, the Palestinian media in East Jerusalem, representatives of the foreign media who understood the potential of demonstrations, and the PLO in Tunisia (the "external PLO"). While the "Tunisians" were not in control of the events they remained in close contact with media.
10. There were a number of interesting commercial initiatives, such as the course in media training organized by Daud Kutab, a leading Fatah activist and top-notch

reporter, and the arranging (for a fee) of press conferences in which Palestinians bitterly complained of the destruction of homes and expulsion of local residents by the Israeli authorities.

11. A prime case was the execution of a drug-user on the main street of the Shabura Refugee Camp in Rafiah. The photographer was a Palestinian employed by AFP, the French news agency.
12. As stated, the Israeli government portrayed the events for the home and neutral audiences as "disturbances" in order to stress their transitoriness, but the effort failed, and the media adopted the Arabic term for the uprising—"Intifada."
13. Some of the most prominent personalities were Professors Yeshayahu Leibowitz, Yisrael Shachak, and Yehoshafat Harkabi, the attorney Felicia Langer, and Major General (res.) Matti Peled.
14. The primary reason for interviewing Americans was most likely the convenience of conversing with them in English.

9 The Israeli Information Mechanism

1. In the book *By Way of Deception*, Victor Ostrovsky notes that the Mossad's psywar unit devised cover stories for Israel's actions. CIA documents that the Iranians captured during their takeover of the United States Embassy in Tehran contain information on the Mossad's psywar unit that hunted down terrorists and former Nazis and was involved in character assassination and black propaganda. Naturally Ostrovsky's material should be treated gingerly.
2. These bodies included the World Zionist Organization and its most important branch, the Jewish Agency (that is active in Jewish communities outside Israel) with its large information department; the Ministry of Tourism, whose role is to encourage tourism to Israel and provide touristic information; the Histadrut (Israel's General Federation of Labor) is involved in large international projects (for example, the Afro-Asian Institute that promotes economic ties and study programs with developing countries); and political parties and student organizations.
3. The question of who is responsible for shaping a country's propaganda policy—the foreign ministry, prime minister's office, or presidency—remains open.
4. On November 30, 2003, the foreign minister stated that Israel's hands were tied in the *hasbara* struggle. Because it respected the right of privacy it refused to publish gory pictures of the victims of terrorist attacks. Thus Israel kept to its official policy not to publicize ultra-sensitive images, or to put it less euphemistically, not to engage in atrocity propaganda. However, the Arab world saw things in a completely different light. During the Second Intifada (2000–2005), Palestinian television broadcast pictures of Palestinian fighters waving internal body organs of compatriots killed in battle with Israel. The al-Jazeera TV station showed images of shredded bodies—Iraqis and Americans—in the Second Gulf War (2003) which irrevocably altered the rules of the game.

5. Ibid., p. 101.
6. Moshe Yeger, *The Foreign Ministry's Hasbara Activity*, Foreign Ministry, Jerusalem, 1981, p. 30.
7. *Government Yearbook 1989*, Hasbara Center, Jerusalem, p. 218.
8. This part is based mainly on IDF publications distributed at the company commander level and higher (security classification: "restricted") during the Intifada. Reservists used them outside the army in order to influence events. In the absence of other sources we may assume that these documents really did reflect the IDF's official approach, since it is unlikely that orally issued orders to commanders ran counter to widely circulated written instructions. An analysis of the documents reveals the IDF's perspective on the Intifada and the way it trained its forces to cope with the Palestinians' psywar. Another valuable source is the interviews that IDF officers gave to the press, but these were carefully screened since both sides used the media as a weapon in psychological warfare.
9. *The Use of Physical Force—Instructions from the Chief of Staff Regarding Operations in the Territories*, Headquarters of the Chief of the Education Corps, Lessons for the Commander, November 1988.
10. At the same time the Central Command/Operations published in February 1988 the rules of engagement in rock throwing incidents.
11. *Psychological Aspects of the Commander and Units Operations in the Territories*, Psychological Branch, Field Psychology and Organizational Advice Section, July 1988.
12. In June 1988 the education corps circulated a brochure entitled "The Arab Population in Judea and Samaria—Village, City, and Refugee Camp" that described the Palestinian social structure
13. "After the Events in Judea, Samaria, and the Gaza Strip," Head of the Education Corps, February 28, 1988.
14. The Center of Alternative Information was temporarily closed when it was revealed to be a front for the PFLP (Popular Front for the Liberation of Palestine). Other organizations were more circumspect and focused only on injustices that Palestinian civilians had to suffer. The most effective of these organizations was the PHRC (Palestinian Human Rights Committee) that worked in conjunction with Israel's best organized group—B'Tselem. The Palestinians also used organizations such as Amnesty International and the International Red Cross.
15. Foreign reporters felt that the liaison officer escort was an interference and counterproductive.
16. An officer in the Spokesperson's Unit suggested that high-ranking officers be coached on their appearance on television and interviews by instructing them in effective communication skills. Official approval was not forthcoming and the suggestion was consigned to the bottom drawer.
17. "Facing the Camera in the Territories," Headquarters of the Chief of the Education Corps, Doctrine and Hasbara Branch, IDF Spokesperson's Unit, June 6, 1988.

18. The IDF introduced a number of changes, such as admitting that a secret counter-terrorist unit (mistaravim) operated in the territories and agreeing to let reporters accompany patrols.
19. This arrangement existed for years but became known only during the Intifada. The tension was so great that in one case a soldier fired a live warning shot at an Israeli photographer standing next to him.

10 Planning Psywar, Defining its Goals

1. The Palestinians recognized that the theme "inevitable victory" meant different things to different target audiences. It is very common in psyops to address the enemy with: "Since you're going to lose in the end, why prolong unnecessary suffering?"
2. Israelis too, Jews and Arabs, tuned on Jordanian TV's English- and Hebrew-language news programs during the Intifada to view the gruesome pictures that Israel censored.
3. Two of these figures were Uri Avnery, whose book, *My Enemy, My Brother*, describes his secret meetings with members of the PLO in Europe; and Abie Nathan, a longtime peace activist who garnered a great deal of media attention. In addition, many Israelis were in contact with Palestinian intellectuals and academics as a result of the growing political divide in Israeli society especially after the First Lebanon War.
4. Israel invested considerable resources in tours as a means of persuasion. The Foreign Ministry (Visitors Department), Government Press Office, Jewish Agency and its associated groups Israel Bonds (money collection for Israel), Keren HaYesod (United Israel Appeal), and the Jewish National Fund—coordinated the visits of Jewish and nonJewish individuals and delegations, taking them on private tours that emphasized Jewish history, the Jewish people's return to its homeland, and modern Israel's spectacular achievements in various fields. The highlight of the tour was an up-close look at Israel's security problem via a visit to the Golan Heights (across from Kuneitra), Tel Fahar (overlooking the Hula Valley), Mt. Zion (dominating the Old City), and so forth.
5. Two main Palestinian channels for conveying messages to Israelis were the Israeli press and Israeli political activists who opposed the government's policy and supported the Palestinians. (It is impossible to know whether the publications were the initiative of the PLO or Israeli reporters and leftwing activists.)
6. In similar clashes the government defined printing leaflets a crime and threatened severe punishment to anyone caught disseminating them. The revolutionary organizations devised innovative methods for distribution and planned their circulation as a multi-pronged operation in order to confound surveillance. Israel tried to block the distribution of the leaflets by rooting out the clandestine printing houses, but it was a case of mission impossible because of their number and the

quantity of photocopy and fax machines in the territories. An analysis of the leaflets shows that after a few weeks they were aimed at Israelis and neutral audiences, not just the home audience. The PLO and the Unified National Leadership realized that Israel's intelligence agencies and international media were also perusing the leaflets.

7. Military intelligence and the Shabak probably taped telephone conversations and intercepted messages, but the traffic was immense and almost impossible to oversee effectively. Also, the Palestinians were aware they were being tracked and tended to use codes when they faxed messages to the Israeli press.
8. G. Sharp, *The Politics of Nonviolent Action* (Boston: Sargent Publishers, 1973).
9. The rules of evidence made it very difficult for the courts. For example, according to military law, when a reservist arrested a Palestinian demonstrator he had to identify the accused even after his tour of duty was over. Therefore, in many cases the reservists preferred to let the demonstrators go rather than deal with complications after the reserve service.
10. An interview with a senior foreign ministry official, Jerusalem, August 2002.
11. The most famous *shahid* in Palestinian history was Izz a-Din al-Qasam, a Muslim preacher who organized a rebellion against the British Mandatory Government and was killed in 1935 after a long pursuit. He still serves as a role model for Palestinian youth and his name has become a recruiting cry for many organizations.
12. The subtext was that Israel is doing to the Palestinians what the Nazis did to the Jews. The Palestinians have contended that Western support for Israel stems from guilt feeling over the Holocaust.
13. Palestinian women did indeed suffer injuries in violent clashes when they confronted Israeli troops arresting Palestinians captured after a chase. Tear gas could cause an abortion if sprayed in a closed room. These things may have happened, but they were a far cry from IDF policy.
14. The decision to implement this activity was made at the highest level of government and secret services therefore the information is still classified. The only sources are the mutual accusations of both parties.
15. The Palestinian report that the IDF produced eighty bogus leaflets seems highly exaggerated and may be a reflection of the internal Palestinian struggle. As far as is known, the military unit dealing with psyops consisted of a few soldiers under the command of a lieutenant-colonel. See: www.fresh.co.il, April 2003.

11 The Second Intifada (2000–2005)

1. The use of violence for attaining political goals does not apply to psychological warfare, which, by its definition, is non-violent. This and other chapters analyze the Palestinians' use of terror and guerilla warfare not on the military level but as a means of conveying messages with a psychological impact on core beliefs of target audiences.

2. The main bodies were military intelligence and the civilian police. On the West Bank there were the Preventive Security Force (commanded by Jibril Rajoub), the Palestinian General Intelligence (commanded by Tawfik Tirawi), and national security. The important bodies in the Gaza Strip were the Preventive Security Force (directed by Mohammad Dahlan), General Intelligence (commanded by Amin al-Hindi), and national security. Next to them operated the armed militias, the main one being the Tanzim in the West Bank (headed by Marwan Barghouti).
3. Anti-apartheid groups successfully employed a divestment campaign against the South African regime. This consisted of a call to boycott companies doing business with the regime and threats to undermine their stocks if they refused to heed the demands of the public. The Palestinians applied this principle in the United States, through the leadership of Naim Ateek, a Palestinian Anglican priest and head of the Sabeel Ecumenical Liberation Theology Center—a Palestinian organization whose aim is to recruit the Christian world against Israel. The campaign won the support of the Presbyterian Church, whose investment fund is estimated at billions of dollars. The fund announced it was liquidating its holdings in the Caterpillar Company.
4. The use of demonization was widespread in all of the great wars of the twentieth century. For example: Britain used it against Germany in World War I; the Nazi propaganda machine, headed by Goebbels, developed the technique of the "great lie" before and during World War II; the Soviet Union applied it against the United States at the end of the Cold War.
5. Three years later, a British cartoonist criticized Prime Minister Tony Blair because of his support of the occupation of Iraq by portraying him in the image of a Palestinian waving his two blood-drenched hands in the air.
6. Bergman, 2002.
7. Lev, 2005.
8. Attempts made to clarify the legal international status of the West Bank between 1949 and 1967 largely fell on deaf ears. Regarding the West Bank, the 1967 War did not occupy a sovereign entity. The West Bank was occupied Jordanian territory, given that its boundaries were cease-fire lines determined in 1949. Jordan's annexation of the territory in 1950 was largely unrecognized internationally. http://www.sixdaywar.org/content/jordanianocuupationjerusalem.asp
9. The 9/11 terrorist attack led to only a very brief respite in the Palestinians' struggle to tarnish Israel's image. They soon diverted discussion from Saudi involvement in financing international terror to the long-standing issue of Israel's brutality in the territories.
10. There are always life-threatening situations in wartime, but officers stress to the troops that even in such cases they have a chance, even if slight, to return from the mission alive.
11. The entire affair still simmers under a heavy pall of doubt. First, the body of a boy named Mohammad al-Dura was brought to a morgue in Gaza a few hours before the event at Netzarim Junction. The IDF's investigation committee,

headed by the physicist Nahum Shahaf, found that it was impossible to hit the spot where the boy and his father were crouching from the angle of the Israeli position. The fatal shot was in the boy's stomach—but the medical pictures from Gaza show a blow to the head. In the photos the boy is seen in four different positions after reportedly being killed (see pictures). In other scenes in the same clip, Palestinians appear in the middle of the junction standing nonchalantly in the midst of the so-called "murderous crossfire."

12. Islam has strict prohibitions against suicide, though it encourages martyrdom in holy wars. Religious scholars with a political agenda interpret the injunctions to mean that death while carrying an explosive device is equal to fulfilling the commandment for jihad.
13. *B'Tselem Report*, November 2001.
14. The documentary's basic problem is that it is filmed after the events. Therefore producers employ supplementary techniques, such as interviews, atmospheric background shots, archival clips, and the announcer's authoritative voice. The genre's halo of popularity comes from the presentation of the film as a credible document, especially given the great amount of time and effort gone into covering a particular subject.
15. One of the most common methods to attack an enemy in psychological warfare is to emphasize only one of an issue in the expectation that the target audience will focus on this aspect rather than the "marginal" ones. Thus, the Palestinians accused Israel of using nuclear power against them. They exploited the fact that some tank shells are sometimes covered with diluted uranium that increases their penetration of enemy armor. Countering with precise information is ineffective in this case, and the side that initiates the accusation benefits by using eye-grabbing, attention-stealing words such as "nuclear weapons."
16. At first the Palestinians termed the fence the "Berlin Wall," but soon realized that the neutral audience "wasn't buying it" so they changed the name to the "apartheid wall." The name served as a metaphor and was quickly picked up in Western media.

    The Palestinian photos showed only the concrete sections of the fence, but according to foreign ministry statistics only 4% of the fence is concrete, which was used to block the field of vision for potential snipers in areas close to the border. The Palestinian reports ignore the fact that the vast majority of the barrier is the same type of fence that surrounds tennis courts.
17. The warrant for Major General (res.) Doron Almog's arrest was in September 2005, that is, after the disengagement when public opinion in Europe toward Israel temporarily changed. This illustrates the power and impact of international law on IDF officers. (Almog had been general of the Southern Command during the first three years of the Second Intifada). The warrant was issued by anti-Israel elements in Britain (the Center of Palestinian Civil Rights) because of Almog's alleged involvement in war crimes, especially the assassination of Salah Shehade. When General Almog learned of the warrant he stayed on the plane and flew back to Israel.

18. Wide circles in the Israeli public seem to harbor strong opposition to the right of return since it would spell, they believe, the loss of Israel's Jewish nature. Aware of this, and in order not increase the opposition, the Palestinians downplayed this issue and focused on the main political theme—garnering Israeli support for the establishment of an independent Palestinian state.
19. The center conducts polls, publishes position papers, and organizes conferences. It specializes in assistance to journalists and the production of documentary films on the Palestinian struggle (see: www.jmcc.org).
20. Thus, for example, they conveyed the first pictures of the liquidation of the Hamas leader Abd al-Aziz Rantissi in Gaza in April 2004.
21. See the position paper on this subject written in guarded diplomatic language by the former vice chairman of *hasbara,* Moshe Yeger—"Comments on Israel's Foreign Service," Position Paper No. 160, Ariel Center for Policy Research, June 2005.
22. In an ABC News report: "In the two years of the renewed Israeli-Palestinian conflict, Iraq has given Palestinian families more than $10 million, all according to a well-known scale. Families of suicide bombers get $25,000 each and families of those killed in confrontations with Israel get $10,000. Those who houses are destroyed by the Israeli military get $5,000 and those wounded by Israelis get $1,000." http://abcnews.go.com/WNT/story?id=129914
23. See, for example, "The PA Received 50 Million Dollars from the United States and then Calls for the Murder of American Soldiers,"—www.pmw.org.il—September 6, 2005.

12 The Psyop War

1. Harel, 2000.
2. Arnon Regular, "The IDF Uses Leaflets against Wanted Individuals in the West Bank," *Ha'aretz,* October 21, 2002.
3. Amira Hass, "The First House Destroyed in Beit Jala," *Ha'aretz,* May 24, 2001.
4. Amos Harel, "Another Suspect Arrested for Participation in the Lynching," *Ha'aretz,* April 25, 2001
5. Rotternet - http://www.rotter.net/, the Makor Rishon (Primary Source) newspaper - http://global-news.info/makor-rishon-%D7%9E%D7%A7%D7%95%D7%A8-%D7%A8%D7%90%D7%A9%D7%95%D7%9Fhebrew/, and MEMRI - http://www.memri.org/
6. www.birzeit.edu—the site's name is a slap in the face to Israel because the ending "edu" is given to institutions of higher learning in the United States. The Palestinians made a great effort to obtain a political ending for their sites—ps—a singular achievement since the average web surfer regards such an Internet ending as tantamount to de jure statehood.

13 Psychological Warfare in Operation "Cast Lead"

1. The technique is reminiscent of Iraqi psychological warfare in the First Gulf War, as a result of which the Americans built up an enormous force several times larger than what was needed to get the job done—so too in the case of Gaza. Aggrandizing the danger to IDF troops was done with the long-term view of future confrontations. Excessive mobilization is a burden on the Israeli economy, erodes society's motivation, and reduces the chances that Israel will embark on another round of fighting.
2. www.palestine-info.info, www.aqsatv.ps
3. Report, 9 December 2008, "Gilad Shalit Hurt in Bombing," http://news.walla.co.il?w=/9/1406802
4. Following the Tzoran High Court decision regarding the removal of transmission antennas close to the Jewish settlement of Tzoran in the center of the country, Israel was no longer able to broadcast to the Arab public. This shortcoming has yet to be amended.

14 The Mavi Marmara Affair

1. http://www.iwar.org.uk/iwar/
2. On a visit to the Gaza Strip, Tony Blair's sister-in-law announced that Gaza is the world's largest concentration camp. This statement was made while she was being photographed in a grocery store packed with produce. See "Blair's sister-in-law: Gaza, the world's largest concentration camp" http://pajamasmedia.com/blog/tony-blairs-sister-in-laws-gaza-media-show/
3. The smuggling stopped when the Moslem Brothers (of which Hamas is the Gaza Branch) lost favor with the Egyptian government.

Bibliography

Amit, Meir. *Rosh b'rosh: Mabat ishi al iruim gedolim v'parshiyot alumot* [Head to Head: A Personal Look at Great Events and World Affairs]. Or Yehuda: Hed Artzi, 1999.

Avnery, Uri. *My Friend, the Enemy*. Westport, CT: Lawrence Hill, 1987.

B'Tselem. "Collaborators in the Occupied Territories during the Intifada: Human Rights Abuses and Violations." January 1994 [Hebrew]. http://www.btselem.org/publications/summaries/199401_collaboration_suspects

Bergman, Ronen. *V'hasherut netuna* [Authority Granted]. Tel Aviv: Yediot Books, 2002.

Brenner, Lenni. *Zionism in the Age of Dictators*. London: Croom Helm, 1983.

Buchnik, Rafi. "Mechadel hashidurim baAravit" [A Mess-up in Arabic Broadcasts]. *Haaretz*, September 18, 2003. http://www.haaretz.co.il/misc/1.911315

Ellul, Jacques. *Propaganda: The Formation of Men's Attitudes*. New York: Vintage, 1973.

Harel, Amos. "Ne'etzar shoter falestini b'chashad l'me'oravut b'lynch" [Palestinian Officer Arrested for Suspected Participation in Lynching]. *Haaretz*, April 24, 2001. http://www.haaretz.co.il/misc/1.696198

Harel, Amos, and Avi Issacharoff. *Hamilchama hashviit* [The Seventh War]. Tel Aviv: Yediot Books, 2000.

Hasbara Center. *Government Yearbook 1987*. Jerusalem: Hasbara Center.

———. *Government Yearbook 1989*. Jerusalem: Hasbara Center.

Hass, Amira. "Habayit harishon sh'neheras b'Beit Jala" [The First House Destroyed in Beit Jala]. *Haaretz*, May 24, 2001. http://www.haaretz.co.il/misc/1.703654

IDF Education Corps. *After the Events in Judea, Samaria, and the Gaza Strip*. February 28, 1988.

———. *Facing the Camera in the Territories*. June 6, 1988.

———. *The Use of Physical Force—Instructions from the Chief of Staff regarding Operations in the Territories*. November 1988.

IDF Psychological Branch. *Psychological Aspects of the Commander and Units Operations in the Territories*. July 1988.

Karsh, Efraim. *Arafat's War: The Man and His Battle for Israeli Conquest.* New York: Grove, 2004.

Katz, Shmuel. *Battleground: Fact & Fantasy in Palestine.* Tel Aviv: Karni, 1973.

Kiernan, Thomas. *Yasir Arafat: The Man and the Myth.* London: Abacus, 1976.

Kramer, Martin. "Hezbollah's Vision on the West." Policy Paper no. 16. Washington, DC: Washington Institute for Near East Policy, 1989.

Lev, Uzrad. *Betoch hakis shel ha'rais* [Inside Arafat's Pocket]. Or Yehuda: Kinneret Zmora-Bitan, 2005.

Linebarger, Paul Myron Anthony. *Psychological Warfare.* Washington, DC: Combat Forces Press, 1954.

Melman, Yossi, ed. *CIA Report on Israel's Intelligence and Security Services.* Tel Aviv: Erez Press, 1982.

Nawi, Eliyahu. *Sipurei hamizrach hatichon hayashan: chochma, zima, vimusar heskel* [Stories from the Old Middle East: Wisdom, Lechery and Lessons to be Learned]. Tel Aviv: Tamuz Publishers, 2000.

Ostrovsky, Victor. *By Way of Deception: The Making and Unmaking of a Mossad Officer.* New York: St. Martin's Press, 1990.

Palestinian Media Watch. "The PA Received 50 Million Dollars from the United States and then Calls for the Murder of American Soldiers." September 6, 2005. www.palwatch.org.il

Regular, Arnon. "Tzahal mefitz keruzim neged mevukashim bashtachim" [The IDF Uses Leaflets against Wanted Individuals in the West Bank]. *Haaretz,* October 21, 2002. http://news.walla.co.il/?w=/9/297193

Roetter, Charles. *Psychological Warfare.* London: Batsford, 1974.

Saleh Abd al-Jawad. "Les Faux tracts." *Revue D'Etudes Palestiniennes,* no. 48 (1993), 69–97.

Schiff, Ze'ev, and Ehud Ya'ari. *Intifada.* Jerusalem and Tel Aviv: Schocken, 1990 [Hebrew].

Sharp, Gene. *The Politics of Nonviolent Action.* Boston: Porter Sargent, 1973.

Taylor, Philip M. *World Encyclopedia of Propaganda.* New York: Sharpe Reference, 1998.

Tlass, Mustafa. *Haplisha haYisraelit leLevanon* [The Israeli Invasion of Lebanon]. Tel Aviv: Maarachot, 1988.

US Army. *FM 33-1-1—Psychological Operations Techniques and Procedures.* Washington, DC: Government Printing Office, 1994.

———. *FM 46-1—Public Affairs Operations.* Washington, DC: Government Printing Office, 1997.

———. *FM 3-13—Inform and Influence Activities.* Washington, DC: Government Printing Office, 2013.

Webman, Esther. "Anti-Semitism as a Corollary of Anti-Zionism: Basic Tenet of Hezbollah Ideology." *Justice,* no. 6 (August 1995): 17.

Yahav, Nir. "Gilad Shalit niftza b'hapetzatzot" [Gilad Shalit Hurt in Bombing]. *Walla News*, December 9, 2008. http://news.walla.co.il?w=/9/1406802

Yegar, Moshe. *The Foreign Ministry's Hasbara Activity*. Jerusalem: Foreign Ministry, 1981.

———. *Toldot hahasbara haYisraelit* [The History of Israel's Foreign Hasbara System]. Tel Aviv: Lahav Publishers, 1986.

———. *L'toldotecha shel Maarachat Hasbarat Hachutz shel Yisrael* [The History of Israel's Foreign Hasbara Campaign]. Tel Aviv: Lahav Publishers, 1996.

———. "He'arot al Sherut Hachutz shel Yisrael" [Comments on Israel's Foreign Service]. Position Paper no. 160. Ariel Center for Policy Research, Israel, June 2005.

Index

www.ingramcontent.com/pod-product-compliance
Lightning Source LLC
Chambersburg PA
CBHW051314270125
20917CB00004B/234
9781137467027